# Making Ends Meet in Contemporary Russia

# Making Ends Meet in Contemporary Russia

Secondary Employment, Subsidiary Agriculture and Social Networks

Simon Clarke

*Professor of Sociology*
*University of Warwick, UK*
*and*
*Scientific Director*
*Institute for Comparative Labour Relations Research (ISITO)*
*Moscow*
*Russia*

Edward Elgar
Cheltenham, UK • Northampton, MA, USA

Published by
Edward Elgar Publishing Limited
Glensanda House
Montpellier Parade
Cheltenham
Glos GL50 1UA
UK

Edward Elgar Publishing, Inc.
136 West Street
Suite 202
Northampton
Massachusetts 01060
USA

A catalogue record for this book
is available from the British Library

**Library of Congress Cataloguing in Publication Data**

Clarke, Simon, 1946-
  Making ends meet in contemporary Russia : secondary employment, subsidiary agriculture and social networks / Simon Clarke.
  p. cm.
  This book is a sequel to an earlier book, 'The formation of a labour market in Russia' (Clarke, 1999).
  Includes bibliographical references and index.
  1. Supplementary employment—Russia (Federation) 2. Labour Market—Russia (Federation) 3. Cost and standard of living—Russia (Federation) I. Clarke, Simon, 1946- Formation of a labour market in Russia. II. Title.

 HD5854.55.R8 C55 2002
 331.12—dc21

                                                                    2002028589
 ISBN 1 84064 262 9

Printed and bound in Great Britain by MPG Books Ltd, Bodmin, Cornwall

# Contents

| | |
|---|---|
| List of tables | vii |
| Acknowledgements | xi |
| 1 Household subsistence in the Russian economic crisis | 1 |
| 2 Secondary employment | 10 |
| Definition and data sources | 10 |
| Scale of secondary employment | 16 |
| Kinds of secondary employment | 26 |
| Characteristics of secondary employment | 41 |
| The incidence of secondary employment | 61 |
| Income from secondary employment | 79 |
| Secondary employment as an element of a household survival strategy | 85 |
| 3 The Russian dacha and the myth of the urban peasant | 113 |
| The Russian crisis and the rise of self-sufficiency | 113 |
| How extensive is the use of land by urban households in Russia? | 114 |
| How much of Russia's food is home-grown? | 118 |
| Deciding to use a dacha | 125 |
| Testing the hypotheses | 131 |
| Why do people use dachas? | 144 |
| Dachas and the domestic production of food | 150 |
| The dynamics of dacha use | 158 |
| The costs and benefits of domestic food production | 159 |
| The myth of the urban peasant? | 167 |
| Conclusion | 176 |
| 4 Social networks and private transfers | 178 |
| Are gift networks symmetrical? | 185 |
| How much do households rely on the help of others? | 188 |
| Private transfers: charity or reciprocity? | 195 |
| Conclusion | 206 |

5  Do Russian households have survival strategies?                     236
    The notion of a 'household survival strategy'                     237
    Do households have *survival strategies*?                         239
    Do *households* have survival strategies?                         247
    Do households pursue distinctive survival strategies?             252
    The gender dimension of survival strategies                       256
    Conclusion                                                        266
References                                                            271
Index                                                                 279

# Tables

2.1    Incidence of secondary employment and desire for
       additional work                                                    18
2.2    Incidence of secondary employment and individual
       economic activity by employment status                            19
2.3    Scale of secondary employment, 1993–97                            22
2.4    Percentage engaged in secondary employment by
       employment status                                                 24
2.5    Branch distribution of secondary employment, 1997–2000
       and primary employment, 1999                                      42
2.6    Percentage of respondents with their second job in the same
       branch as their first and distribution of first and second
       jobs by branch                                                    43
2.7    Forms of secondary employment 1994–99                             44
2.8    RLMS 1998–2000 distribution of secondary occupations by
       sphere of occupational activity                                   45
2.9    Percentage distribution of secondary employment by
       employers' area of activity                                       46
2.10a  Incidence of secondary employment by occupational
       status in primary job (men)                                       48
2.10b  Incidence of secondary employment by occupational
       status in primary job (women)                                     49
2.11   How is your secondary employment formalised?                      50
2.12   Type of registration by sector of secondary employment            51
2.13   Distribution of hours worked in the previous month in
       second job by employment status                                   52
2.14   When do you normally engage in your secondary
       employment?                                                       54
2.15   Professional demands of supplementary job                         58
2.16   Skill demands of supplementary job                                58
2.17   Intensity of supplementary job                                    59
2.18   Percentage of household income contributed by
       supplementary earnings, by household income ranking               82
2.19   Percentage of household money income contributed by
       supplementary earnings, by household income ranking               83

2.20   Percentage of household money income contributed by
       supplementary earnings, by household income ranking          84
2.21   Who has secondary employment? (couple-based
       households in which both partners are working)               91
2.22   OLS regressions – dependent variables: log of earnings in
       main job and log of hourly earnings in second job            97
2.23   OLS regression – dependent variable: log of hours
       worked last month in supplementary job                       99
2.24   Multinomial logistic regression – probability of having
       permanent, regular or occasional secondary employment;
       those with a primary job                                     101
2.25   Multinomial logistic regression – probability of having
       permanent, regular or occasional secondary employment;
       those without a primary job                                  103
2.26   Logistic regression – probability of having a second
       job and individual economic activity                        105
2.27   Multinomial logistic regression – probability of having
       regular or occasional secondary employment; those
       with no primary employment                                   108
2.28   Multinomial logistic regression – probability of having
       regular or occasional secondary employment; those
       with primary employment                                      110
3.1    Percentage of population of urban census districts in each
       region with each type of plot and median size of plots       115
3.2    Land holding in four large cities                            117
3.3    Percentage of urban and rural households using land          117
3.4    Percentage of agricultural production by value by
       category of producer at current prices                       119
3.5    Number of producers, land under cultivation and
       production of various products on personal plots             120
3.6    Percentage of households buying some or all of their
       needs and average percentage produced themselves
       for food products                                            124
3.7    Logistic regression – dependent variable: probability of
       having a dacha                                               133
3.8    Logistic regression – dependent variable: probability of
       possessing a plot of land (All-Russia, urban population)     135
3.9    Logistic regression – dependent variable: probability of
       household using land in the last year                        137
3.10   Reasons cited for having and for not having a dacha          145

| | | |
|---|---|---|
| 3.11 | Mean household income per head by main reasons for having or not having a dacha | 148 |
| 3.12 | Hours worked on the dacha and amount produced by hobbyists and subsistence producers | 149 |
| 3.13 | Methods of provisioning | 151 |
| 3.14 | Logistic regressions – probability of home-production of at least 50 percent of consumption of various products | 155 |
| 3.15 | Expenditure on food of households with and without a dacha | 165 |
| 3.16 | OLS regression – dependent variable: proportion of potatoes in oblast home grown | 174 |
| 4.1 | Private transfers of money and goods | 180 |
| 4.2 | Percentage distribution of help provided to households | 182 |
| 4.3 | Percentage distribution of help provided by households | 183 |
| 4.4 | Characteristics of relatives and friends who are recipients and donors of help. | 184 |
| 4.5 | Number of significant others identified by individual household members who were also in help relationships with the household | 185 |
| 4.6 | Median percentage of household income given and received as gifts and loans by households which are net donors and net recipients, by income quintiles | 190 |
| 4.7 | Percentage of households receiving help and net help received by net beneficiaries | 191 |
| 4.8 | Impact of private transfers on the incidence of poverty | 193 |
| 4.9 | Percentage of total transfers given and received by household income quintiles, 1992–2000 | 194 |
| 4.10 | Logistic regression – probabilities of being a recipient, both recipient and donor and being a donor of all forms of help | 209 |
| 4.11 | Logistic regression – probabilities of being a recipient, both recipient and donor and being a donor of money | 212 |
| 4.12 | Logistic regression – probabilities of being a recipient, both recipient and donor and being a donor of food | 215 |
| 4.13 | Logistic regression – probabilities of being a recipient, both recipient and donor and being a donor of goods | 218 |
| 4.14 | Logistic regression – probabilities of being a recipient, both recipient and donor and being a donor of loans | 221 |
| 4.15 | Logistic regression – probabilities of being a recipient, both recipient and donor and being a donor of help | 224 |

4.16    Logistic regression – probabilities of household being
        a lender, lender and borrower or borrower               227
4.17    OLS regressions – gross value of help and of
        loans given and received                               231
4.18    OLS regressions – value of all forms of help given and
        received and variable means                            234
5.1     Actions taken by respondents in the past twelve months  241
5.2     Actions taken by respondents in the past twelve months  242
5.3     Actions taken by respondents in the past two years       243
5.4     Steps taken by members of households which had
        experienced financial difficulties in the past two years 244
5.5     What you would do if you had to increase your earnings?
        (Percentage distribution of responses of those in work) 245
5.6     Assessment of the material situation of the household
        by household heads                                      245
5.7     Did you consult with members of your family when
        you left your last job?                                 249
5.8     OLS regression – weekly hours worked by high and
        low earners, couple-based households                    250
5.9     OLS regression – monthly hours worked by high and
        low earners, couple-based households                    251

# Acknowledgements

This book is based primarily on the results of qualitative and survey research on employment and the development of a labour market in Russia conducted in collaboration with my colleagues in the regional affiliates of the Institute for Comparative Labour Relations Research (ISITO), based in Moscow. The research has been funded at various stages by the British Overseas Development Administration, Economic and Social Research Council, Department for International Development and INTAS. We are very grateful to these bodies for their support. Needless to say, they bear no responsibility for any of the opinions expressed in this or other works based on the research.

This book is a sequel to an earlier book, *The Formation of a Labour Market in Russia* (Clarke, 1999b), based on the same research projects, which focused on the primary labour market. Other commitments have delayed the completion of this volume. A third anticipated volume, on the segmentation of the Russian labour market, will probably never see the light of day.

As always, I am very grateful to my ISITO colleagues on the basis of whose work this book has been written, and particularly to Valery Yakubovich, Veronika Kabalina, Irina Kozina, Marina Karelina, Tanya Metalina, Sergei Alasheev, Sveta Yaroshenko, Tanya Lytkina, Inna Donova and Lena Varshavskaya, whose work and ideas have provided an invaluable resource in writing this book.

# 1. Household Subsistence in the Russian Economic Crisis

In the Soviet Union all adults had the right and obligation to work, while those who were unable to work by reason of age or infirmity or the need to care for the young (women caring for young children or households which had lost their 'breadwinner') received appropriate social benefits, with allowances being provided for children of school-age and stipends being provided for students. This meant that, at least in principle, each household member contributed sufficient to the household budget to cover their subsistence in the form of a wage or social benefit, the average pension being about one-third of the average wage. In 1985, on the eve of perestroika, wages on average accounted for three-quarters of household incomes, with social transfers accounting for a further one-sixth.[1]

Wages and benefits were generally fairly low, but the costs of housing, energy, utilities, public transport, vacations and basic foods were heavily subsidised and health care, child care and education were free, so that most households could count on having enough to meet their basic subsistence needs (the 'traditional poor' were those households with at most one breadwinner supporting disabled members or a large number of children). Those able to earn higher wages could save money towards more substantial purchases or to provide for their retirement, the average household having savings in the State Savings Bank in 1985 amounting to about seven months' household income. Consumption was constrained as much by the shortage of goods as it was by the shortage of money in the hands of the population.

There were very limited opportunities for households to increase their money incomes. Those who stayed in the same workplace could expect to increase their income over time as they gained seniority or were promoted to higher positions, although differentials were low.

---

[1]  Unless otherwise indicated, all statistical data in the text is derived from the *Russian Statistical Yearbook*, published annually by the Russian State Statistics Committee, Goskomstat Rossii.

*1*

People could, and did, change jobs in the hope of increasing their wages (or of getting better access to scarce goods and services), and could earn higher wages by going off to work in the more remote regions, often with a view to buying a home to retire to. Many people took on second jobs to earn additional spending money, and there was a thriving 'second economy' based on the mutual exchange of goods and services between friends and neighbours, although to do such private work for payment was illegal. It was illegal to earn money through trading ('speculation') or by employing others, but collective farmers were able to sell their own produce on the *kolkhoz* markets.

The period of perestroika was marked by a substantial growth in household money incomes, which increased by 50 percent between 1985 and 1990, unmatched by an increased supply of consumption goods, resulting in growing shortages and the accumulation of monetary savings which culminated in inflation, largely suppressed until 1991. Perestroika also offered increased opportunities for income-earning activity, with the legalisation of 'individual labour activity', co-operatives and eventually private enterprises. However, the vast majority of the population at the end of the period of perestroika still relied on wage income and social benefits, which made up almost 90 percent of household incomes in 1990.

The 'transition to a market economy' following the collapse of the Soviet Union was supposed to stimulate the growth of an economy freed from the stultifying constraints of the Soviet system of centralised management, but in fact led to an economic collapse unprecedented in world economic history. According to the best available data, GDP fell by about half between 1990 and 1998. Many commentators have argued that such statistics exaggerate the scale of the economic decline to which the Russian population has been subjected because they do not take account of the qualitative changes in the composition of economic activity. Thus, a large part of the decline in GDP is accounted for by the collapse of unproductive military production and the decline in investment, which make no direct contribution to the living standards of the population. Nevertheless, this collapse has still implied a drastic decline in the employment and earnings of those who had been working in these sectors, while consumer goods industries have hardly prospered: the production of light industry fell by more than any other sector, to 12 percent of its 1990 level in 1998, while agricultural output was halved, as the market for food, clothing and consumer goods was swamped by imports, paid for by the export of fuels, metals and minerals freed from domestic use by the collapse of industry, the trend only being partially checked following the collapse of the rouble in August 1998.

While macroeconomic aggregates might exaggerate the extent of the decline of the Russian economy, there is no doubting the impact of that decline on the incomes and employment of the Russian population. The collapse of the traditional economy led to a massive destruction of jobs by no means matched by the anticipated job creation in new sectors of the economy, and to falling wages for those lucky enough to have work. This disaster was compounded by widespread temporary lay-offs ('administrative leave') and short-time working and by the extensive non-payment of wages. Between 1990 and 1998 total employment in the Russian economy fell by almost a quarter, with about half of that number dropping out of the labour force and the other half being considered to be unemployed. However, in 1999 fewer than 14 percent of those unemployed according to the ILO definition (actively seeking and available for work) were actually registered with the Employment Service and eligible for unemployment benefit, many of those registered not receiving any benefit because of the lack of money in the Employment Fund.

Meanwhile, money wages lagged seriously behind prices, losing about a third of their value in each successive wave of inflation, so that by the end of 1998 real wages due (though not necessarily paid) had fallen to less than half the 1985 level, not much more than their level in 1964, when Khrushchev was removed from power as a result of the failure of his efforts at economic reform. Even this understates the impact of the crisis on many households, since wage inequality increased from Scandinavian to Latin American levels, the wage Gini coefficient increasing to 0.48. The minimum wage, which had set a meaningful floor to wages in the Soviet period at about half the average wage, was eroded by inflation so that by 2000 it amounted to only one-twelfth of the officially recognised basic adult subsistence minimum. Goskomstat's 1999 wage survey found that 42 percent of wage-earners received less than the adult subsistence minimum, while two-thirds did not earn enough to support one other person at the minimum subsistence level. Many of those owed such meagre wages never received them. In the last quarter of 1998 almost two-thirds of all wage-earners reported delays in the payment of their wages to the Russian Longitudinal Monitoring Survey (RLMS) and almost a third reported having received nothing at all the previous month. The remonetisation of the economy after the 1998 crisis meant that the situation with the non-payment of wages improved considerably, but still in the RLMS in the autumn of 2000, almost 20 percent of wage-earners had not been paid their wages the previous month and almost a third were owed money by their employer (for discussion of the aggregate data on employment and wages see Clarke, 1999a, 1999b, 2000).

The decline in pensions and welfare benefits broadly parallels that of wages. The average pension, which still comfortably exceeded the appropriate subsistence minimum in 1992, had fallen to three-quarters of the pensioner's subsistence minimum by 2000, while the minimum retirement pension had fallen from well over half to one-sixth of the subsistence minimum, although the political weight of pensioners meant that delays in the payment of pensions were less substantial than delays in the payment of wages and other benefits. Child benefit in 2000 amounted to only six percent of the child's subsistence minimum and student grants had fallen by well over half in real terms. Finally, the substantial savings which many families had accumulated were wiped out by the massive burst of inflation in 1992 and again by the financial crisis of August 1998.

Interpretation of the data on income and employment is difficult because of the dubious quality of some of the official statistics and because there have been such radical changes in the structure of the economy. Although wages have lagged far behind the consumer price index, the range and quality of goods available has undoubtedly improved considerably, so that monetary measures may exaggerate the extent of the decline in the standard of living, or at least in the quality of life. Some commentators, clutching at straws, herald de-industrialisation and falling incomes for their contribution to the health of the population as a result of a sharp reduction in industrial pollution and an improvement in diet, as vegetables replace fatty meat – the consumption of meat and dairy produce fell by more than 40 percent between 1990 and 2000. Nevertheless, such wry optimism is somewhat undermined by the dramatic decline in life expectancy, especially of men (the life expectancy of men in Russia is now less than that of men in India), and increased incidence of infectious diseases, most notably TB and HIV.

Despite all such qualifications, the impact of the economic catastrophe on the traditional sources of household incomes is undeniable. The incidence of poverty rose to between one-third and half the population, depending on the measure selected, and something like 10 percent of households are in persistent chronic poverty, with incomes which are consistently less than half the subsistence minimum, less than the minimum food budget (for a review and discussion of the data see Clarke, 1999a, 1999b). According to the RLMS data, in the autumn of 1998, 60 percent of households had a total money income from wages and benefits that was less than the regional subsistence minimum. Even following the modest recovery of the economy, according to the RLMS data for the autumn of 2000, 46 percent of households had a money income that was less than the subsistence minimum. According to a report prepared for the Ministry of Labour, 2.9 percent of the population was in extreme poverty at the beginning of 2001, with incomes so low that they risked starvation, too poor even to buy enough bread and potatoes to survive. A further 8.1 percent had enough to cover minimum food costs, but not to pay for their housing and utilities and 14.6 percent could pay for basic food, housing and utilities but could not meet their basic needs for clothing (SOTEKO, 2000, p. 35).

Many western commentators still insist that the situation is not as bad as it looks. The Russians whom most western visitors encounter in the hotels, bars and restaurants in the centre of the main cities appear to be surviving very well. The obvious conclusion is that they have hidden sources of income, which do not appear in the official statistical data because they are not reported to the authorities. Thus it is widely believed that many Russians have well-paid jobs that are not officially registered, while many of those even in officially registered jobs receive significant additions to their declared wages in the form of fringe benefits and payments off the books.[2]

There is no doubt that some people are working in unregistered jobs, their income and employment not being reported to the statistical authorities, and some people (mostly in professional and managerial positions) earn substantial unreported supplements to their official wages, but the statistical authorities make allowance for such unreported income and employment in their published data and such

---

[2]     This complacent picture is supported by the official statistical data, which supplements the sum of reported wages in the National Income Accounts by more than 30 percent to allow for 'hidden wage payments' (until 1995 this was included in 'property, entrepreneurial and other income', the estimate for which by that year exceeded total wage incomes). However, this is an accounting fiction to balance the extremely dubious books, which is not based on any evidence that such hidden wage payments actually exist (Clarke, 2000, p. 183).

people do not seem to be shy about reporting their income to survey interviewers. While much economic activity may escape official reporting, there is no reason to believe that people systematically conceal their income and employment from interviewers conducting social surveys and the survey data is remarkably consistent, both between surveys and with the published official data.[3]

Survey data suggests that the extent of unregistered primary employment has been greatly exaggerated. In a Supplement which we attached to Goskomstat's Labour Force Survey in the Komi Republic and Kemerovo Oblast in 1997 we asked respondents, where was their labour book? Over 99 percent of those employed in state and former state enterprises said it was in their main place of work, but over 10 percent of those employed in new private enterprises or working in family firms and almost half those working for private individuals said that their labour book was somewhere else. This would imply that the scale of 'unregistered employment' is very much less than is often assumed, amounting to much less than 5 percent of total employment, and is largely confined to individual labour activity and unregistered individual and family enterprises. Ninety-seven percent of the RLMS 2000 respondents said that their job was officially registered. Three-quarters of those with unregistered jobs worked in enterprises employing fewer than 25 people, around half earned less than the subsistence minimum and more than 80 percent were denied the basic legal entitlements to paid vacations, sick leave or maternity leave, supporting the conclusion that unregistered jobs are mostly low-paid and insecure jobs in small private firms.

There is no evidence that the reported decline in wages, benefits and employment exaggerates the depth of the crisis which has been experienced by Russian households. Every autumn through the 1990s experienced international aid agencies, which are not prone to exaggeration, warn of the risk of mass starvation in Russia in the winter to come and yet, at least up till now, such warnings have turned out to have been false alarms. Of course, Russians take pride in surviving. The older generation love to tell their children and grandchildren that they don't know the meaning of hardship, regaling

---

[3]    The official data, including estimates for unreported employment, published until 1998 certainly overestimated the level of employment in the economy, the Labour Force Survey data suggesting that employment is about 9 percent less than is officially reported (Clarke, 1999b, Chapter 6). Goskomstat has recognised this and now publishes the figures derived from the Labour Force Survey as its official employment data.

them with their stories of stoical survival of famine and wartime suffering. But tens of millions of Russians did not survive famine and war – those who lived to tell the tale are the lucky ones. The question that westerners repeatedly ask is, how do Russians survive the loss of their main sources of income?

The most frequent answers given to this question refer to the alternative possibilities of obtaining subsistence that are available to Russian households. Many of those in low-paid jobs or suffering lay-offs or short-time working are supposed to have second jobs which supplement their primary incomes. The less fortunate have the option of reverting to subsistence production, growing their own food on the plots of land attached to their 'dachas' (despite the romantic image evoked by the word, most dachas are little more than a potting shed on a small allotment). Finally, the Russian traditions of hospitality and communality (the *obshchina*) persist, so that those who really fall on bad times can call on the support of their friends and relatives. However, there has been no systematic attempt to assess the significance of these alternative sources of subsistence, nor of their role in securing the survival of impoverished households.

There is no doubt that secondary employment, subsistence agriculture and private transfers are significant sources of household subsistence in Russia. However, it is important to establish more precisely how significant they are and to look beyond an assessment of their absolute scale to investigate their incidence. If we are concerned with explaining how Russian households survive the crisis, we have to ask to what extent these sources of income and subsistence provide a means by which the impoverished can supplement their household incomes, rather than merely providing additional resources for those who are already comfortable. In particular, we have to ask to what extent these sources provide the potential elements of a 'survival strategy' of impoverished households, so that those who suffer misfortune can compensate by tapping these alternative sources.

We do not have to rely on anecdotes and observations in city-centre bars and hotels to identify the sources of household subsistence and the characteristics of 'household survival strategies' in Russia. Although its quality is variable, there is ample survey and official data on which to base an assessment and it is this data that will primarily be used in this book. The principal sources that will be used are the official statistics published by Goskomstat, the data of the regular surveys of the All-Russian Centre for Public Opinion Research

(VTsIOM), of the Russian Longitudinal Monitoring Survey (RLMS) and of a household survey conducted in four cities in May 1998 by the Institute for Comparative Labour Relations Research (ISITO).[4]

Most research into 'household survival strategies' has been ethnographic research, based on extended interviews with and observation of a small number of respondents, usually drawn from a fairly restricted circle, and we have ourselves conducted such research in the course of a series of projects on the Russian labour market. While such research provides an invaluable insight into the contours of household decision-making and provides an essential foundation for the formulation of hypotheses regarding household subsistence, it is very difficult to identify from respondents' narratives the structure of constraints and opportunities underlying their decisions, and so the real scope for strategic decision-making, and it is not possible to generalise from such evidence to the population as a whole. It is therefore essential to complement such ethnographic data with the analysis of the data of official statistical reporting and sample surveys.

The analysis of survey and official data can, in the first instance, provide us with evidence on the scale and extent of the various sources of household subsistence. Because the quality of much of the data is suspect, it is expedient to analyse data from different sources in order to distinguish consistent findings from those which might be due to idiosyncrasies of the data sources. However, the analysis of the data enables us not only to identify the scale and extent of various phenomena, but also to investigate their incidence. In particular, we can identify the extent to which secondary employment, domestic agriculture and private transfers are means by which the poorest households are able to sustain themselves, as opposed to means by which those who are already comfortable are able to increase the size and security of their incomes. Moreover, we can go some way towards identifying the significance of these phenomena in 'household survival strategies' by discovering the extent to which households which have fallen on hard times are able to avail themselves of these sources of subsistence. If these phenomena are elements of household survival strategies, we would expect members of households which have experienced a fall in their income, loss of employment, short-time working, lay-offs or the non-payment of wages to be more likely to

---

[4]     For details of these data sets see Clarke, 1999b, Chapter 6. The RLMS data is available from www.cpc.unc.edu/rlms. The ISITO data and details of the survey are available through www.warwick.ac.uk/russia.

engage in these activities than households which have not suffered such misfortunes. If members of such households are not more likely to engage in these activities in response to misfortune, the presumption must be that such households had already taken advantage of all the opportunities available to them and that objective constraints have limited their ability to realise a survival strategy based on increasing their sources of income and subsistence. The only survival strategy available to the majority of households in such circumstances would be to cut their expenditure in accordance with their depleted income.

In the following three chapters of this book I will use the available data to look in detail at the principal alternative sources of household subsistence: supplementary (secondary) employment, domestic agricultural production and reliance on social networks for private transfers. In each case the analysis will draw on a range of survey and official data to establish the scale and incidence of these phenomena and to assess their contribution to household subsistence. In particular, I will ask to what extent each of these phenomena serve as elements of a 'household survival strategy', a means by which impoverished households are able to augment their household resources.

In the concluding chapter I will review the evidence as a whole to question the usefulness and appropriateness of explaining the economic circumstances of Russian households and the behaviour of household members in terms of the notion of a 'household survival strategy'.

# 2. Secondary Employment

The phenomenon of secondary employment is inextricably bound up with the idea of the informal economy: there is a popular belief, propagated by the mass media as well as by academics and politicians, that a large number of those with little or no apparent source of primary income as a result of unemployment, low wages, lay-offs, short-time working or the non-payment of wages in fact have second jobs in the informal economy which bring in the income they need, if not to live comfortably, at least to survive. In this chapter I will look not at such popular beliefs, but at the available data, in an attempt to paint a realistic picture of the scale, forms and significance of secondary employment as a source of income for Russian households. The chapter is based on research reports (including Donova and Varshavskaya, 1996; Donova, 1998; Varshavskaya and Donova, 1998; Varshavskaya and Donova, 1999), field notes prepared by the ISITO research teams and on analysis of the data of ISITO and other surveys.

## DEFINITION AND DATA SOURCES

Secondary employment was extensive in the Soviet Union. However, since it was frowned on ideologically and restricted legally it was barely researched and there is virtually no statistical information on secondary employment in the USSR. In the literature of the Soviet period, secondary employment and overtime working were treated almost exclusively as evils of the capitalist system, symptoms of the poverty and overexploitation of the working class in the capitalist world which had been banished under socialism.

Secondary employment only began to be studied in the perestroika period, in the second half of the 1980s, but for a long time the only comprehensive review of secondary employment was a book by Shvetsov (Shvetsov, 1989). The only official data on secondary employment was the administrative reporting of the number of people employed in officially registered second jobs, *po sovmestitel'stvu*, and, more recently, the number employed on a contractual basis to carry out specific pieces of work. In the Soviet period, when everybody had to have an officially registered place of work, such employment would normally have been secondary. Nowadays many people working on this basis might not have any other job.

More systematic research became possible when the All Russian Public Opinion Research Centre (VTsIOM) began to ask about secondary employment in its regular polls from 1993, with more detailed questions being asked from 1997. Since then a number of articles have been published using this and other survey data (see, in particular, Khibovskaya, 1995, 1996; Klopov, 1996; Perova and Khakhulina, 1997, 1998), although based only on tabulations, without any multivariate analysis of the data. The Labour Force Surveys, conducted regularly by Goskomstat, have asked about supplementary employment since 1992, but the primary data is not available to independent researchers. The Russian Longitudinal Monitoring Survey has been asking about secondary employment in its two waves of panel surveys since 1992 and there has also been a number of independent surveys which have included questions about secondary employment.

My colleagues in ISITO have asked about secondary employment in three surveys: one, a *supplement* attached to the Labour Force Survey in October 1997 in Kemerovo oblast and the Komi Republic, the second, a *work history survey* of a sample of 800 current employees of 16 state and former state industrial enterprises in April 1997, which involved both questionnaire and qualitative interviews, the third a *household survey* of all the adult members of 4 000 households in April–May 1998, both the latter surveys in four large Russian cities (Samara, Kemerovo, Syktyvkar and Moscow). These will be the principal data sources used in this chapter.

There is an immediate methodological problem of defining just what we mean by secondary employment. On the one hand, many people are involved in a range of activities which may not bring in any money income: the most common is work on their garden plots, but they may provide a whole range of services for family, friends and neighbours, such as repairs, building or decorating work, which are not paid directly but which may be reciprocated. This is common in any society, but was especially widespread in the Soviet Union, where the provision of such services for payment was illegal until 1987. By convention, such activities, like domestic labour, are excluded from the definition of employment. It is important to remember them however, because a substantial part of the growth of paid secondary employment in Russia consists of the monetisation of the provision of services which had formerly been provided on a non-monetary basis.

On the other hand, in Russia people still have the Soviet concept of primary employment as involving registration in a full-time job: a person's main job is normally understood as a full-time job in a place which keeps their labour book, in which their work record is officially recorded.[1] Those who do not have any registered employment will frequently say that they do not work, even if they are in fact working long hours in some unregistered activity, so reinforcing the identification of secondary employment with informal employment.[2] Thus, for example, in surveys, a higher proportion of those who define themselves as unemployed than of those who say that they have a job report that they have supplementary employment. These people are not captured by those surveys, such as Goskomstat's Labour Force Survey or RLMS, which only ask people who have already reported that they have some paid employment about any supplementary employment. The researchers of the Institute of Population of the Russian Academy of Sciences have proposed using the concept of 'multiple employment', rather than the value-laden concept of secondary employment (ISEPN RAN, 1998), but this approach annihilates the distinction that is very real to respondents between a 'real job' and 'supplementary work'. In the ISITO surveys, as in those of VTsIOM, we have asked all respondents about additional employment.

For the purposes of the discussion in this chapter we are interested in secondary employment as an additional source of money income, as opposed to the use of household labour for subsistence agricultural production that will be considered in the next chapter. We therefore define secondary employment as any form of employment, apart from an individual's primary occupation, which yields a money income. We regard as secondary (supplementary – we will use the terms

---

[1]   All Russian citizens still possess a labour book, which is deposited in an enterprise or organisation that is thereby defined as their principal place of work, even if they never actually go there. This is where their length of service, which qualifies them for pension and other social benefits, is recorded. When Russians are asked about their main job they will normally understand by this the place of work at which they are formally registered in this sense. Secondary or additional employment is then understood in relation to this main job, even if it actually takes up more time and brings in more money than the main job.

[2]   In the ISITO household survey 1 percent of the adult respondents who said that they did not have a job had in fact been working full-time in the previous month in what they defined as supplementary work and about 90 percent of these were in unregistered employment.

interchangeably) employment, not only the second jobs of those in work, but also the reported employment of those who consider themselves to be unemployed, on leave, retired or engaged in domestic labour as their primary occupation. In the Russian case we have to qualify the definition to include those cases in which the money income is in fact paid in kind, is paid only with a delay or may even remain unpaid indefinitely. This definition does not include additional income earned through working overtime in the primary job, although the second job may be for the same employer and at the same place of work as is the primary job.[3] We include all forms of 'self-employment' within the definition of secondary employment, as well as waged employment at an enterprise or for a private individual.

Secondary work is usually undertaken outside the normal working hours of the primary job, although sometimes it is possible to receive additional earnings for work done during normal working hours, whether by taking on two jobs simultaneously or by working on the side in the normal place of work, often using the equipment, parts and materials provided by the employer (*kalym*).[4] Those engaged in secondary employment may have their employment formally registered, either in the traditional form as a registered second job, *po sovmestitel'stvu*, or according to a labour contract or agreement, or their employment may be unregistered and off the books. Self-employment may equally be formalised, with the individual normally being registered as an 'entrepreneur without juridical status',[5] but it is more commonly informal and unregistered. The principal significance of registration is that the employer pays social insurance dues and the

[3] Paid (legal) overtime is still much less common in Russia than in capitalist countries, and to some extent second jobs can be seen as a substitute for overtime working: in some cases a person is employed in a second job to do exactly the same as in the first one. This enables the employer to evade the legal limitation of the working day and to avoid the obligation to pay the legally prescribed premia for overtime working. In the new Labour Code, which came into effect in February 2002, overtime working is defined as additional work undertaken on the initiative of the employer and must be paid at increased rates. Work as internal *sovmestitel'* is work undertaken on the initiative of the employee and separately contracted and imposes no obligation for payment at a higher rate.

[4] Theft from the workplace is endemic in Russia and the sale or use of such stolen materials can be the basis of secondary economic activity and an important source of household income.

[5] An 'entrepreneur without juridical status' might in fact work for an individual or enterprise on a contractual basis, in which case what is in reality a wage relation appears in the form of self-employment, the employee avoiding tax and the employer avoiding social insurance dues. Until 2002 those working on a labour contract were not protected by the provisions of the Labour Code.

employment is included within the systems of state taxation and statistical reporting.

The definitions of secondary employment used in the various data sources vary from one to another, the differences being expressed in the different wording of the questions asked. The way in which primary employment is defined affects the measures of secondary employment (see ISEPN RAN, 1998, pp. 128–33 for a comparison and reconciliation of the different data sources). There have also been some changes in the wording of the questions over time. The Goskomstat Labour Force Survey of all adults between the ages of 15 and 72 has sought to capture as 'employed' all those with any source of labour income, so that only those with more than one source of income will be considered to be in secondary employment. Respondents are first asked if they have done any kind of work or had any kind of employment or self-employment, paid in money or in kind, even if for only one hour, or unpaid work in a family enterprise or been on leave from a paid job in the week prior to the survey.[6] Those who reply that they have had such employment are later asked whether they have had any other paid work or employment (including the provision of services) or worked unpaid in a family enterprise in the previous week. In the ISITO supplement to the 1997 Labour Force Survey in Kemerovo oblast and the Komi Republic we repeated this question to those who had said that they did not have any work, finding that the incidence among these people was as high as among those who said that they did have employment.

In the first phase of the RLMS surveys (1992–94), respondents who had said that they 'now work at some enterprise, organisation, firm, collective farm, state farm or co-operative, or firm' were later asked if they 'work *additionally* in some enterprise (some organisation) that pays you wages'. In addition, all adult respondents were asked if they engaged in any kind of 'individual economic activity', examples offered being as a private driver or tailor, agricultural activity, hunting or fishing for sale. In the second phase (1994–2000), respondents'

6    Until 1997 respondents were also asked whether they had been engaged in any kind of agricultural activity, hunting, fishing, or gathering mushrooms or berries with the aim of selling some of the produce. As a result of the findings of the ISITO supplement to the 1997 Labour Force Survey, Goskomstat changed the wording of its principal question to include reference to 'any kind of supplementary earnings' from 1998 to try to catch all those with any form of employment, although this rewording appears to have had no significant effect on the reported levels of primary and secondary employment. Since 1999 all respondents have also been asked about the domestic production of goods and services.

primary employment status was defined by asking them baldly if they now worked, were on paid or unpaid leave, or did not now work. Those working or on leave (including maternity leave) were later simply asked if they had 'some other kind of work' and whether they had been engaged in this in the past 30 days, and all respondents were asked if they were involved in 'individual economic activity', examples of which now did not include agricultural activity, but did include, in addition to driving and sewing, helping others with apartment or car repairs, purchasing or delivering food or looking after a sick person, or 'something else that you were paid for'. In 1998, all respondents were also asked if they had found supplementary work in the previous year as a means of responding to economic difficulties and in 2000 if they had worked an extra job in the course of the previous twelve months.[7]

VTsIOM starts by simply asking people who say that they are 'working now' about their 'main' job, before asking all respondents whether they had had any other kind of work or occupation, apart from their main occupation, bringing in additional income in the previous month. In fact, many people say that they do not work but go on to say that they do have additional employment. In principle, this would be a primary job on the Goskomstat survey and a secondary job on the VTsIOM survey. In recent years VTsIOM's respondents have usually been offered the alternatives of having regular additional employment or of having irregular additional earnings, this form of the question eliciting a substantially higher positive response.

In the ISITO work history survey of industrial employees, we simply asked respondents if they had any kind of regular or periodic supplementary earnings and whether they had such earnings currently and in the previous year. In the ISITO household survey we asked all adult respondents if they had had any kind of (additional) paid work or employment, excluding work on their garden plots, in the previous 12 months, whether this work was permanent, regular or 'from time to time' and whether they had had such supplementary employment in the previous month.

---

[7]   In 1998, 5 percent of those not working said that they had found supplementary work in the previous year and in 2000 7 percent of those not working said that they had worked an extra job during the previous year, suggesting that, like Goskomstat, RLMS misses a lot of secondary employment by not questioning further those who initially say they are not working.

## SCALE OF SECONDARY EMPLOYMENT

Although frowned on, secondary employment was widespread in the Soviet period, and was often the only way in which workers could be found to do the less desirable jobs or householders could get repairs done and personal services provided.[8] About 2 percent of the working population did additional work as an officially registered supplementary job (*po sovmestitel'stvu*) in 1982, either during their vacations or after hours, and by 1987, when the legal framework was more favourable, this had more than doubled, with 4.7 million people working on this basis in the Soviet Union. These figures were roughly in line with rates of secondary employment in the USA (5 percent) and the EU (2–3 percent) (Khibovskaya, 1995).

In addition to registered supplementary jobs, there was certainly a great deal of unregistered (and, until 1987, illegal) secondary employment in the Soviet Union, but there are no accurate estimates of its extent. In the ISITO work history interviews with industrial employees, we found very few who had had additional earnings in the Soviet period. When the researchers asked them why, many reacted with bewilderment: work at the factory gave decent earnings and they were fully occupied. The underlying sentiment was generally that 'in the past there was not enough time and there was enough money': the problem in the Soviet period was not so much the inadequacy of money income as the shortage of goods to buy.

There is considerable disagreement about the scale of secondary employment in post-Soviet Russia. The Federal Employment Service estimated in the middle of 1994 that about 11 percent of the working population was involved in secondary employment. According to the estimates of the Russian Tax Inspectorate, 35–40 percent of the adult population have second jobs (Simagin, 1998). According to a Presidential representative, addressing the State Duma on the theme in 1998, 90 percent of Russian citizens have second jobs (cited Varshavskaya and Donova, 1999). However, these estimates are purely speculative.

One source of harder data is the statistical reporting of enterprises and organisations, which report the contractual status of their employees to Goskomstat. This provides data on the number of people

---

[8]     Shlapentokh estimated that, in the Soviet period, half of all shoe repairs, 40 percent of apartment repairs and 30 percent of all electrical appliance repairs were carried out by the 'private sector' (Shlapentokh, 1989, p. 191).

officially registered as being employed *po sovmestitel'stvu* and on the number employed on the basis of a civil code contract or agreement to carry out a particular piece of work, in addition to the number registered as regular (usually full-time) employees. This data will underestimate the extent of secondary employment to the extent that the latter is unregistered and unreported (although Goskomstat makes estimates for non- and under-reporting on the basis of its own sample surveys and data from sources such as the tax inspectorate). On the other hand, many of those employed on this basis will not be engaged in secondary employment since employment *po sovmestitel'stvu* is nowadays a typical way in which people are employed part-time, while contracting is a typical way of formalising a short-term employment relationship and/or avoiding payroll and income taxes. With those reservations, from this data it was estimated by Goskomstat that 2 percent of the working population did secondary work on the traditional basis in 1994 (Vychislitel'nyi tsentr, 1994). In May 1998, 2.1 percent of those employed in medium and large enterprises were reported to be working as external *sovmestitel'i* and 1.8 percent were working on civil code contracts, a total of 1.8 million people out of a working population of around 58 million (Goskomstat, 1998c).[9] In 2000, 8.1 percent of those employed in small businesses were reported to be working as *sovmestitel'i* and 5.3 percent were working on civil code contracts, a further 1.0 million people (Goskomstat, 2001). However, it is not possible to determine what proportion of these people were engaged in secondary employment and how many of them were working on this basis in a primary job (Goskomstat estimates that this is a second job for 70–80 percent of these people (Goskomstat, 1996a), which would indicate an incidence of these forms of secondary employment of about 4 percent).

Sample surveys provide the only comprehensive sources of data on secondary employment. Goskomstat has published the findings of the Labour Force Survey on secondary employment since 1996, but this data shows an extremely low incidence of multiple job holding, with substantially more people seeking additional work than currently have second jobs (Table 2.1). A further 4.8 percent of the labour force in 1999 and 4.6 percent in 2000 (mostly in rural districts) was involved in domestic agricultural production for sale (in whole or in part) and 0.1

---

[9]   In 1994 Goskomstat estimated that large and medium enterprises, which account for 80 percent of primary employment, account for less than 50 percent of secondary employment (Popov, 1995, p. 28).

percent in both years was involved in the domestic production of other goods and services for sale, an approximately equal number of people without other jobs also being involved in these activities (Goskomstat, 2000g).

*Table 2.1:    Incidence of secondary employment and desire for additional work (adults, 18–72; Labour Force Survey data, 1996–2000).*

| Percentage of labour force | Have second jobs | | | Looking for more work | | |
|---|---|---|---|---|---|---|
| | Total | Men | Women | Total | Men | Women |
| March 1996 | 1.30 | 1.25 | 1.34 | 2.49 | 4.73 | 2.26 |
| October 1997 | 1.18 | 1.23 | 1.13 | 5.05 | 9.62 | 4.59 |
| October 1998 | 1.11 | 1.04 | 1.18 | 5.26 | 9.99 | 4.87 |
| Average 1999 | 2.21 | 2.25 | 2.16 | 7.23 | 7.68 | 6.73 |
| Average 2000 | 1.80 | 1.80 | 1.80 | 5.76 | 6.02 | 5.45 |

*Source: Goskomstat, 2000c, 2000g. The figures refer to the survey week for 1996–98 and the previous month from 1999.*

Goskomstat's specialists have difficulty in understanding why the Labour Force Survey yields such a low figure for secondary employment and have frequently modified their questions, making comparison of the data over time impossible. Part of the reason was that much secondary employment is episodic and until 1999 the Labour Force Survey question referred only to the week prior to the survey, while other surveys refer at least to the previous month, but even the addition of a question referring to the previous month has not increased the reported incidence substantially (in 2000 1.3 percent had had second jobs in the previous week and a further 0.5 percent in the previous month). It may be that there is a greater reluctance on the part of respondents to admit to a representative of an official body that they have secondary employment which may not be declared to the tax authorities, a supposition supported by the fact that the Labour Force Survey finds many fewer people working in typically unregistered forms of employment (casual employment or self-employment) than do other surveys.

In the Supplement that ISITO attached to the Labour Force Survey in Kemerovo and Komi in October 1997 we were able to probe a bit more deeply into the secondary employment of the respondents. We found that as many of those without a primary job had supplementary employment as did those with a primary job, 1.8 percent of the adult population of those regions having such work, and twice as many people said that they had had additional work in the course of the year, although only 10 percent of those who had worked in the previous week said that they did so on a permanent basis, 16 percent did it periodically and 74 percent only episodically.

*Table 2.2:* Incidence of secondary employment and individual economic activity by employment status (RLMS data, 1992–2000).

| Percentage of respondents in each category | Working | | Maternity leave | | Paid leave | | Unpaid leave | | Does not work |
|---|---|---|---|---|---|---|---|---|---|
| | Sec (last month) | IEA | Sec | IEA | Sec | IEA | Sec | IEA | IEA |
| July–October 1992 | 3.4 | 2.1 | | | | | | | 2.8 |
| December 1992–March 1993 | 3.6 | 1.4 | | | | | | | 2.9 |
| July–October 1993 | 3.6 | 1.6 | | | | | | | 3.0 |
| October 1993–January 1994 | 3.2 | 1.5 | | | | | | | 2.7 |
| October 1994 | 4.7 (4.2) | 7.7 | 4.7 | – | 1.8 | 9.1 | 2.4 | 14.6 | 7.1 |
| October 1995 | 4.1 (3.8) | 5.4 | 3.9 | 4.6 | 2.5 | 2.5 | 14.3 | 14.3 | 8.0 |
| October 1996 | 4.3 (4.0) | 5.8 | 1.5 | 2.8 | 2.4 | 7.3 | 5.4 | 10.8 | 6.9 |
| October 1998–January 1999 | 4.6 (4.1) | 5.7 | 0.9 | – | 11.1 | 7.4 | 13.2 | 13.2 | 8.2 |
| September–December 2000 | 5.0 (4.5) | 6.0 | 3.4 | 3.4 | 10.8 | 10.8 | 7.7 | 23.1 | 11.0 |

The RLMS surveys, like those of Goskomstat, only ask those who say that they are now working if they also have 'some other kind of work', although they do not restrict the question to the previous week (since 1994 respondents have been asked if they have other work and then if they have engaged in it in the previous month) and all respondents are also asked about any 'individual economic activity' in the previous month. Although the form of the questions makes it difficult to interpret this data, it has the advantage of being a panel survey so that we can, at least in principle, identify changes in and determinants of the extent, forms and incidence of secondary employment in individual biographies. This data (Table 2.2) show that around four percent of people in work reported having second jobs, but in the second phase of the survey, with a reworded question, substantially more people admitted to being involved in individual economic activity, particularly if they were on paid or unpaid leave (not much can be read into the precise figures, since the numbers are rather small, with around 200 of the 7000 adult respondents on leave in each round, and the wording of the questions changed between the two phases of the survey). In total around 8–10 percent of adults were reported to have had some form of supplementary employment in each of the surveys over the period 1994–2000, many more than are reported by Goskomstat. Just over half of those involved in individual economic activity had no other paid work.

In 1998 RLMS, 7 percent of all respondents said that they had found supplementary work in the previous year.[10] Just over a third of these respondents had said that they did not have a primary job, and so had not been asked if they had had supplementary work in the previous month, suggesting that, like the Labour Force Survey, RLMS misses a substantial number of those who have some employment but do not consider it to be their main job. In total, just over 10 percent of those in work reported that they had had secondary employment in the previous month or had found supplementary work in the previous year.

In 2000, 9 percent of all RLMS respondents said that they had worked an extra job in the previous 12 months, 40 percent of whom

---

[10]  The question did not make clear whether it referred to having undertaken *any* supplementary work or having found *new* supplementary work in the previous year. Seventeen percent of those who reported supplementary work in the previous month said that they had not found supplementary employment in the previous year. Just over a quarter of the respondents who said that they had found supplementary work in the previous year and had also been in the previous round of the survey had also reported secondary employment in 1996.

had said that they did not have a primary job. Eleven percent of those who had reported primary employment reported that they had undertaken supplementary work either in the previous month or in the previous year. Respondents were also asked if they had engaged in a series of individual economic activities in the previous year (selling home produced goods; selling, trading or importing other goods; performing various services for pay) and 7 percent reported that they had done one or another of these, a further four percent of urban households and 22 percent of rural households reporting that they had grown crops or raised livestock for sale. In total, excluding agricultural production for sale, 18 percent of all respondents reported some kind of secondary activity either the previous month or during the past year.

The RLMS is a panel survey, mostly returning to the same people each time, enabling us to examine the stability of secondary employment. Only about a quarter of those involved in individual economic activity in any one round and a third of those with a second job reported that they had such activity in the subsequent round of the survey, so that only five of almost 5000 respondents who were in every round of the second phase of the survey, from 1994 to 2000, had a second job in every round and only seven were involved in individual economic activity in every round.[11] Moreover, more than half of those who were engaged in secondary employment in successive rounds seem to have changed their occupation between rounds, so that only three people had the same secondary occupation through 1994 to 1998, all three having the same occupation in 2000.[12] Those who gave up their second jobs had not been conspicuously less committed to secondary employment: between 1994 and 1996 they had worked significantly longer hours and earned significantly more in

[11] The turnover is more or less the same between 1996 and 1998 and between 1998 and 2000 as over the single years that span previous rounds, and indeed is more or less the same when we compare any two rounds. Thus the turnover is more likely a reflection of the occasional character of much secondary employment, rather than of permanent movements into and out of the secondary labour market. Respondents are only asked about their individual economic activity in the previous 30 days, so those who work irregularly (three-quarters of respondents say that their IEA is only incidental work) may report one year but not the next. As noted above, in 1998 and 2000 about twice as many reported activity in the previous year as in the previous month. Fewer than a quarter of respondents who were in every round ever reported any secondary employment, the majority on only one occasion.

[12] It is difficult to know how much of these reported changes of occupation reflect instability of employment and how much is instability of response or coding. There is quite a lot of inconsistency between rounds of RLMS, as is not unusual with panel data.

the previous year than those who maintained their secondary employment, and in 1996 and 1998 there was no difference in earnings or hours between those who subsequently kept up their second jobs and those who did not. This all suggests the conclusion that secondary employment tends to be episodic and unstable rather than providing a regular activity and steady source of income.

*Table 2.3: Scale of secondary employment, 1993–97 (annual averages of published VTsIOM data).*

|                  | 1993 | 1994 | 1995 | 1996 | 1997 | 1998 | 1999 | 2000 |
|------------------|------|------|------|------|------|------|------|------|
| Yes              | 12.5 | 15.0 | 16.7 | 15.6 | 13.8 | 12.1 |      |      |
| No               | 87.5 | 85.0 | 83.3 | 84.4 | 86.2 | 87.9 |      |      |
| Yes, regular     | 7.0  | 5.8  | 5.1  | 5.0  | 3.9  | 2.3  | 2.5  | 3.7  |
| Yes, occasional  | 13.0 | 12.2 | 12.2 | 11.4 | 10.8 | 8.0  | 9.8  | 9.6  |
| No               | 80.0 | 82.0 | 82.6 | 83.6 | 85.2 | 89.6 | 87.7 | 86.7 |

*Source: Bi-monthly issues of VTsIOM Bulletin,* Ekonomicheskie i sotsial'nye peremeny: monitoring obshchestvennogo mneniya *and Perova, 1999. 2000 data relates to May, September and November surveys only. The first two rows report responses to a bald 'yes or no' question, the subsequent three rows report responses to the question with three alternatives.*

VTsIOM has regularly asked all of its respondents, aged 16 and over, whether they had additional work in the previous month.[13] There are some problems with interpreting the VTsIOM data. On the one hand, the quality of the VTsIOM data is not consistent and the application of weights to correct for the socio-demographic bias of the achieved sample has a significant impact on the results (unless otherwise stated, weighted data is hereafter used for tabulations, using VTsIOM's weights, and unweighted data for regressions). On the other hand, a bald question asking people whether or not they have had any other job, in addition to their main occupation, in the previous month elicits a lower positive response than if respondents are offered the possibility of having engaged in either regular or occasional supplementary work, which has been the more common form of the question in recent years.[14] The annual averages in response to the two

[13]   I am very grateful to VTsIOM for making the relevant data for the period March 1993 to May 1998 available to me. Unless otherwise stated, reported findings relate to this data set.
[14]   When asked elsewhere in the questionnaire whether they or members of their family have taken any steps to improve their material position, a consistently higher proportion say that they have additional sources of income (Maleva, 1998, n. 6, p. 38).

questions are summarised in Table 2.3. This data suggests that there was a small but statistically significant increasing trend in the incidence of secondary employment between 1993 and 1995, with a significant decline between 1996 and 1998,[15] although the RLMS data shows no trend in the incidence of secondary employment over time.

A survey conducted for the Ministry of Labour by the Institute of Population of the Russian Academy of Sciences in 1997 found a rather higher incidence of secondary employment than have the VTsIOM surveys, partly because they proposed replacing the concept of 'secondary employment' with the concept of 'multiple employment', but also because they did not confine their attention to the previous month. This survey found that 51 percent of those who worked had only one job, 32 percent had two jobs, 14 percent had three jobs and 3 percent had four or five jobs (ISEPN RAN, 1998, p. 124).

The data considered so far derives from All-Russian samples. The national survey data suggests that the incidence and role of secondary employment is greater in the large cities that should be the motor of development of the market economy. The ISITO surveys have all been conducted in such cities, which gives the results more than purely illustrative significance. Although the ISITO surveys can only claim to be representative of the population of the cities in which they have been carried out, for analytical purposes there are advantages to having a more homogeneous sample and, as we will see, the findings of these surveys are not dramatically different from those of the national surveys and in some respects serve to supplement the latter.

Thirteen percent of respondents in the 1997 ISITO work history survey of industrial employees currently had secondary employment and 30 percent had had secondary employment in the course of the previous year, exactly the same as Khibovskaya's estimate, on the basis of the VTsIOM data for the whole adult population, that around 30 percent of the Russian population were engaged in some kind of secondary employment at some point during the year (Khibovskaya, 1996).[16] Nine percent of respondents said that they had at some time

---

[15]  The tax authorities waged quite an aggressive campaign in 1998 to encourage citizens to register their secondary employment for tax purposes and this might have discouraged respondents from confessing that they had such employment.

[16]  It appears from this sample that the secondary employment of industrial workers is much more stable than is suggested by the RLMS data. Ninety-five percent of those engaged in secondary employment at the time of the survey in April 1997 had also been involved during 1996, while 80 percent of those not engaged at the time of the survey had not been involved the previous year either, and almost 50 percent had never been involved in secondary employment.

had regular additional earnings and a further 43 percent said that they had been involved periodically, although almost half of these people reported no involvement in the previous year.

In the ISITO household survey, 18 percent of people in jobs said that they had had some kind of additional paid employment in the previous 12 months – rather fewer in Lyubertsy on the edge of Moscow – and half of the people who had engaged in secondary employment in the previous year had also been active the previous month (Table 2.4). As in the other surveys, a substantial proportion of 'non-working' adults, particularly of those who reported that they were 'unemployed', also reported that they had 'additional' work. In this survey, over a third of the registered unemployed and over 40 percent of those receiving unemployment benefit reported having had supplementary employment in the previous month.[17] Almost 60 percent of people had had only one second job in the previous 12 months, but 15 percent reported having had five or more (in some cases this would probably be the same type of work for different clients).

*Table 2.4:    Percentage engaged in secondary employment by employment status ( ISITO household survey, May 1998).*

|  | Working | Non-working adult | Non-working pensioner | All adults |
|---|---|---|---|---|
| Worked in second job last year, of whom: | 17.7 | 33.0 | 4.4 | 16.5 |
| Work permanently | 4.5 | 4.2 | 0.7 | 3.5 |
| Work regularly (periodically) | 2.6 | 4.4 | 0.8 | 2.4 |
| Work episodically | 10.5 | 24.1 | 2.9 | 10.4 |
| Worked last month | 9.6 | 12.5 | 2.7 | 9.5 |
| N | 5 028 | 1 053 | 1 913 | 7 994 |

These figures correspond quite closely to those found by the VTsIOM surveys, despite the fact that the sampling frame is very

---

[17]    An April 1994 survey conducted by VTsIOM for the EDI of the World Bank of 316 respondents from the normal VTsIOM sample who were unemployed, working short time or on administrative leave found that 19 percent of these worked an average of 22.5 hours in 'second' jobs, working predominantly in self-employment (49 percent) or the private sector (23 percent) (Yemtsov, 1994).

different. RLMS and VTsIOM data suggest that the incidence of secondary employment is not very different across different types of urban population centre, although it is significantly higher in Moscow and Saint Petersburg and lower in the countryside. The VTsIOM figures for inhabitants of large cities (over half a million population) indicate that around 6 percent had regular secondary employment and around 12 percent irregular secondary employment during 1997–98 (my calculation from VTsIOM data).

It is very likely that this is an underestimate of the extent of secondary employment in the population. the ISITO interviewers reported that some people were reluctant to allow the interviewer to record that they had second jobs, particularly because the ISITO survey was at the end of the tax year when all those with such jobs are supposed to fill in declarations.[18] We also asked household heads whether the household had any income from secondary employment, and while two-thirds reported that it did not, 11 percent of the heads of households in which no individuals had reported any secondary income said that such earnings were an important part of household income.[19] Moreover, in 8 percent of households in which the head had said that there was no secondary income, at least one household member reported secondary earnings. The implication is that 38 percent of households had at least one member who had some income from secondary employment. This would imply that the incidence of secondary employment at individual level might be as much as twice that which is reported here. Nevertheless, this would still mean that 85 percent of the adult population – 80 percent of the population of working age – does not have regular secondary employment while almost half of all households are not involved in secondary employment at all.

The consensus that emerges from a review of the survey data is that

[18] According to our interviewers, the reluctance of respondents was to recording specific details of secondary employment. The interviewers did not report any reluctance of household heads to acknowledge the fact of secondary employment in more general terms. Nor is there any particular reason to doubt the responses on income from secondary employment given by those who had admitted the fact of secondary employment (or the 1 percent of cases who reported income from secondary employment immediately after saying that they did not have any such employment).

[19] These households had significantly higher household incomes net of secondary earnings and had significantly higher household expenditure relative to the declared income of household members than other households, suggesting that they were more likely to have undeclared income. The coefficient on a dummy variable inserted into our regressions to mark these households is negative, as we would expect, but is not statistically significant.

around 5 percent of the adult population works regularly in supplementary employment, with around twice as many people involved in occasional secondary employment in any one month. This figure is in line with levels reported for the United States (5–6 percent) and the EU (3 percent), and for other transition countries in the first half of the 1990s: in Hungary 2.5 percent had additional forms of employment, in the Czech Republic 4.5 percent and in Poland 8.5 percent (Klopov, 1996). Even if this estimate were doubled, as the ISITO survey data suggests it might be, it would not approach some of the wilder estimates put forward.

The incidence of supplementary employment among the non-working population appears to be about the same as that among the working population. Some of this work is regular employment or self-employment which is not reported as a primary job by respondents because it is unregistered or because it is only part-time.

Secondary employment tends to be unstable and irregular. Moreover, the fact that the Labour Force Survey data suggests that about three times as many people would like to work longer hours than in fact have supplementary employment suggests that additional work is not so easy to find, so that the possibilities of secondary employment are constrained by the availability of such work. This means that a substantial proportion of the adult population may engage in some kind of supplementary economic activity at some time or another but that relatively few households can rely on supplementary earnings to sustain the household budget consistently. The evidence suggests that around a third of urban households have some income from secondary employment, but at least half the adult population has never had a second job.

## KINDS OF SECONDARY EMPLOYMENT

Secondary employment is quite a heterogeneous phenomenon, ranging from a formally registered regular second job to occasional street trading, casual labour or home-working. In this section we will look at the main types of secondary employment that we have identified on the basis of our qualitative research and work-history interviews, most of which were conducted during our research on employees of state and former state industrial enterprises and small businesses in the new private sector during the second half of the 1990s, starting with the formalised secondary employment inherited from the Soviet period.

## Formalised Supplementary Work (*po sovmestitel'stvu*).

According to the VTsIOM data, about forty percent of all secondary employment of those with a primary job is formally registered as such, *po sovmestitel'stvu*, divided about equally between internal and external *sovmestitel'i*, depending on whether the second job is in the same or a different enterprise from the first. This is very close to the findings of the ISITO household survey, in which around a quarter of all secondary employment of those with a primary job was as internal *sovmestitel'* and about 20 percent as external *sovmestitel'*.

This was the traditional kind of formalised secondary employment that had developed from the end of the 1920s and was always quite widespread in the Soviet period, even after a 1959 Council of Ministers' resolution restricting it. It arose as a result of the chronic labour shortage, which meant that enterprises and organisations were not able to fill all their vacancies, and from the Soviet (dis)organisation of production, which meant that there were many jobs which had to be fulfilled but which did not make heavy demands (for example, foremen of small production sections, time- and record-keepers, office managers and other office employees, maintenance workers). Such jobs were always filled by internal *sovmestitel'i*, that is, workers of the same enterprise who would officially take on the job in addition to their own, either during normal working hours or at the end of the working day or on days off, depending on the character of the job. In industry it was usually the line managers and specialists and sometimes office workers who took on these jobs. In the public services, secondary employment *po sovmestitel'stvu* has always been particularly widespread in education, compensating for labour shortages and allowing the low-paid to supplement their incomes.

There are also traditional low-skilled jobs which can either easily be divided up or which do not involve much work (cleaner, caretaker, security guard and so on), providing a basis for part-time employment. People from all occupational groups, except for managers and skilled specialists, have always done this kind of work. Enterprises either gave this work to their own employees, or took people from outside who were willing to do the jobs for low pay.

This kind of work was not usually well-paid, traditionally being paid at only half the scale rate, but it is convenient because it can easily be fitted around normal working hours and it is usually stable and secure. It is therefore especially attractive for those who could not otherwise undertake supplementary employment or those, such as the elderly or disabled or those with caring responsibilities, who are unable to undertake full-time work. This is probably why, compared to other forms of secondary employment, women are twice as likely as men to work as internal *sovmestitel'i* and the low-paid and over 50s are substantially more likely than the better-paid and younger age groups to do so (VTsIOM data).[20] According to the ISITO household survey data, managers are much more likely to have such positions, while professionals, unskilled workers and lower white-collar workers are much less likely to work as *sovmestitel'i*.

According to the industrial workers in the ISITO work history interviews this kind of additional work does not provide a substantial addition to their wages, increasing them by not more than 30–50 percent. However, in their opinion, the advantage of this kind of additional work is the fact that it provides a regular and relatively stable source of additional earnings.

> I have an additional job as a section foreman on 0.3 of a full salary. The section is small, but if there is to be such a production unit there has to be a foreman, somebody has to be responsible for health and safety (senior foreman, plastics factory).

> I have an additional job as a polisher in my own shop. It is organised officially as *sovmestitel'*. There is not enough work for a whole person, but there is some work all the same – so I do it (foreman, engineering factory)

It might be expected that this kind of additional work would be in decline as the conditions that gave rise to it have disappeared. On the one hand, employers do not face a labour shortage and are no longer constrained by the bureaucratic regulation of staffing levels, although health, education and public services have problems filling jobs because of the low wages. On the other hand, there are many more and better-paid opportunities for secondary employment elsewhere. There has been a tendency in industrial enterprises for many of these jobs to have been either liquidated or turned into the principal jobs for workers who have moved into them as a result of staff reductions.

> Earlier I earned extra as a technician – I washed the floors in the entrances… And I would continue to do it today, but in the housing administration they say: 'we need full-time technicians' (female operative, plastics factory).

[20]  To compare the different types of secondary employment a series of logistic regressions was run, with the probability of undertaking that particular form of secondary employment, against all other forms, as the dependent variable. Those differences reported in the text are statistically significant, controlling for other relevant factors, at least at the 95 percent level.

However, there has been a counter-tendency to expand this form of secondary employment as a means of holding on to valued workers in impoverished state and former state enterprises by giving them an additional source of income, and according to the VTsIOM data the incidence of this form of secondary employment has been increasing over time. Sometimes supplementary work is imposed on the workers by the shop management.

> Once a week I clean the mixing chambers, this is an extra two hours' work. The work is rather heavy, but it does not take a lot of time, and it adds 200 thousand roubles [$35 at that time] to my salary for the month. The addition is insignificant, the chief of shop asked me and I could not refuse, it is not difficult for me (woman worker, chocolate factory).

Fear for their jobs and the increased dependence of workers on middle management forces them to take on such undesirable additional work.

In the ISITO data, internal *sovmestitel'* is much less likely to be the form of secondary employment chosen by, or offered to, those working in privatised enterprises or the new private sector, and is most common among those working in public services. Those who earn relatively high wages are much less likely to work as *sovmestitel'*, probably because it does not pay well enough, but it is also much less commonly found in enterprises which pay below average wages and among those workers who have had a spell of administrative leave. In the least successful enterprises we would expect people to look for their additional work somewhere else, where they would expect to be better paid and might have a better prospect of actually receiving the money earned. In the ISITO and VTsIOM data this form of secondary employment pays less than other forms, but the difference is not large enough to be statistically significant. In both sets of data, those undertaking this kind of secondary employment also work on average fewer hours, and so their total supplementary earnings are rather less than those of other forms of secondary employment, boosting their pay packet on average by just over half.

It is as common to work *po sovmestitel'stvu* at another enterprise as at one's primary place of work. This is not surprising, since many of those undertaking this form of secondary employment are trying to compensate for low or unpaid wages in their primary place of work and so are more likely to get better earnings elsewhere. Quite often people will find second jobs in small enterprises which lease their premises from the enterprise in which they have their main job, access to a skilled labour force often being one reason for small enterprises choosing to locate on the territory of a particular traditional enterprise. However, the self-employed are also significantly more likely to choose this over other forms of secondary employment, presumably because it enables them to secure themselves a stable source of income. According to the VTsIOM data, working as an external *sovmestitel'* is a favoured form of secondary employment for those in their 40s, but unmarried men and skilled workers are less likely to choose this form of secondary employment, all of which reinforces the conclusion that this is attractive for those who want a relatively stable form of secondary employment. Those working as external *sovmestitel'* earn more in total than those working as internal *sovmestitel'*, but mainly because they tend to work longer hours, boosting their basic pay by about three-quarters.

## Kalym

*Kalym* (literally 'bride-price') is the word used by most of the ISITO respondents to describe additional work which is done at their own enterprise during normal working hours, often using the factory's equipment, parts and raw materials. In this case the ability to make supplementary earnings is conditional on formal employment in the enterprise. Although *kalym* usually involves the theft of the enterprise's resources, it has traditionally been regarded as the entitlement of the worker, its forms and extent regulated by well-established informal norms, although it can amount to large-scale theft when it is linked to the involvement of outside criminal organisations. According to the results of the ISITO surveys this kind of secondary employment is quite rare, accounting for only 5 percent of cases in the ISITO work history survey (those who reported that they 'had worked in their normal place of work, during working hours (*kalym*)') and around 8 percent of secondary work of those in employment in the ISITO household survey,[21] although this is probably an underestimate since respondents are not always completely frank in answering about this kind of work on the side, so we can guess that *kalym* is rather more widespread than this (and certainly outright theft from the workplace is ubiquitous). *Kalym* was extensive in a large automobile

[21] This is the number of those reporting that they had 'provided services or produced commodities, using the possibilities of my enterprise'. Some of these people might have been working on officially formalised contracts.

factory in which we conducted a case study, where it was integrated into criminal networks, which made respondents (particularly the line managers who organised the work) very reluctant to discuss it with outsiders.

*Kalym* usually involves fulfilling orders for various kinds of standard items in regular demand (from bolts, nails, angles and other 'trifles' to garage gates, coffins, metal doors and gratings). Our observations suggest that the possibilities of doing this kind of supplementary work are the greatest for workers in the auxiliary shops (repair, tool-making, transport and so on).

> From a researcher's field notes: 'Manufacturing of everyday necessities during working hours using factory materials is a fairly widespread phenomenon among the adjusters, fitters and other workers who have spare time during the working day. There was even a certain specialisation: in one shop they make knives, drills with attachments, in another shop – piano hinges, in a third – taps and rubber seals for them, in the joiner's shop – laths, beads, wooden items; in the watch-producing department they repair watches.'

*Kalym,* more than any other form of self-employment, is predominantly a man's kind of activity. It does not necessarily only involve the individual doing the work. Quite often the foreman (or other line managers) will share in the income for the fact that 'they do not see more than they should'. In some cases *kalym* takes on a semi-formalised status, similar to working on contract, as foremen or line managers make informal agreements to supply more substantial pieces of work for cash payment, which is distributed among all those involved in the work. Such work is sometimes for outside customers, but in some cases it is for other sections of the same enterprise. This practice became quite common in enterprises which did not have the money to pay wages for regular work, since it made it possible to hang on to skilled workers by providing them with work which could be paid in cash. When it is well-organised, *kalym* can provide a very substantial income.

The equivalent of *kalym* for professionals and white-collar workers is the use of their employers' facilities, such as computers and telephones, to enable them to carry out consultancy work, to do some typing or even to organise their own business on the side, often doing such work at their desks during normal working hours. Medical personnel frequently use the facilities of their polyclinic or hospital to provide private medical services.

The rural equivalent of *kalym* is the use by agricultural workers of land, fodder and agricultural machinery owned by a state or collective farm to raise their own stock or grow their own crops. This is how rural domestic producers are able to produce half the meat, wool and milk produced by the whole agricultural sector on only 2 percent of the total area under pasture (Goskomstat, 2000e). According to the Labour Force Survey, 18–19 percent of the employed rural population work on their own account to produce agricultural products for sale (Goskomstat, 2000g).

### Work on short-term labour contracts (agreements)

Work on labour agreements is a form of subcontracting in which the individual is employed to carry out a particular piece of work. In the past this was traditionally used to employ people on temporary or seasonal jobs, particularly in agriculture, the construction industry, leisure and tourism, but nowadays it has been extended to a wide range of professional and commercial services. As against work *po sovmestitel'stvu*, which assumes the fairly constant and long-term additional employment of the worker, work on labour contracts is in most cases a short-term form of secondary employment, usually limited to the time required for the fulfilment of a certain order (or volume of work), which is especially attractive to employers in unstable economic conditions.[22] It is very commonly used for the employment of financial and technical specialists, for example in the preparation of business plans and investment projects, and in the construction industry, for both primary and secondary jobs.

According to the Labour Force Survey data, this accounts for about a quarter of all secondary employment, over a third in construction and half the second jobs in finance and insurance. In the ISITO household survey labour agreements accounted for 10 percent of all secondary employment, and about 20 percent of those whose second job was in a state enterprise or a private corporation. In the ISITO data, this kind of secondary employment is most common in industry, construction and public services. Many more people do the same kind of work without any form of contract, on the basis of a verbal agreement, particularly when they are working for a small or a new private enterprise,

[22]    Goskomstat data suggests that work on contract declined relatively in the second half of the 1990s. In 1994 more than twice as many people were employed on contract than as *sovmestitel'i* in large and medium enterprises (Popov, 1995, p. 28), but by 1998 the latter outnumbered the former both in large and medium enterprises and in small businesses, with about 1.7 million in total working as *sovmestitel'i* and 1.3 million on contract (Goskomstat, 1998b, 1999a).

although a verbal agreement has no legal status. According to the Labour Force Survey data for 2000, 20 percent were working in their second jobs on the basis of a casual agreement and 25 percent were working on fixed-term contracts (Goskomstat, 2000g).

Hiring people to work on a contract to carry out a specific piece of work has the advantage for the employer of avoiding all the liabilities of an employer, including taxation, health and safety and employment protection (because this kind of contract is regulated by the Civil Code, not by the Labour Code, a loophole that has been blocked in the new Labour Code which came into force in February 2002), and often eliminating managerial responsibility for the work in question. For the employee it has the advantage of independence and flexibility and, in many cases, good earnings. Among the most widespread kinds of such work for industrial workers are things like the manufacture and installation of various metal constructions (doors, railings, garages etc.), construction and repair work, preparation of welfare projects (children's camps, factory vacation centres and sanatoria for the spring and summer season, housing and municipal services for the winter) and transportation services (mostly driving and loading). Professionals, such as service and repair engineers, computer specialists, accountants and lawyers, are very likely to undertake secondary employment on this kind of contractual basis. This kind of work can be undertaken by people with a wide range of occupational or professional skills, while many of the jobs require little or no skill at all.

In the past this kind of work would often be done by people who had no other job and many of those working under contract, particularly in the construction industry and in market trading, may still do this as their only work. However, an employer who brings in outsiders to earn good money when the establishment is at a standstill and the regular employees are earning little or nothing is asking for trouble. Thus, employers will very often first of all offer this work to their own employees, concluding an appropriate labour contract with them (if the work is to be carried out outside their normal working hours), thereby giving them the opportunity of getting additional earnings. In one of the ISITO case study enterprises, which faced a shortage of skilled workers and substantial fluctuations in production, a core labour force was retained and when the company received a large order it concluded labour agreements with its own employees (line managers as well as workers) to carry out the work as a form of overtime, the miserable wages on their own not providing a sufficient incentive. According to the workers, such additional work could amount to between two and seven shifts a month.

> To earn extra money we often have rush jobs, and sometimes also the overhaul of the equipment. Earlier in the producing shops there were 10–12 repairmen, but now at best 2–3 people remain. What can they do?! They only patch holes. And our equipment wears out in any case – sometimes it works, sometimes it doesn't. So we repair it after work under agreements. During normal working hours there is only enough time for running repairs (repair mechanic, plastics factory).

> We now cook our resins under labour agreements. We began to do it at the end of 1993, when the factory began to work on particular orders. But they come rather irregularly. Therefore it is unprofitable to keep superfluous people. And it is good for people too – there is the opportunity to earn extra money to live (shift foreman, plastics factory).

Some enterprises which are working far below capacity may try to take advantage of opportunities for outside contracting to provide work for their own employees and a source of income for the enterprise, establishing specific procedures for such outside contracting (which distinguishes it from *kalym*, because it is regularised). However, in our experience such attempts were generally unsuccessful. Sometimes, the equipment and the organisation of the production process in the enterprise turned out not to be well-adapted to the fulfilment of small volume orders, but more generally such schemes failed because the overheads imposed by the enterprise made the jobs unattractive for both customers and workers, both of whom preferred to make their own independent arrangements.

> Pensioners frequently come, one of them comes to the chief of shop with a paper which has been made out by the factory management, he presents a bottle in a trembling hand – 'here's to you, guys, you work well, I have paid my whole pension'. And we cook up something like a cover for his cellar for him, and he inspects it minutely and sniffs all around it – 'hey, something here is askew, yes, it should be curved here' ... In general, we only take on such work under pressure from the chief. And there is nothing left for pay, kopecks, and the bother... And so when somebody comes from outside with an order, without any paper, yes with his own hardware – that is a godsend. And I do not care how he got in here, how he has got his materials in and how he will get them out (foreman, mechanical engineering factory).

> For example, the order for welding iron garage gates at the 1994 price came to 500 thousand. From this, wages had to be deducted: ITR – 40 thousand, two workers – 80 thousand each. The rest of the money went upstairs as overhead charges (deputy chief of welding shop, mechanical engineering factory).

The welders preferred to organise such work on their own account, taking on various kinds of repair and construction work as a specialist team, reminiscent of the *shabashniki* (moonlighters – wandering construction brigades) of the Soviet period:

> We are a permanent company, we are like a moonlighting brigade, we look for work on our own or through friends, and after work, or on free days, or during vacations, we work. What do we do? We make everything! Iron doors, balconies, railings, repair the heating, we strengthen garages. How else could I have bought two automobiles? (foreman of a welding section of mechanical engineering factory).

Work under labour contracts tends to be much better paid than regular or even than overtime work,[23] since the size of earnings under a labour contract is usually the result of a bargain between the two parties to the contract rather than being based on the meagre regular pay scale. According to the workers we interviewed in industrial enterprises, the additional earnings from work under labour agreements is usually equivalent to at least a month's basic wage, otherwise they would probably refuse to take on the work offered. Moreover, the money earned under a labour agreement is paid with smaller delays than main wages, because it is financed from a specific order, and this makes it even more attractive for the workers. The arrangement is favourable to the enterprise as well, since it allows it to smooth the zigzags of the production programme and not to have to maintain a reserve of people in case of the arrival of a large order. This arrangement can also be used to get the work off the books and so reduce the social insurance and income tax liabilities of the employer and the employees.

This kind of work increases the dependence of workers on their line managers (above all on shop and section chiefs), who usually decide who will participate in an agreement and who drum up and distribute the money for completed work. Moreover, work under agreements is used by shop management as a means of holding on to the workers necessary for the division, as it allows the latter substantially (quite often by two or three times) to increase their earnings. Because of this, these kinds of additional employment are mostly undertaken by those

---

[23] During the late perestroika period it was not uncommon for more lucrative work and pay to be channelled through co-operatives or private 'small enterprises', sometimes with the same work being double-counted as the person worked simultaneously for both, legal status attaching to the job in the state enterprise but the bulk of earnings attaching to the job in the small enterprise. This system continued to be used through the 1990s to avoid taxation and accountability to shareholders.

with a high level of qualification who are also deeply embedded in the system of informal social relations (these are above all skilled workers and shop managers with long service at the given enterprise).

Work on contract is not only typical of industrial employees but is also a very common form of primary and secondary employment for those with scarce professional skills, such as lawyers, accountants and computer specialists. Small enterprises do not need, and often cannot afford, to provide full-time permanent employment for such specialists but hire them on a temporary part-time basis under a labour contract to carry out a specific piece of work.

As might be expected, according to the VTsIOM data this form of secondary employment is associated with those who earn higher wages in their first jobs, and is relatively much more common in large cities than in towns and rural districts. It has also increased relative to other forms of secondary employment over the past few years. Those working in this form of secondary employment earn about 50 percent above the average rate per hour for second jobs, but work rather shorter hours than average, although still sufficient on average to double their monthly earnings.

### Self-employment: private services and commercial activity

In the Soviet period a wide range of services was provided privately by individuals for one another. Small construction and decorating jobs, repair of radios, televisions and washing machines, clothing repairs, looking after the sick or disabled, cooking and making preserves, dressmaking, private transport and private tuition were all services which no state enterprise would provide. Until 1987 it was illegal to do such odd jobs for financial reward. Usually they would be done on the basis of reciprocity with friends or relatives, maybe in exchange for a bottle of vodka or a bucket of potatoes. As times got hard and the legal environment became more permissive, people increasingly used their skills, resources and experience as a means of earning a bit of extra money. Many of these activities require some kind of skill, but very often these are skills picked up, in the case of men, during their military service, or, in the case of women, from their mothers or grandmothers, rather than being skills associated with the primary job or in which the individual has a formal qualification. Sometimes such secondary employment becomes effectively primary not only in the size of the income received, but also because it begins to impose constraints on the primary job (its schedule, intensity of labour and so on), with people sometimes taking unpaid leave from their main job to concentrate on more lucrative supplementary work. This kind of work is the most likely to be under-reported since it tends to be unregistered and is the easiest to conceal from the tax authorities.

We have already seen that this kind of unregistered occasional self-employment – 'individual economic activity' – is the most common form of supplementary employment, and the most common form of self-employment is the traditional provision of private services: construction and repair, motor transport, sewing, cleaning and so on, which account for about two-thirds of the cases of self-employment. There is little that the ISITO respondents do not do: they repair apartments and automobiles, they build houses, dachas and garages, they sew and knit to order, clean buildings and prepare food, transport goods and people and so on. Usually their services are much cheaper, often of higher quality and, most important of all, in the neat expression of one of the participants in the ISITO survey, 'they are always here and now, instead of somewhere else and tomorrow, as are the state services'.

> I sew at home, it is very important for the family budget. There is always a lot of work. I live in a hostel and know a lot of people. And it is much better to sew a thing than to buy one (confectioner, confectionery factory).

> I repair footwear. I do the heels – they are beautiful! I put heels to rights for all our girls (setter, typography).

> Well, I am an electrician by trade, so at home I do the wiring for the neighbours. And I also do wallpapering and paint ceilings for money (mechanic–sanitary technician, construction materials factory).

While some self-employment is skilled and quite well-paid, some of it is literally scraping the barrel: scavenging in rubbish tips to find returnable bottles and saleable materials, for example. The production of goods for sale is relatively rare, the bulk of it accounted for by sewing, woodworking and the preparation of foodstuffs. The notorious street and shuttle trade employs only about one in ten of those whose secondary activity takes the form of self-employment, the vast majority doing this only on a casual basis, while most of those working in trade do so working for somebody else.

According to the VTsIOM data, the provision of personal services is most common in industrial cities and is much less often done by single men, with women and married men being involved about three times as often as single men. It pays at around the average rate, but the hours worked are a little below average so that the total secondary earnings of those providing personal services are a little below average, but still sufficient to boost pay by almost three-quarters. Those offering construction and repair services tend to be prime-age men with lower levels of education who are in workers' jobs as their first job, if they have one. The self-employed and the unemployed are especially likely to undertake this form of additional employment. Surprisingly, their rate of pay appears to be significantly below the average.

Those who describe themselves as brokers and commercial intermediaries for their second jobs in the VTsIOM data claim to earn almost three times as much as the average for secondary employment, both per hour and in total. Men are three times as likely to do this kind of activity as women, and it is especially favoured by young people, under 24, and by those with high household incomes and with high earnings in their primary job. This kind of secondary employment is not very common and it seems to be in decline as private individuals can no longer compete with specialist companies.

Providing private lessons is most common in cities and has been on the increase over the last few years. Women, who dominate the teaching profession, are three times as likely to choose this form of secondary employment as are men.

## Trading

Despite popular impressions, trading is by no means the dominant form of secondary employment. In both the VTsIOM and the RLMS data it accounts for about 12 percent of all secondary employment, and in the Labour Force Survey it has declined from about 20 percent to 14 percent of all secondary employment, which is similar to the proportion of primary jobs accounted for by the branch, although in the ISITO household survey data it accounts for almost a quarter of the total number of second jobs. The idea that trade is a testing ground for entrepreneurial skills is somewhat misleading, since the majority of those whose secondary employment is in trade are not trading for their own account but are working for somebody else, usually a private individual or an individual or family business (Clarke and Kabalina, 1999). In the Labour Force Survey data, fewer than one-third of those engaged in secondary employment in trade and catering are self-employed or working as entrepreneurs, only marginally more than in industry.

According to the ISITO work history interviews, the majority of industrial workers either do not participate at all in shuttle trading or running stalls and kiosks, or their participation is only incidental (mostly during administrative leave or on free days when working short-time) and is limited to various kinds of auxiliary work (helping friends and relatives to sell, helping to protect them, helping with transport). The majority of those questioned believed that to work successfully in this sphere you needed capital, connections, particular individual psychological qualities and skills which they did not possess.

I had to earn extra money once, last year, when they sent everyone from the line on administrative leave, my husband was also without work at the time. I tried to trade in children's socks. Some relatives of a neighbour came and brought some children's knitwear at a low price, which they offered to sell. I stood in the market with these socks for about a week, I sold a few, but did not make any profit, I only wasted my time, either the goods were not fashionable, or I do not know how to trade (woman worker, chocolate factory).

They suggested that I sell cosmetics, but I could not decide, and I didn't have the money to start up (computer operator in offset shop, typography).[24]

My husband and I got involved in the distribution of our home-produced knitwear. As direct-sales representatives we only sold them in offices... But it is so chaotic. Some kind of opening appears – there is nothing left but to get involved. We succeeded in this respect. Compared to what we had at the factory, sometimes we would earn as much in one day. But the work was not really for us. I felt very nasty – it seemed to me like the total end of the world (engineer-technologist, electronics factory).

I earned a bit extra in commerce, I traded in the radio market... To some extent it was profitable. I bought some things. Why did I give up this work? Well, because it was not for me (welder, construction materials factory).

Apart from the continuing widely held prejudices against involvement in trade, which are particularly strong in smaller towns, the developing professionalisation of this sphere means that commercial activity demands full-time employment and hence makes it impossible to combine it with (non-fictitious) work in a primary job.

Some employees are forced to engage in trade by the fact that they are paid their wages in kind, sometimes in the produce of their own enterprise and sometimes in barter goods. The employee then has to sell the goods in order to obtain a money income, with the possibility

---

[24] Pyramid selling, particularly of cosmetics, has become widespread in Russia, with many of the leading western pyramid-selling companies active in the market.

of making some additional income if the goods have been obtained at wholesale factory prices. This situation does not appear to be very common: although in the ISITO household survey payment in kind was not uncommon, the goods received tended to be for the household's own consumption: it was much rarer for the worker to sell the goods received.[25]

> I sometimes take my salary in the form of our shop's products – film, polyethylene covers, basins, buckets. I take all this to my relatives in the country (they still do not have these things at the moment) and I sell them. I make a profit and people benefit... But not many of our workers do it. They say: 'We do not know how to trade, but you have talent – you could even sell snow in the tundra in winter' (female operative, plastics factory).

Sometimes enterprises which receive payment in barter may offer large consignments of these barter goods to their own employees (mainly line managers with long experience of work at the enterprise, 'tested cadres') for sale on favourable terms (for example, with extended cheap credit). This may provide that employee with the opportunity to set up in business as a trader, perhaps with a partner to handle the selling, or to make money as an intermediary with a trading organisation. This kind of secondary employment can easily lead into a dangerous entanglement with criminal organisations, as can the sale of goods stolen from the enterprise.

Although the image of the street trader is of the pensioner standing on the street corner selling her heirlooms, in fact, according to the VTsIOM data, street trading is much more commonly the choice of the under-40s and those whose first job is as a lower-level non-manual worker (clerical, service and sales personnel) – those in their 30s are three times as likely to be involved as are the over-50s. Women are almost twice as likely to be involved as men and this is the favourite supplementary occupation of the unemployed. There has been a slight tendency for street trading to decline over the years as a second job for those in work, although there is no such tendency when we include those who do not have a primary job. Street trade pays a bit above average, but the difference is not statistically significant, although those involved in trading work long hours, so that on average they increase their earnings by 80 percent over their pay in their first job.

[25]    Although 17 percent of those in work in the ISITO household survey had at some time been paid in kind, 95 percent mainly kept the goods received for their own use and only 4 percent mostly sold them. Not one respondent identified the sale of the products of their own workplace as their main form of secondary employment in the previous month.

# CHARACTERISTICS OF SECONDARY EMPLOYMENT

'Secondary employment' is quite a heterogeneous phenomenon, ranging from the regular employment in a second job *po sovmestitel'stvu* inherited from the Soviet period, to self-employment and entrepreneurial activity taking advantage of the new opportunities presented by the market economy. In this section we will look more closely at the characteristics of secondary employment on the basis of the analysis of the survey data.

## The branch distribution of secondary employment

The popular image of secondary employment is of street trading and the private provision of service and repairs in the 'shadow economy', but for many people a second job is just that, waged work for a second employer. If we look at the branch distribution of secondary employment, we find that the pattern of secondary employment is not radically different from that of primary employment, although the traditional forms of secondary employment are concentrated in public services and the new forms of secondary employment in trade, services and repairs. The Labour Force Survey reports the branch of the economy in which secondary employment is carried out (Table 2.5), although it should be noted that this source probably considerably underestimates the scale of unregistered and informal secondary employment and so understates the extent of secondary employment in trade and services.

The Labour Force Survey data brings out clearly the coexistence of new and traditional forms of secondary employment. Although second jobs have, at least until recently, been found disproportionately in the spheres of trade, catering, services and construction, the public services (particularly education, culture and science) are also heavily dependent on the use of secondary employment.

Opportunities for secondary employment in the new private sector appear to be in decline as a result of the professionalisation of the sector. This is reflected in Goskomstat estimates of employment in small enterprises, which showed an increase of 6 percent in the number of permanent employees between 1994 and 1995 (almost all the increase in the private sector) but a fall of 30 percent in the number working on contract and 10 percent in the number working *po sovmestitel'stvu* (Goskomstat, 1996d). The definition of a small enterprise was changed in 1996, but the number reported employed in small businesses on contract and as external *sovmestitel'i* continued to fall sharply. Having accounted for 44 percent of all employment in small enterprises in 1994, they had fallen to 13 percent of employment in small businesses in 2000 (Goskomstat, 2001).

*Table 2.5:    Branch distribution of secondary employment, 1997–2000 and primary employment, 1999 (Labour Force Survey data).*

| Branch | 1997 | 1998 | 1999 | 2000 | 1999 Primary |
|---|---|---|---|---|---|
| Industry | 17.6 | 17.3 | 17.6 | 17.7 | 26.4 |
| Agriculture and timber | 8.0 | 6.2 | 9.7 | 9.0 | 11.0 |
| Transport and communications | 6.5 | 6.4 | 7.3 | 6.4 | 9.1 |
| Construction | 8.6 | 7.1 | 10.1 | 9.9 | 6.6 |
| Trade and catering | 21.3 | 19.1 | 16.6 | 14.1 | 12.5 |
| Public and private services | 4.5 | 7.4 | 4.9 | 6.8 | 3.8 |
| Health and social services | 8.7 | 7.2 | 8.9 | 9.1 | 7.3 |
| Education | 14.8 | 17.5 | 14.2 | 16.6 | 9.7 |
| Culture, art and science | 4.5 | 4.7 | 4.5 | 4.0 | 2.6 |
| Finance and insurance | 0.4 | 0.5 | 0.5 | 0.6 | 1.3 |
| Public administration | 2.3 | 2.5 | 2.6 | 2.5 | 7.8 |
| Other | 2.7 | 4.1 | 3.1 | 3.2 | 2.0 |
| Total | 100.0 | 100.0 | 100.0 | 100.0 | 100.0 |

*Source: Goskomstat, 2000c; Goskomstat, 2000g.*

In the public services, secondary employment has traditionally been a response to low wages in primary employment: on the one hand, providing employers with the means of making up for labour shortages resulting from low pay; on the other hand, providing employees with an opportunity to supplement their miserable wages. In trade and catering and construction, secondary employment provides employers with a flexible casual labour force and employees the chance to supplement their incomes and get some experience of working in the market economy. The marked decline in secondary employment in trade and catering probably reflects both changes in the demand for secondary labour, as the industry becomes more professionalised, and in the supply of labour, as the supply of more stable jobs and the payment of wages picked up in the economic recovery following the August 1998 crisis.

*Table 2.6:* *Percentage of respondents with their second job in the same branch as their first and distribution of first and second jobs by branch (ISITO Household Survey).*

| Percentages | Both jobs in same branch | First job | Second job |
|---|---|---|---|
| Agriculture, mining and manufacturing | 37 | 27 | 17 |
| Construction | 37 | 6 | 3 |
| Transport, storage and communication | 43 | 9 | 6 |
| Trade, hotels, catering and repairs | 65 | 20 | 37 |
| Finance, insurance, business and personal services | 48 | 4 | 6 |
| Public administration, community and public services | 74 | 33 | 32 |
| N=414 | | | |

The branch distribution of secondary employment according to the ISITO household survey is shown in Table 2.6. This indicates a greater concentration of secondary employment in trade, catering and repairs than does the Goskomstat data, which is to be expected since the latter seems to under-report more informal secondary employment. There is quite a strong tendency for people to do their second jobs in the same sector and branch as their first job, which is not surprising since around a quarter do the second job at the same workplace as their first job. Almost two-thirds of those who worked in a state enterprise or organisation also did their second job in such an establishment, while the majority of those whose first job was in the private sector also worked in the private sector in their second jobs. The VTsIOM data for 1996–98 shows the same tendency, although fewer of those working in the state sector, only 41 percent, also had their second jobs in state enterprises or organisations.

It is equally striking in the VTsIOM data (Table 2.7) that the predominant forms of secondary employment remain those traditional in the Soviet period, of working *po sovmestitel'vu* in a regularly contracted second job, either at the main place of work or elsewhere, and the provision of services, with a relatively small number of people involved in street and shuttle trading, which belies the popular image of Russia's market economy. Only one in eight of those with supplementary work was involved in trading, and the vast majority were only so involved on an occasional basis. The reason for this is primarily that street and shuttle trading has become a sphere of full-time primary employment, often working very long hours, in which there is relatively little space for the casual employee. Secondary employment in this sphere often involves helping out friends and relatives rather than being a regular source of supplementary income.

Table 2.7:　Forms of secondary employment 1994–99.

| | 1994–96 | 1997–99 | | | | | | | | | | |
|---|---|---|---|---|---|---|---|---|---|---|---|---|
| Percentage distributions | | All | 1 | 2 | 3 | 4 | 5 | 6 | 7 | 8 | 9 | 10 |
| Sovmestitel' at main place of work | 14 | 13 | 30 | 70 | 40 | 60 | | | 21 | 29 | 23 | 23 |
| Sovmestitel' elsewhere | 13 | 12 | 47 | 53 | 50 | 50 | | | 38 | 23 | 18 | 7 |
| Services: construction, repair, sewing | 20 | 23 | 9 | 91 | 5 | 95 | 32 | 32 | | 11 | 13 | 31 |
| Professional services on contract or order * | 6 | 7 | 26 | 74 | 53 | 47 | | 6 | 18 | 10 | | |
| Personal services # | 6 | 8 | 22 | 78 | 13 | 87 | 11 | 19 | | | | |
| Street trade, shuttle trading | 11 | 12 | 15 | 85 | 26 | 74 | 27 | 17 | | | 9 | 7 |
| Production of consumer goods for sale | 5 | 3 | 8 | 92 | 18 | 82 | 9 | 1 | | | | |
| Tutoring, private lessons | 2 | 3 | 29 | 71 | 26 | 74 | | 1 | | | | |
| Broker, intermediary activities | 4 | 3 | 13 | 87 | 17 | 83 | | 3 | | | | |
| Other | 12 | 10 | | | | | | | | | | |
| Difficult to say | 10 | 8 | | | | | | | | | | |

Notes:
* e.g. computer programming, translation, writing, lecturing.
# e.g. child care, nursing, cleaning, cooking etc.

Key to column labels: 1 Regular; 2 Occasional; 3 Registered; 4 Unregistered; 5 Pensioners; 6 Unemployed; 7 Managers; 8 Specialists; 9 Clerks; 10 Workers

Source: 1994–6, my calculations from VTsIOM data (April 1994, May 1995, March 1996), 1997–9 from Perova, 1999.

There have been no dramatic changes over time in the forms of secondary employment in the VTsIOM data. However, there was a marked decline in the proportion of people doing their supplementary work in a state enterprise or organisation over the period 1997–99 and a corresponding increase in the proportion doing it in a private enterprise. This is probably partly but not completely a reflection of the continuing privatisation of state enterprises.

*Table 2.8:* RLMS 1998–2000: distribution of secondary occupations by sphere of occupational activity.

| Percent | Second job | Individual economic activity | Total secondary employment |
|---|---|---|---|
| Agriculture | 2 | 9 | 8 |
| Textiles and clothing | 2 | 12 | 10 |
| Other Industry | 7 | 7 | 7 |
| Motor and electrical service and repair | 3 | 8 | 7 |
| Construction | 8 | 17 | 15 |
| Trade | 9 | 12 | 12 |
| Catering | 1 | 1 | 1 |
| Transport | 6 | 14 | 12 |
| Commercial services | 10 | 4 | 5 |
| Professional and technical services | 8 | 1 | 2 |
| Education, art and culture | 16 | 2 | 5 |
| Health | 5 | 3 | 3 |
| Clerical | 3 | 0 | 1 |
| Service personnel | 3 | 5 | 4 |
| Security | 5 | 2 | 2 |
| Cleaners | 12 | 4 | 5 |
| N | 387 | 1 562 | 1 949 |

*Source: Author's calculations from 1998 and 2000 RLMS data: occupational coding of secondary occupations.*

*Table 2.9:    Percentage distribution of secondary employment by employers' area of activity.*

| Percentage distribution | Total | State | Private company | Self-employment | Individual private enterprise |
|---|---|---|---|---|---|
| Agricultural | 1 | 1 | 0 | 4 | 0 |
| Industrial, of which | 15 | 8 | 23 | 24 | 8 |
| (1) Production of food | 1 | 0 | 0 | 2 | 2 |
| (2) Production of clothing | 5 | 0 | 0 | 16 | 2 |
| Construction services | 2 | 2 | 4 | 0 | 1 |
| Trade | 24 | 1 | 31 | 13 | 44 |
| Service and repair of cars | 1 | 0 | 1 | 2 | 0 |
| Commercial and financial services | 4 | 1 | 5 | 10 | 3 |
| Transport related | 5 | 4 | 3 | 9 | 5 |
| Sport, leisure, hotels and catering | 2 | 7 | 0 | 0 | 2 |
| Security services | 2 | 4 | 4 | 0 | 0 |
| Professional services | 3 | 0 | 5 | 2 | 5 |
| Education, culture and arts | 13 | 35 | 6 | 6 | 5 |
| Health and welfare services | 9 | 22 | 4 | 2 | 2 |
| Housing repairs and communal services | 9 | 8 | 9 | 3 | 12 |
| Services to households | 8 | 4 | 4 | 11 | 11 |
| Service and repair | 2 | 1 | 0 | 9 | 0 |
| Personal services | 1 | 0 | 0 | 5 | 0 |
| N | 390 | 91 | 75 | 93 | 131 |

*Source: ISITO household survey, those with secondary employment last month, excluding internal* sovmestitel'i.

Table 2.8 shows the occupational distribution of secondary employment according to the RLMS data and Table 2.9 shows a more detailed branch breakdown of the ISITO household survey data. The ISITO data in particular shows very clearly the extent to which, in the state sector, the health and education services rely on secondary employment to cover their staffing needs (this is particularly marked among internal *sovmestitel'i*, of whom 22.5 percent were doing their second jobs in educational institutions and 20 percent in the health service). Self-employment commonly involved making clothes, providing individual services and various kinds of service and repairs, while those working for individuals or private companies were most commonly engaged in trade. Trade was much less commonly undertaken on the basis of self-employment.

In the ISITO work history survey, two-thirds of those who were self-employed were involved in providing private services and only 8 percent in street trading, 6 percent producing commodities for sale, 4 percent producing agricultural goods, 6 percent providing intermediary services, 4 percent other kinds of intellectual labour and 5 percent various kinds of manual labour.[26]

Reviewing the data on the branch distribution of secondary employment as a whole, we can clearly identify the dominance of the two distinct types of secondary employment that we have discussed above. First, the traditional forms of secondary employment involving registered employment in an enterprise or organisation, usually as a *sovmestitel'*, to provide professional services or to do unskilled work (cleaning, security), particularly in the public sector. This kind of work is much more likely to be undertaken on a regular basis and to be formalised. Second, the new forms of secondary employment, dominated by self-employment and work for small private and family businesses in trade, catering, services and repair. Many of the activities undertaken in the latter form of secondary employment are by no means new. Secondary self-employment is dominated by the traditional activities of making and repairing clothing, servicing and repairing domestic appliances, repairing and decorating apartments, private tutoring and private 'taxi' services. The novelty is that these services are now performed openly for money. Trade and catering is the newest sphere of secondary employment, though not as dominant as popular imagination has it, performed primarily in small private companies.

## The occupational distribution of secondary employment

The incentives and opportunities to engage in secondary employment differ quite substantially between different occupational categories. We would expect those with physically or intellectually demanding

---

[26] In Goskomstat's Labour Force Survey data for 1999, 26 percent of those working in second jobs in trade were self-employed, against 18 percent of all those with second jobs. Trade accounted for less than a quarter of all self-employment in second jobs.

primary jobs to be less inclined to take on additional work, while we would expect those with scarce technical or professional skills to have many more opportunities to undertake additional employment. Tables 2.10a and b show the incidence of secondary employment by major occupational groupings for men and women across the three data sets. The variation between the data sets is quite substantial, but from the regression coefficients in Tables 2.25, 2.26 and 2.28 (at the end of the chapter) we can see that differences between occupational groupings are barely statistically significant, although senior professional staff and, amongst men, technicians are generally more likely to engage in secondary employment.

*Table 2.10a: Incidence of secondary employment by occupational status in primary job (men).*

| Percentage with second jobs | RLMS 1994–2000 | | | VTsIOM 1993–98 | ISITO |
|---|---|---|---|---|---|
| | Second job | IEA | Total | | |
| Senior administrators and managers | 5.3 | 4.9 | 8.9 | 18.9 | 4.8 |
| Middle and low managers | 4.4 | 7.0 | 11.2 | 16.5 | 20.4 |
| Professionals, upper specialists | 12.0 | 10.2 | 20.3 | 26.8 | 29.2 |
| Technicians, low specialists | 7.2 | 8.0 | 13.9 | 21.4 | 23.9 |
| Upper non-manual workers (admin/commerce) | 6.3 | 7.7 | 13.4 | 17.8 | 17.4 |
| Lower non-manual (clerical/sales/services) | 5.2 | 7.9 | 12.2 | 19.6 | 21.2 |
| Skilled manual workers | 3.1 | 9.2 | 11.9 | 16.8 | 20.6 |
| Semi/unskilled manual workers | 2.7 | 6.1 | 8.5 | 13.5 | 15.8 |
| Total | 4.6 | 8.4 | 12.3 | 18.3 | 20.6 |

*Source: RLMS, VTsIOM and ISITO Household Survey data.*

Only the RLMS data has detailed information on the occupations of both primary and secondary jobs. In this data, one-fifth of respondents worked in exactly the same occupation in their second job as they did in their first job and about half in the same occupational category, skilled workers and professionals being the most likely to work in the same occupational category in their second job. One-third worked in secondary occupations higher up the scale than their primary job and a fifth in a lower status occupation. About a fifth of skilled manual workers, clerical workers and junior technicians worked as semi-skilled or unskilled manual workers in their second jobs, while a quarter of unskilled workers did skilled workers' jobs for their second jobs (two VTsIOM surveys in 1996 produced very similar results).

*Table 2.10b: Incidence of secondary employment by occupational status in primary job (women).*

| Percentage with second jobs | RLMS 1994–2000 | | | VTsIOM 1993–98 | ISITO |
|---|---|---|---|---|---|
| | Second job | IEA | Total | | |
| Senior administrators and managers | 0.0 | 2.0 | 2.0 | 17.3 | 8.3 |
| Middle and low managers | 7.0 | 4.9 | 10.6 | 11.4 | 9.6 |
| Professionals, upper specialists | 7.7 | 5.0 | 11.7 | 16.2 | 20.5 |
| Technicians, low specialists | 3.0 | 4.6 | 7.1 | 11.9 | 18.3 |
| Upper non-manual workers (admin/commerce) | 3.8 | 2.8 | 6.4 | 11.2 | 12.2 |
| Lower non-manual (clerical/sales/services) | 2.9 | 3.5 | 6.2 | 10.2 | 11.7 |
| Skilled manual workers | 2.8 | 6.3 | 8.8 | 10.5 | 14.2 |
| Semi/unskilled manual workers | 4.2 | 3.4 | 7.4 | 10.2 | 13.1 |
| Total | 4.5 | 4.1 | 8.1 | 12.3 | 15.2 |

*Source: RLMS data 1994–2000 (N=22 334); VTsIOM data 1993–8 (N=65 886); ISITO household survey (N=4 888).*

## The formalisation of secondary employment

Traditional forms of secondary employment, as *sovmestitel'*, involve regular registered employment with an enterprise or organisation, while the new forms of secondary employment are more often casual and informal and involve working independently or for a private individual or small business (Table 2.11). The difference in the formalisation of employment is partly a matter of size: 85 percent of those working for a company employing 10 people or fewer, but only 14 percent of those working for a company employing more than 100 people, did so on a verbal agreement. Those who work only episodically are much more likely to work on a verbal agreement than those working on a more regular basis. In education, in 2000, according to the Labour Force Survey, 85 percent of second jobs were working for an enterprise or organisation and 53 percent were permanent jobs, while in trade and catering and in construction only 31 percent of jobs were working for an enterprise or organisation, as opposed to self-employment or working for a private individual, and only 23 percent of second jobs in trade and catering and only 11 percent of jobs in construction were permanent (Goskomstat, 2000g).

*Table 2.11: How is your secondary employment formalised? (ISITO household survey, April-May 1998).*

| Percent | Total | State enterprise or budget organisation | Joint-stock company | Limited liability company | Individual or family business | For a private individual |
|---|---|---|---|---|---|---|
| Indefinite employment without a contract | 13 | 35 | 14 | 8 | 5 | 1 |
| Permanent contract | 8 | 12 | 14 | 13 | 12 | |
| Contract of one to five years | 2 | 5 | 6 | | | |
| Contract of less than one year | 4 | 7 | 6 | 5 | 5 | 1 |
| Agreement to carry out particular work | 13 | 22 | 25 | 13 | 10 | 2 |
| Verbal agreement | 60 | 20 | 36 | 63 | 69 | 96 |
| N | 306 | 86 | 36 | 40 | 42 | 102 |

*Source: ISITO Household survey data, excluding those self-employed or working in their own enterprise.*

In the VTsIOM data (Table 2.6), those working as *sovmestitel'i* or in professional services and those working regularly in their supplementary job were much more likely than those working in trade or in providing personal services or those only occasionally engaging in supplementary work to have their employment officially registered, and correspondingly reported to the tax and statistical authorities.

The Labour Force Survey and RLMS tend to show a higher proportion of secondary employment as being registered than do the other two data sets, reinforcing the impression that they capture relatively less of the more informal forms of secondary employment than do the latter. According to the Labour Force Survey data, in 1999–2000, about three-quarters of respondents worked for a wage in their second jobs, of whom almost half the women and a quarter of the men had permanent second jobs, with about a third of the men and one in ten of the women working on a casual basis, the remainder having some form of temporary contract. Almost three-quarters of those asked by RLMS in 1998 and 2000 replied that their second job was registered and fewer than a quarter that it was unregistered, although only 11 percent of 'individual economic activity', three-quarters of which is incidental rather than regular work, was formalised according to an agreement, official contract or licence.

In the April 1997 ISITO work history survey most secondary employment in state and former state enterprises and organisations was registered, while the vast majority of secondary employment in the new private sector and almost all self-employment was unregistered (Table 2.12).

*Table 2.12: Type of registration by sector of secondary employment (all reported second jobs).*

| Percentage | State and municipal | Privatised | New private | Self-employed | All cases |
|---|---|---|---|---|---|
| In my own workplace | 11 | 12 | 4 | | 5 |
| Registered in my own enterprise | 15 | 40 | 0 | | 11 |
| Not registered in my own enterprise | 20 | 19 | 1 | | 8 |
| Registered somewhere else | 37 | 24 | 20 | 4 | 18 |
| Not registered somewhere else | 17 | 4 | 75 | 96 | 57 |
| N | 54 | 67 | 81 | 108 | 313 |

*Source: ISITO work history survey, April 1997. Total includes 3 cases who worked additionally for social or non-commercial organisations.*

## The time demands of secondary employment

For most people, a second job involves at most working a few evenings a week, or working over the weekend, although a small minority work very long hours, particularly if they are not currently working in a primary job.

Those with regular second jobs tend to work longer hours than those whose supplementary employment is only occasional and, as we might expect, those without primary employment work longer hours than those for whom supplementary employment is in addition to their main job. The longest hours are worked by those who run their own business as their supplementary employment. The distribution of hours worked in the ISITO household survey data is shown in Table 2.13.

The distribution of working hours reported by the other data sets is broadly similar to that reported by the ISITO household survey, although the Labour Force Survey reports rather shorter hours worked in secondary employment than the other data sets, amounting on average between 1996 and 2000 to between 12 and 16 hours a week, with two-thirds working fewer than 16 hours a week, but 2 percent working more than 40 hours a week. A third of those working long hours in their second job were temporarily not working at their primary job and a further 20 percent were working less than full-time in their main job.

*Table 2.13:  Distribution of hours worked in the previous month in second job by employment status.*

| Percentage | Workers with permanent or regular second job | All workers | Non-working adults | Non-working pensioners | Total |
|---|---|---|---|---|---|
| 1-20 hours | 27.3 | 33.8 | 23 | 9 | 31.1 |
| 21-40 hours | 18.5 | 21.0 | 11 | 18 | 18.8 |
| 41-80 hours | 26.6 | 23.6 | 22 | 27 | 23.4 |
| 81-160 hours | 18.8 | 14.8 | 26 | 36 | 17.6 |
| More than 160 hours | 8.8 | 6.8 | 18 | 9 | 9.0 |
| Mean hours | 66 | 56 | 93 | 85 | 65 |
| Median hours | 50 | 40 | 70 | 80 | 44 |
| N | 319 | 385 | 103 | 11 | 499 |

*Source: ISITO household survey, April–May 1998*

Half the RLMS respondents over the period 1994–2000 had worked for less than 30 hours in the previous month in all forms of secondary activity, one quarter had worked for ten hours or less, but around a quarter had worked for more than 70 hours in the previous month and as many as 10 percent worked 160 hours or more, more than was worked by the average respondents in their primary jobs. The majority of those working full-time in secondary economic activity did not have or were not working in their primary jobs. One in eight of those who said that they did not work in October 1998 and one in five of those who said they did not work in 2000 had in fact worked full-time (more than 160 hours) in individual economic activity the previous month.

Half the respondents in the ISITO work history survey had done no more than 140 hours work over 36 days in the course of 1996, but around 5 percent had worked effectively full-time in their second jobs for the whole of the previous year, probably because they had been laid off or had taken voluntary leave, and a third of respondents had worked for eight or more hours per day when they worked at their second jobs, most probably working on their days off.

There has been a statistically significant tendency for the number of hours worked in secondary employment to decline over the years in the VTsIOM data, although there was a significant increase in the first half of 1998. The median number of hours worked per week fell from 14–15 in 1993–95 to only ten in 1996–97, increasing to 13 in the first half of 1998. While about a third of respondents worked less than ten hours a week – a couple of hours at the end of the working day, or one day over the weekend – about one in ten worked full-time or more in their second job, as in the RLMS data, indicating that their primary job, if they had one, made only formal demands on their time and energy.[27] Those with regular second jobs worked on average about 50 percent longer than those whose supplementary work was occasional, and those who had their own business worked on average more than twice as long as those who worked for a wage or who were self-employed.

VTsIOM, with its large data set, allows us to explore the determinants of working hours in more detail (Table 2.23). There is little variation in the hours worked by age, pensioners only working significantly shorter hours when they get well into their seventies, and no significant variation between primary occupations or between those working in state or in private enterprises. Men, especially if they are married, work considerably longer hours than women. The fact that men both earn substantially more and work longer hours means that their secondary earnings are on average about 90 percent more than those of women. Those with a relatively lower household income per head also work longer hours, but those who earn at a higher hourly rate work shorter hours, suggesting that people tend to work the number of hours necessary to generate their target income. The same inverse relationship between the wage earned and the hours worked in

---

[27]  VTsIOM does not regularly ask the hours worked in the main job, but the working week is currently an average of 39–40 hours.

supplementary employment is found in each round of the RLMS survey and in the ISITO household survey, although in the latter it is not strong enough to be statistically significant.

Table 2.14 summarises the ISITO data on when people do their secondary employment (in the household survey only those currently working in a primary job were asked this question). In the Labour Force Survey Supplement data working women were much more likely than men to work in their second job during normal working hours at their main workplace (19 percent against 6 percent) and non-working women more likely than men to work during time free from domestic responsibilities (44 percent against 26 percent). Differences between men and women in the household survey data were not sufficient to be statistically significant.

*Table 2.14: When do you normally engage in your secondary employment?*

| Percentage distribution | LFS | | Household Survey |
|---|---|---|---|
| | Working or on leave | Not working | |
| During normal working hours at main workplace | 11 | 3 | 15 |
| During regular vacations | 9 | 4 | 1 |
| During administrative leave | 3 | | 3 |
| On free days or when working short-time | 5 | | 14 |
| At weekends and public holidays | 14 | 4 | 13 |
| At the end of the working day | 43 | 7 | 45 |
| While looking for a permanent job | 8 | 47 | <1 |
| During time free of domestic responsibilities | 7 | 35 | 8 |
| N | 149 | 74 | 425 |

*Source:1998 ISITO household survey data; 1997 LFS supplement data, Kemerovo oblast, Komi Republic.*

**Earnings from secondary employment**

There is a great deal of variation in the rates of pay for secondary employment, which means that the coefficients in wage regressions are generally not significant, but some people are able to earn good money in their supplementary employment. Table 2.22 (at the end of the chapter) reports the findings of regressions for primary and secondary earnings using the VTsIOM data. The coefficients in regressions using the other data sets are consistent with these, but are generally not statistically significant.

On average, people with second jobs earn about three times the hourly rate of their primary jobs, although around a quarter earn less in their second jobs than in their first ones. The determinants of wages in secondary employment are very similar to the determinants of wages in primary employment, although the returns to education are slightly higher in secondary employment. The lowest pay tends to be earned by those working in a regular second job in their own enterprise or those providing personal services, while those in occasional secondary employment tend to earn at higher hourly rates. Those working in trade and services in their second jobs earn significantly more than those in the productive sphere or in public services. The highest earnings, but also the biggest variation, tends to be in trading, entrepreneurial and commercial activity and providing professional services. Those with higher educational qualifications and professional skills earn much more than do ordinary workers. Earnings increase steadily with educational level, graduates earning about twice as much as those with incomplete secondary education. Senior managers and specialists earn at twice the hourly rate of skilled manual or white-collar workers, who in turn earn almost twice as much as unskilled or clerical workers. Hourly earnings are progressively lower for older age groups, and fall quite rapidly for older people, so that younger people earn more than twice as much as those who have reached pension age. Men earn about a third as much again per hour as do women, controlling for other variables.

Although people usually work shorter hours in their second jobs, up to a quarter of people earn as much or more from their second as from their first jobs, while between half and two-thirds of people earn less than half as much in their secondary as in their primary employment. The median earnings from secondary employment of those in the ISITO survey who had a second job in May 1998 were 250 roubles ($41 at the exchange rate at the time) against a median wage of 800 roubles ($130). The median earnings the previous month of those who had a second job in the RLMS in the autumn of 2000 was 700 roubles ($25) and for individual economic activity was 300 roubles ($11), when the average wage received in the previous month in the sample from a primary job was 1034 roubles ($37).

Those with supplementary employment who do not have a primary job are a disparate group. Those who are not working by choice tend to earn much more and the unemployed a bit more in their supplementary employment than do those for whom this is a second job, while pensioners and students earn on average much less. Overall, in the ISITO household survey, those who did not have main jobs earned on average only a little over half the hourly rate of those in regular employment, but since they tended to work longer hours their total earnings were about the same, and this is also broadly the case in the RLMS data.

We have seen that the concept of 'secondary employment' covers a wide range of different practices and activities, with the sharpest contrast being between work as *sovmestitel'* and the contractual provision of professional services, which are more likely to be undertaken on a regular basis and are much more likely to be legally formalised, and trading and the provision of other kinds of services, which are more likely to be undertaken on an irregular basis and are much less likely to be formalised. Self-employment is nearly always unregistered and casual employment in the new private sector is rarely registered. The data sources differ somewhat in their estimation of the balance between these different types of secondary employment, probably above all because of the different forms of the questions asked. In general, the different sources are pretty consistent in their estimates of the scale of registered secondary employment, but seem to differ in the extent to which they capture the more informal and casual kinds of secondary employment which are usually unregistered and to which respondents may be more cautious to admit.

Since secondary employment tends to pay at a much higher rate than primary jobs for those in work, we might ask why people who feel that they are not earning enough do not simply change jobs, rather than taking on additional work? The obvious answer would be that the primary job, even if poorly paid, is more secure than the kind of activities in which people engage for their second jobs, not least because it includes entitlements to various social and welfare benefits and the accumulation of pensionable service. It does seem to be the case that some of those with second jobs minimise their commitment to their primary job, or even take leave from their primary job, to concentrate their efforts on their secondary employment, and some have clearly dropped their primary job altogether, regarding themselves as unemployed, while making their secondary employment their only income-generating activity. Thus it might well be, as some commentators have argued, that secondary employment serves as a stepping stone to another job, allowing a dissatisfied employee to explore the possibilities of labour mobility.

## Secondary employment and labour mobility

Secondary employment is usually regarded by economists and employers as a negative phenomenon, since it reduces the commitment of the employee to the principal place of work without replacing it with a commitment to what is predominantly a casual employment relationship in the second job. However, some commentators have suggested that secondary employment provides a way of easing the labour market transitions that are the inevitable consequence of large-scale employment restructuring. Individuals can 'try out' a new and risky endeavour and develop the appropriate skills and experience without having to make an irrevocable commitment to it. In this sense, secondary employment would be a form of 'graduated labour mobility' (Klopov, 1996).

Against this interpretation it should be emphasised that a substantial proportion of secondary employment does not involve experience of a different profession or the acquisition of new skills. For around a quarter of those in work, the second job is not even done in a different workplace, while a substantial proportion of regular second jobs are to be found not in the new private sector, but in state and former state enterprises and organisations. Secondary employment does not appear to make any special demands for new skills, although in the ISITO, but not in the RLMS data, those who had undergone additional training in recent years were significantly more likely to have supplementary employment than those who had not.

Tables 2.15 to 2.17 summarise the very similar findings of the three surveys regarding the professional demands of supplementary employment. Around a third of such jobs made no particular professional or skill demands, while well over half required skills which the employee already had. Only a very small proportion of secondary jobs required the employee to learn new skills or to exercise a higher level of skill than in his or her primary job. Moreover, secondary employment hardly prepares the employee for the rigours of capitalist work discipline, since two-thirds of respondents said that the intensity of work in the second job was about the same or less than in the primary job. For the majority, therefore, supplementary employment involves working longer hours to secure additional income without providing any opportunity to master a new profession or to upgrade their skills.

*Table 2.15:    Professional demands of supplementary job.*

| Percentage | VTsIOM Sept 1996; July 1997 | ISITO work history | ISITO household Survey |
|---|---|---|---|
| Same profession as in main job | 36 | 27 | 41 |
| Another profession I have | 28 | 31 | 19 |
| A profession acquired for the job | | 6 | 7 |
| No professional skill required | 28 | 35 | 32 |
| Other/No answer | 7 | 2 | |
| N | 600 | 310 | 559 |

*Table 2.16:    Skill demands of supplementary job.*

| Percentage | VTsIOM Sept 1996; July 1997 | ISITO work history | ISITO household Survey |
|---|---|---|---|
| More skill | 14 | 7 | 6 |
| About the same skill level | 37 | 31 | 46 |
| Less skill | 38 | 27 | 11 |
| Not comparable skill | | 20 | 37 |
| Other/No answer | 11 | 15 | |
| N | 599 | 362 | 559 |

*Source: VTsIOM survey data; ISITO work history survey; ISITO household survey.*

Overall we can conclude that in at least one-third of cases of secondary employment we observe the deskilling and dequalification of workers in their second jobs. Even if their original professional skills have been outdated with the virtual elimination of scientific and technological research and the liquidation of Russia's most technologically advanced industries, secondary employment rarely offers the opportunity to develop new skills since a substantial proportion of second jobs are casual and make very limited skill demands. Although secondary jobs often do not demand any particular skills, employers nevertheless prefer to take on highly qualified and experienced employees even for unskilled manual jobs (Chernina, 1996). Women, who have a higher educational level than men, have been the particular victims of deskilling through secondary employment, with a significantly higher proportion of women than men saying that their second jobs require less skill than their primary jobs or no skill at all, probably because women are more likely than men to work as unskilled sales personnel or to undertake menial work such as cleaning. Skilled workers and specialists are very likely to have to take a job at a lower level of skill, while managers and senior specialists are more likely to be able to find additional work in their own profession, often as consultants.

*Table 2.17: Intensity of supplementary job (ISITO Household Survey).*

| Percentage | |
| --- | --- |
| About the same as in main job | 25 |
| Higher than in main job | 33 |
| Lower than in main job | 42 |
| N = 428 | |

The overwhelming majority of industrial workers interviewed by us did not consider their additional work as a kind of 'insurance' in case they lost their main job, and did not consider the possibility of their additional work becoming their principal job. For them it was primarily a temporary, situational phenomenon allowing them to get through financial difficulties or to provide the family with a higher level of consumption. When we asked people in the ISITO household survey what they would do if they lost their main job, 45 percent of respondents who had second jobs nevertheless expected to get another job in their own profession, 17 percent in another profession but only 6 percent (11 percent of those who had regular second jobs) replied that they would concentrate on their second job. Just as many said that they would look for a variety of supplementary jobs.

The RLMS survey data enables us to follow employment changes over time, although it is difficult to identify job changes unambiguously in the data before 1998, when a direct question was included for the first time. On this data, those who had second jobs in any one round were about 20 percent more likely to change jobs than those who did not have a second job, a statistically significant but not a dramatic increase. However, having a second job did not seem to serve as a stepping stone to a job change – where the secondary occupation is recorded, only one in seven of those changing jobs took a job in the same profession as their previous secondary occupation.

Even if supplementary employment is not necessarily a stepping stone to a new job, it may play a role in easing labour mobility for those who are already seeking to change their jobs, even if it plays this role only for a minority. In the VTsIOM data, those who said that they were planning to change jobs in the near future were almost twice as likely to have second jobs as those with no such intention (conversely, 30 percent of those with second jobs, but only 18 percent of those without, were thinking of changing their main job). We would expect this to be particularly likely to be the case with the transition from the security of a state enterprise to the less secure, but often better-paid, alternatives of self-employment or work in the new private sector. This may be one reason why there appears to have been a decline in the incidence of secondary employment, as many people decide to move into new spheres of employment on a permanent basis, the professionalisation of the latter then reducing the opportunities for secondary employment.

Intending to change jobs and actually doing so are very different matters, with many more people declaring a desire to change jobs than actually do so. In the RLMS data, those who had second jobs in 1996 were twice as likely to say that they would like to find different work, while those who had said that they would like to change jobs were twice as likely to have done so by 1998, but the second job seems not to have been very significant in the change since those with second jobs in 1996 were not significantly more likely subsequently to have changed jobs than those without (men, those working in very small enterprises and in non-state enterprises and those with shorter job tenure were substantially more likely to have changed jobs, none of many other variables, including wage delays, administrative leave and payment in kind being statistically significant), nor were those who did not work in 1996 but had individual economic activity significantly more likely than those without such activity to be working in 1998, controlling for other socio-demographic factors.

The weight of the evidence points to the conclusion that secondary employment does not have an unambiguous impact on labour mobility: for some the second job may be a stepping stone to a new career, for others it may be a way of remaining in a job which pays low wages but may have other compensating advantages, with the two factors more or less balancing out, but for most people the decision to undertake secondary employment is more a situational than a strategic decision.

# THE INCIDENCE OF SECONDARY EMPLOYMENT

We have investigated the available data on the scale and forms of secondary employment. In this section we will look more systematically at the incidence of secondary employment. In exploring the incidence of secondary employment we are looking not simply at abstract individuals with particular socio-demographic characteristics, but at particular individuals making employment decisions within a dense network of social relations and social institutions. In this section we will discuss the various opportunities and constraints affecting the probability that people will engage in secondary employment and formulate and evaluate a series of hypotheses on the basis of regressions using the available datasets.

## Incentives, opportunities and constraints

Surveys consistently show that more people would like to have an additional job than in fact have one at present: having a second job is not just a matter of wanting an additional source of income, but it is also a matter of having the opportunity to have one. Goskomstat's Labour Force Survey shows that about four times as many people would like more work, half of whom would like to work longer hours and half of whom would like a second job, than actually have supplementary employment. VTsIOM has asked respondents on a number of occasions whether they would like to continue or to find additional work in the next three months. On average, a quarter of respondents said that they would like to have additional work, against one-eighth who in fact had it. In November 1997, of those who said that they did not want additional work, only 13 percent said that it was because they did not need it. Almost half said that they were not able to take on any additional work and almost a third that they could not get good work or work that brings in enough money. In the VTsIOM data, significantly more people without than with second jobs said that they did not have the time to work any more hours. To undertake supplementary work it is necessary to have the time to do so and the skills, experience and resources necessary to find additional employment.

We noted above that most of the industrial workers we interviewed had not been involved in secondary employment in the Soviet period. They had had plenty of money, considering how little there was to buy, while they did not have the time or energy to work further at the end of a normal working day. Industrial workers, like the rest of the Russian population, have felt the full weight of falling real wages against increasing demands and opportunities for expenditure in Russia since 1992. At first people began to find themselves short of money, but the workload at their main place of work had not been reduced significantly and this limited the extent to which they could try to supplement their incomes through secondary employment. Wage delays further increased the pressure on the household budget, but those not being paid their wages were still usually expected to put in a full working week, while the inability of the employer to pay limited the possibilities of secondary earnings at the main place of work. However, as enterprises began to cut back on production, rather than accumulate unsold stocks, and to put workers on short-time or send them on mass long-term 'administrative leave' (which would often last for several months) 'there was plenty of time but now there was not enough money'. This gave a powerful push to the development of secondary employment amongst industrial workers. It was precisely at this time that workers who in the past had not thought about other work were compelled to begin to search for it, and most got it by the traditional methods, through friends and relatives:

> When the shop stopped for three months, I worked as a loader in a greengrocery – my wife works there. It was unofficial, I was not registered, they simply paid cash (foreman, mechanical engineering factory).

> The first time I began to search for work was in January when they released us for three months of factory leave. Actually, it turned out to be only a month, but I had time to work 14 shifts as a seller in a kiosk. And in half a month I earned more than twice as much as I earned in a month at the factory. In the kiosk they recruited friends, the place was brisk, they asked me to stay there. I could and I wanted to, but after a while they called the shop back to work, I had no time to get used to trade (record-keeper, mechanical engineering factory).

> For seven months, I earned extra as a watchman in a state shop (my shop was not working at that time), because the console of the security indicator system was being repaired. I also worked there in an additional job as a driver (using my own automobile) and as a loader. I found this work very simply: my sister is the director of this shop (foreman, mechanical engineering factory).

As delays in the payment of wages escalated from 1995 there was less and less point in taking on additional work in a depressed enterprise: 'Now it is possible to find work, but it is more difficult to find money', so people began to look beyond the factory gates for an alternative source of income. As one respondent in a depressed enterprise explained:

> In general, earning extra at the factory is now ineffective: well, I could pick up the orders for seven jobs, but all the same there isn't any money – not for one job and not for seven.

> Now it is possible to earn extra here, doing repairs, for example, but there is not much sense, because there isn't any money.

Although our interviews suggested that industrial workers began to look for second jobs as they suffered from wage delays and lay-offs, the survey data seems to show that wage delays do not have a significant impact on the likelihood of people engaging in secondary employment, presumably for the reason already noted, that such people are still having to work in their primary job and so do not have the time and opportunity to undertake additional work.[28] In the VTsIOM data, the likelihood of those with wage delays having second jobs even declined over the period 1994–97 as wage delays became more extensive. Those who had not experienced wage delays also worked significantly longer hours in their second job, according to the VTsIOM data (Table 2.23, at the end of the chapter). Finally, in neither the RLMS nor the ISITO data were individuals with other household members suffering from wage delays significantly more likely to have secondary employment.

It might be expected that the situation would be very different with regard to administrative leave, when people may be laid off for long periods with little or no pay and have plenty of time on their hands. A September 1995 survey of workers on short-time or administrative leave (657 workers interviewed) found that 71 percent of respondents had additional earnings. Forty-five percent were not working at their own profession, 10 percent at their profession in another enterprise and 16 percent in their own enterprise at their own job (although only 2 percent of employers said this was possible). Only 30 percent would stay in their main jobs if they had to go back full-time, but 67 percent would do so if pay were increased (Garsiya-Iser et al., 1995). A May 1994 World Bank survey similarly found that most people on leave

---

[28] In the RLMS data, those with wage delays or part of their wages paid in kind were significantly more likely to engage in individual economic activity. Such forms of activity seem to be more responsive to changes in circumstances than more regular secondary employment.

had secondary employment, half being self-employment (Commander and Yemtsov, 1995).

In the RLMS data those on leave were not significantly more likely to have secondary employment (Table 2.27). The probabilities vary quite a lot from year to year (Table 2.2), but the number on leave in each survey is quite small and RLMS does not clearly differentiate those on compulsory leave from those who have taken leave from their main jobs by choice, either unpaid to concentrate their time and effort on a more lucrative second job while retaining the benefits of being registered in their official place of work, or to look after a sick child or relative, or on paid sick-leave or taking their regular vacation. In the ISITO household survey, one-third of those on unpaid leave (and more in the Goskomstat Labour Force Survey) had taken leave at their own request, the remaining two-thirds being on administrative leave.

Those who had been on administrative leave in the ISITO survey were more likely to have secondary employment, particularly occasional secondary employment, than those in work, while those in the RLMS surveys who had been sent on unpaid administrative leave were significantly more likely to have undertaken individual economic activity, though not to have taken second jobs.[29] In neither the ISITO nor the RLMS data does the existence of other household members who have suffered from administrative leave have any significant impact on the probability of the individual undertaking secondary employment. The VTsIOM data does not include information on leave, but those whose enterprises had seen lay-offs in the past year were slightly (and significantly) more likely to have second jobs than those whose primary employers had not made lay-offs, although those who thought that their own jobs were at risk were not more likely to have covered the risk by taking second jobs.

Although those on administrative leave do seem to find additional work to make up for their loss of earnings, both the interview and survey data suggest that they do not respond immediately to being sent on leave by finding supplementary employment.

---

[29]    RLMS only asks about unpaid administrative leave, but about a third of respondents on administrative leave in the Goskomstat Labour Force Survey report that they were paid during their leave, as required by the Labour Code. Although RLMS respondents are asked if they have ever been on leave, comparison of their responses across rounds indicates that the overwhelming majority in fact refer in their replies only to the previous year or so. Leave more than a year in the past has no significant impact on current secondary employment.

Domestic work takes up a lot of time – domestic work is really additional work. When the shop stopped, I worked in the house, repaired things, and my father and mother helped with money, they are pensioners (fitter, six classes of education, was born in the countryside).

People take some time to get used to their new situation, having a rest, doing things around the home, before they decide, in the face of shortage of money and falling stocks of food, that they will have to find second jobs, and only then do we find that they are more actively involved in secondary employment than their employed colleagues. Thus, in the ISITO work history survey, it was only when people had been on leave for well over two months in the course of the year (not necessarily continuously) that the incidence of secondary employment was significantly increased, with 63 percent of those who had been on leave for more than 80 days in the course of 1996 (10 percent of the sample) having engaged in secondary employment during the year, against 29 percent of those who had been on leave for 80 days or less and 28 percent of those who had not been on leave at all, so it would seem that it is not until people have been on leave for more than about two months that they become significantly more likely to engage in secondary employment. The RLMS data suggest the same: those whose last period of unpaid leave was less than two months were no more likely to have secondary employment than those who had had no experience of leave, while those whose last leave lasted more than two months were about twice as likely to have secondary employment, even if they were no longer on leave. In the ISITO household survey only a small number of respondents (2 percent of those in work) had been sent on administrative leave for more than 80 days in the previous year and the duration of leave had no impact on the probability of engaging in secondary employment.

Overall, the survey data suggests that the non-payment of wages, the payment of wages in kind and short-term lay-offs have little impact on the likelihood of individuals or household members taking on second jobs, although the RLMS data suggests that such people are more likely to engage in 'individual economic activity', doing odd jobs for friends and neighbours, buying and selling or, if they have a car, working as an unregistered taxi service. Those who have been laid-off for a long-period, of two months or more, are more likely to find themselves additional work and to continue to do such work even when they return to their regular jobs.

## Recruitment to second jobs

In order to get a second job it is necessary to have the skills, qualifications and experience that are in demand in an increasingly competitive labour market. However, it is also important to have the right connections because very few people get their second jobs through formal channels. Secondary employment is deeply embedded in the institutional framework of the workplace and the household, with their associated networks of friendship and kinship. The secondary labour market is not an anonymous marketplace in which potential employers meet up with potential employees. We have seen that a significant proportion of second jobs are in the same workplace as is the main job. Moreover, most people get a second job through personal connections and in many cases in the ISITO case study research we found that these personal connections are former workmates or managers who have got jobs elsewhere or set themselves up in business. Those who are self-employed for their supplementary employment similarly depend on personal networks to get access to customers, most people finding customers through friends and relatives rather than advertising their services more widely.

Secondary employment in most cases appears to be situational, in the sense that people do not decide that they need additional work and then go out and look for a job, seeking out advertisements, visiting the employment service or private agencies. Most people get their second jobs through a friend or relative, on the basis of a chance suggestion, or may be offered the job by the employer. This is confirmed by the survey data on the methods of recruitment to second jobs.

Over half of those asked by VTsIOM had got their supplementary job with the help of friends or relatives and only one in eight through an advertisement or an agency. More than 70 percent of the respondents in the ISITO work history survey had found out about their second job through personal connections, and two-thirds had actually got the job through such connections, while 20 percent had created the job for themselves, leaving only 3 percent who had found out about it through an advertisement and none through an agency. Similarly, in the ISITO household survey more than two-thirds of respondents had found their job through connections, 20 percent had created the job for themselves, 5 percent found out about it from an advertisement (second jobs involving pyramid selling are often found through advertisements) and fewer than 1 percent through an agency.

Those who had got the job independently or through an agency earned only a little over a third as much as those who had got the job through a friend or been offered it by an employer, although the best paid were those who had advertised their services or created their own job (the earnings of the latter groups were also much more dispersed so that the difference in earnings is not statistically significant).

One in ten of the respondents in the ISITO work history survey had been offered the job out of the blue, and this is a phenomenon that cropped up repeatedly in the more detailed work history interviews. It appears very commonly to have been the case that it was not the worker who was looking for additional work, but the employer who was seeking out somebody to do the job. While in the primary job market the worker usually looks for a job himself or herself (whether purposefully or casually), in the secondary labour market a significant proportion of workers play a passive role and it is the employers who are active. The employers use the same channels for finding workers as workers themselves use in looking for primary jobs (Clarke, 1999b), first of all making inquiries through current employees, friends and relatives, but in this case the information travels in the opposite direction, from the employer to the potential employee:

> I do additional work from time to time. Usually *they offer me* additional work on the computer, to type in some text. There were two such offers in 1996... In both cases *they offered me* work here. I did not look for additional work myself (senior foreman of offset shop, northern typography).

> I am a specialist on rabbeting machines. *They often call me* in to other printing works... I know a lot of people, if there is work, *they phone me* (rabbeting machine operator, Moscow typography).

> No, I did not look for additional work... How could I look for it? I am at work here all the time. What happened was that *they offered it to me* casually, and I agreed (chief of design office, engineering factory).

> Once a week I clean the mixing chambers... the *shop chief asked*, and I could not refuse, it is not difficult for me (worker, chocolate factory).

> I worked additionally as a cleaner in my own enterprise... *They offered it to me* themselves as *sovmestitel'stvo*. Possibly if they had not offered it to me, I would not have begun to look for additional work myself (personnel officer, northern typography, emphasis added in all cases).

We also quite often found in depressed enterprises that managers try to find supplementary employment for their more skilled and highly valued employees, in the hope that if they can guarantee them a chance to earn some money they will not leave for another job. Sometimes this involves shop chiefs actively looking for contracts and orders from outside to keep the shop working, as we have already seen, or it might involve making contact with other employers who might need some temporary or casual employees.

Most of those we interviewed who had actively sought supplementary work were those who were the least competitive in the secondary labour market, who looked for jobs which are not much in demand (cleaners in public sector organisations, sellers in state shops, tutorial assistants and so on).

> I worked additionally in the kindergarten as a night nurse.... The kindergarten was near my house, right beneath the window. I went and asked them: 'Would you be able to offer me any work?'. The head offered it to me – this job was always vacant, and I just needed to work the second shift, during the day I was at work (woman engineer, 40 years old, engineering factory).

> I worked additionally as a cleaner in the technical college. Immediately after I was dismissed (I worked there before as a guard) I asked the director to keep me as a cleaner (woman auxiliary worker, 54, from a family of refugees, dairy).

Those with a good network of social contacts are well placed to get themselves another job. In the ISITO household survey a number of questions were asked relating to the social network of the household, and we find that those whose household was involved in a more extensive social network were significantly more likely to have supplementary employment (although, of course, having another job may widen one's social network).[30] In view of the role of the new private sector in providing secondary employment it is interesting that there is also a significant tendency for those whose support networks include relatively more people who work in the new private sector to be more likely to have a second job (Tables 2.25, 2.26 at the end of the chapter).

## Opportunities for secondary employment

The ISITO, RLMS and VTsIOM regressions are quite consistent in confirming that those best-placed in the labour market both earn more

---

[30]    The head of household was asked whether or not the household had given or received help in money or in kind to or from up to three others in the previous twelve months. Each adult household member was asked to nominate one person outside the household with whom he or she spent free time, one to whom the respondent turned for advice regarding work problems (only asked of those currently in work) and one to whom the respondent might turn in search of a new job. The household network is defined very crudely as the total number of people nominated by household members in reply to these questions.

from secondary employment and are more likely than those less well-placed to engage in secondary employment. Prime-age well-educated men are the most likely to engage in secondary employment, although the variables age, sex and education are less significant once we control for occupational status and branch of the economy in the primary job. Sex differences are much greater in relation to occasional than to permanent or regular secondary employment and to individual economic activity than to having a second job.

Although those with the lowest incomes may have the greatest need of additional earnings, the very fact that they have low incomes indicates that they are relatively disadvantaged and so have the least opportunity to realise their aspiration for an acceptable standard of living. Those who are more in demand in the labour market as a whole have the best chances of getting additional employment: prime-age men with work experience and professional training or higher levels of education.

Age and educational level, which are partially related to one another, have a significant impact on involvement in secondary employment. Elderly workers tend to have a lower educational level and also tend to be involved in secondary employment less than younger and better educated workers. We would expect younger people to be more likely to change their jobs if they are dissatisfied with their wages than to seek additional employment, while those with a continuous work record would be expected to be more reluctant to give up their jobs.[31] Older people have fewer opportunities of finding supplementary employment and those over pension age have their pension to fall back on. Thus, as we would expect, the incidence of secondary employment increases with age but at a diminishing rate, falling off as retirement approaches.

The likelihood of engaging in supplementary employment also increases with the level of education, controlling for age and occupational characteristics, with those with higher education being the most likely to have a second job, particularly if they have a postgraduate degree. In the ISITO data, but not in RLMS, those who had undergone additional training in the last few years were also more likely to have secondary employment. RLMS has the most detailed information on education, but it does not appear that those with

---

[31] Job tenure does not have a significant impact on the probability of having secondary employment in the ISITO or RLMS regressions. However, those with more than ten years' tenure in their current job were significantly *less* likely to have secondary employment than those with shorter tenure in the ISITO household survey data.

vocational or technical education are more likely to be engaged in secondary employment than are those with more general qualifications. Nevertheless, we would expect those with technical or vocational qualifications that are highly in demand (accountants, computer specialists, building trades) to be more likely to have second jobs, while those with redundant qualifications will be less likely to be able to find supplementary work than those who have the adaptability of a more general education. Not surprisingly, those who have followed professional courses (the examples offered as prompts in the questionnaires are 'tractor driving, chauffeuring, typing, accounting') are particularly likely to have secondary employment.

According to respondents' self-definition of their socio-economic status, the incidence of secondary employment in the VTsIOM data increases as people move up the occupational scale, being highest for managers and lowest for unskilled workers. The proportion in regular secondary employment and in registered secondary employment also increases as the individual ascends the occupational scale (Perova, 1999). However, in general the differences between broad occupational categories are not statistically significant, mainly because the variance within each category is very large: constraints and possibilities depend more on the characteristics of the particular occupation than on its standing within the broader socio-economic classification. As would be expected, secondary employment tends to be most common among highly qualified professionals and, to a lesser extent, among skilled workers (see Tables 2.10a and 2.10b).

We would expect the supply of supplementary jobs to be greater where the market economy is more diversified and more highly developed, and we do in fact find that the incidence of secondary employment is significantly greater in large industrial cities than in smaller towns and in rural districts. There are not very substantial regional variations in the data, although the incidence of secondary employment is higher, but not spectacularly so, in Moscow and Saint Petersburg.

## Constraints

Sometimes the skills that people deploy in their second jobs have been acquired and honed in their primary workplace, so that the character of their primary job conditions the possibilities of secondary employment. The possibility of undertaking secondary employment is also very dependent on having the time and energy to do the additional work at the end of the normal working day, on days off or at weekends. The intensity of work and the work schedule in the primary job will be expected to affect the possibilities of undertaking secondary employment.

Constraints may be as important as opportunities in determining the likelihood of people undertaking additional employment: after all, only a small minority have regular second jobs and the majority of the population has never taken on additional work. We have already noted that the majority of VTsIOM respondents without second jobs say that they are not able to take on additional work. In the Supplement to the October 1997 Labour Force Survey in Komi and Kemerovo we asked the vast majority who had not had any supplementary employment why they had not taken on additional work. A quarter of respondents said they did not have the time, 17–18 percent each said that their health would not permit it, that they did not need to do it and that they could not find such work, while 7 percent said that they did not want to do it and 5 percent (mostly women) said that they were constrained by family circumstances.

Those who work long hours in demanding jobs may not have the time and energy to take on additional work, while those with relatively short working hours and few demands in their main job may be well able to take a second job (or those with a lucrative second job may reduce the hours they work in their main job). There is a significant inverse relation between the hours worked in the primary job and the likelihood of undertaking secondary employment in the RLMS data, but the relationship is weaker in the ISITO household survey data and in the ISITO work history survey of industrial workers there is a significant *positive* relationship between the hours worked in the primary job and the likelihood of having secondary employment. In general, those working a significantly reduced working week in their primary job are much more likely to have a second job, but there is not much variation among those working 40 hours or more in their main jobs.

In the ISITO household survey data there is actually a weak but significant ($p<.05$) *positive* correlation between the hours worked in the primary job and the hours worked in the second job, but there is no significant relationship in the RLMS data (VTsIOM does not have data on hours worked in the primary job). It appears that the hours worked in the first job do not impose a serious constraint on secondary employment: some people simply work extraordinarily long hours in order to earn what they regard as a satisfactory income.

The work regime may be as significant a factor as the actual length of the working week in determining the possibility of undertaking additional employment. Shift working, whether on a single shift ('from eight to five') or on rotating shifts, which is widespread in industrial enterprises, is a barrier to supplementary employment, particularly on a regular basis.

> I work from eight o'clock till five o'clock, when could I do any additional work? There is the child to fetch from nursery, to take for a walk, things to do in the house (foreman, confectionery factory).

> Now my work schedule means that I do not have an opportunity to do additional work. I would like to do additional work, but I cannot find any (foreman, metallurgical factory).

Some people work on 12 (16 or even 24) hour shifts, which is more convenient from the point of view of supplementary work because there is a fair amount of time between shifts. Obviously, the most convenient work regime from this point of view is the 'free' mode of working which does not impose any requirement for regular daily attendance at work, and in the ISITO household survey data those on such a schedule were significantly and substantially more likely to engage in secondary employment, as were those whose primary job was on a sub-contractual basis, than those with any other kind of work regime. It is hardly surprising to find that secondary employment among teachers in higher education and researchers in scientific institutes, who have plenty of time for it, is so widespread.[32] From this point of view the extensive use of administrative leave in industrial enterprises over the past few years has increased their employees' opportunities of taking on supplementary work, as we have just seen.

Those who are not working (or on leave from their jobs) comprise a very disparate group. Needless to say, the unemployed have the greatest incentive and opportunity to take on supplementary work and indeed those who are not employed are more likely to have such work in all the data sets, while the unemployed are much more likely than those with a primary job to have regular supplementary employment. The duration of unemployment has no significant impact on the

---

[32] A survey conducted in Kemerovo by Lena Varshavskaya and Inna Donova found that at least 65–70 percent of university lecturers had additional work. In the RLMS data, university lecturers were more than four times as likely as the average person to have a second job. This is probably one reason why academics tend to over-estimate the extent of and opportunities for secondary employment in the general population.

probability of having additional employment, which would suggest that it is the time freed rather than the income lost by unemployment, whose impact is likely to increase over time, which is the principal factor in determining the increased likelihood of the unemployed taking on additional work.

A further constraint on secondary employment is the fact that the demand for labour in the secondary labour market is concentrated on a relatively limited range of occupations, connected with the specificity of the kind of work involved, which correspond to the professional qualifications of only a limited number of workers. Others, therefore, either have to master a new trade, or find jobs which do not require any special professional training. It is no accident, therefore, that skilled professionals (computer programmers, lawyers, accountants – all of whom are three times as likely as others to have a second job in the RLMS data) and workers of mass universal trades (builders, mechanics, electricians, welders) have practically always had additional employment, even in the Soviet period. Workers with narrow occupational specialisation (miners, metallurgists, chemical industry operatives) objectively have much less chance of finding additional work, as there is virtually no demand for their professional skills in the secondary labour market.

Other objective factors which affect the workers' inclination to seek secondary employment are such characteristics as the physical burden and the degree of responsibility of their primary jobs. Thus, in the ISITO work history survey, only 4 percent of the employees of a bus company (most of whom were drivers) had had additional employment in 1996, against an average of 30 percent across all enterprises. In the RLMS surveys, bus drivers are one-third as likely to have a second job as the rest of the employed population.

> A bus driver must not overload himself too much. Our work involves risk for us and for others, if you get tired and run someone over, no amount of money can make up for it (driver, bus company).

A driver's wife expressed a similar view:

> Additional work? Constantly, you have to make ends meet... My husband does not do any additional work, he is a driver, they pay him a bit better. But then, if he does not rest properly, how will he keep his eyes open and do his work behind the wheel? I was always against him doing additional work (laundress, dairy combine).

When we come to social groups which are characterised by a combination of constraining factors we naturally find that they reinforce one another. For example, miners comprise a narrowly specialised group of workers involved in hard physical work living in small mono-industrial depressed towns and villages. Surveys conducted by ISITO in Vorkuta and Prokop'evsk in 1995–96 found that no more than 3–5 percent of the mineworkers had additional work.

## Secondary employment of workers at enterprises of various types

We might expect those with their primary jobs in the new private sector to be less likely than those working in state and former state enterprises to have second jobs because we would expect them to have higher primary earnings and more demanding jobs, reducing both the incentive and the opportunity to undertake secondary employment ('there is neither time nor energy left for additional work'). In the ISITO survey, those working in the new private sector were much less likely to have permanent second jobs than were those working in state enterprises, but there was no significant difference in the incidence of more irregular secondary employment. In the VTsIOM data there is no significant difference between those working in state and private enterprises in the likelihood of having a regular second job, but those working in privatised or private enterprises were significantly more likely to undertake occasional supplementary employment. This might be connected with the fact that those working in the private sector often have more flexible and informal working arrangements and have better connections with those offering casual employment, and so have more opportunity to undertake occasional secondary employment.

In ISITO case studies of new private enterprises, those engaging in secondary employment normally did so in the same trade or profession as they exercised in their first job. There is a tendency in both the VTsIOM and the ISITO data for people to have their first and their second jobs in the same sector. This is consistent with the idea that secondary employment is institutionally embedded, but runs somewhat counter to the idea that secondary employment provides a way in which people can optimise the balance of security and income-earning opportunities, by having one job in the state sector and the other in the private sector – although a job in the state sector offers precious little security nowadays.

As noted above, there are few differences between branches of the economy in the incidence of secondary employment, although those whose first job was in public services (primarily health and education), the entertainment industry or, to a lesser extent, in trade were significantly more, and agricultural employees significantly less, likely than others to supplement their income with a second job. Almost two-thirds of those working in state enterprises or organisations did their supplementary work as *sovmestitel'i*, equally divided between their own and another enterprise. Those working in state enterprises or those with their own businesses were those more likely to find supplementary employment in street or shuttle trading.

**Domestic constraints and household composition**

Many people who do not have primary jobs are impeded by other responsibilities or disabilities from taking on supplementary employment. Women on maternity and child care leave and people unable to work as a result of disability or ill health are much less likely than others to have a second job. The incidence of secondary employment declines sharply as retirement approaches and non-working pensioners are much less likely than employed people or the unemployed to have additional work (although, in the VTsIOM data, they were more likely than others to have regular supplementary work). Those who defined themselves as housewives (or, much more rarely, househusbands) were also substantially less likely than others to have supplementary earnings.

There is some variation between the datasets in relation to the influence of sex on the probability of undertaking secondary employment, controlling for other variables, perhaps because of the different patterns of secondary employment of men and women and the different forms of secondary employment captured by the different wording of the survey questions. In the VTsIOM data, men are substantially more likely than women to engage in secondary employment, particularly on an occasional basis. In the RLMS data, working men are much more likely than working women to engage in individual economic activity, but the differences in relation to second jobs and for those not working are not statistically significant. In the ISITO household survey data, men are much more likely to have occasional secondary employment than are women. Finally, in the Goskomstat Labour Force Survey data there is no difference between men and women in the incidence of secondary employment (see Table 2.1). In the VTsIOM data men tend to work significantly longer hours in their second jobs than do women, in the ISITO data the difference is not significant and in the RLMS and Goskomstat data there is no difference in the hours worked in their second jobs by men and women.

It seems that the difference between men and women is as much situational as being determined by their sex alone. Among those in work, women dominate in the health and education sectors, where regular secondary employment is the common method of augmenting miserly wages, and many of the jobs available on a casual basis (cleaners, casual sales personnel) are stereotypically women's work. Women may have demanding domestic responsibilities, on top of the demands of their primary job, and this might be expected to inhibit their further participation in the labour market. Women on maternity or childcare leave are indeed much less likely to engage in supplementary employment. Married women, particularly if they already have a primary job, are also much less likely to have secondary employment than those who are not married.

From the ISITO interviews it was clear that the stereotype that in case of material difficulties the man must be the first 'to rush to the barricades' is still strong: 'My husband is earning normally for now. If there isn't enough money, let him worry about it'; 'my husband has always earned good money'; 'my husband does not do badly – why should I work?' While women might expect their husbands to find a second job if the household is short of money, their expectations are by no means always realised. In the ISITO household survey, the heads of 20 percent of non-pensioner couple-headed households said that the household did not even have enough money to buy basic foodstuffs, yet in these households the men were not significantly more likely than their wives to have a second job (in 12 percent of these households only the wife had a second job, in 13 percent only the husband and in 6 percent both had second jobs, while in 20 percent of the less impoverished households only the husband and in 10 percent only the wife had a second job, with both having second jobs in 6 percent of cases).[33] The data is not entirely consistent, but, in general, married men are no more inclined than single men to engage in secondary employment, although married men do tend to work significantly longer hours in their secondary employment than do single men in the

[33]    Of course, this disparity will partly reflect the fact that women tend to earn much less than men, so that their secondary earnings are less likely to lift a household out of poverty.

ISITO and VTsIOM, but not in the RLMS, data (Table 2.23 at the end of the chapter).

In the ISITO and the VTsIOM surveys, the person who was identified as being responsible for bringing the main income into the household (the breadwinner) was substantially more likely to have a second job: a woman breadwinner was much more likely to have regular secondary employment than a man who was not the breadwinner (although, of course, they may have been designated as the breadwinner because they had a second job).[34] On the other hand, there is no evidence that the burden of domestic labour is a serious barrier to secondary employment for women. In the VTsIOM survey in July 1997 women who said that they were responsible for managing the household were not significantly less likely to be engaged in secondary employment than those who did not have that responsibility, although men in such circumstances were less likely to have secondary employment.

In the ISITO household survey women with second jobs devoted significantly (but not substantially – 22 against 24 hours per week) less time to housework than did those without second jobs, but secondary employment had no significant impact on the amount of housework that men did (around an average of 10 hours per week). However, although married women are much less likely than single women to have second jobs, when we control for other factors, the amount of time devoted to housework is not a significant variable in determining the probability of having a second job for either men or women. In the RLMS 1998 data, there is no statistically significant difference in the number of hours devoted to housework between either men or women with and without supplementary work although, controlling for other variables, women who devoted more time to domestic labour (including care for children and the elderly) were slightly less likely to have secondary employment ($p<.05$), while men who had primary jobs were significantly more likely to have secondary employment the *more* time they devoted to housework. It would seem, therefore, that women's obligation to devote an average of 24 hours a week to domestic labour (35 hours, including childcare and care of the elderly, in the RLMS data) is not a barrier to their undertaking supplementary employment: they simply add the hours to those that they already

[34] All adult members of the household were asked to identify the breadwinner in their household in the ISITO survey, the breadwinner for analytical purposes being identified by majority vote. In general, this turns out to be the highest earning member of the household, whether that be a man or a woman (Kozina, 2000).

work, while for men helping with the domestic labour is not an alternative to secondary employment as a claim on their time.

Controlling for other socio-demographic factors, the demographic composition of the household does not appear to be a very significant factor in determining the likelihood of engaging in supplementary employment. There are few significant differences in involvement in secondary employment according to whether the head of household is a man or a woman, nor according to whether there are children nor how many children there are in the household, nor how many pensioners or working members there are in the household. Members of households of one or two people are less likely to engage in secondary employment, those of three, four or five more likely to do so, but members of the largest households are not significantly more likely than average to do so, perhaps because such households will already have well-diversified income sources. While married women are substantially less likely than those who are single to be involved in secondary employment, divorced or separated women are more likely to have a second job than are married men. It would seem that married women are more constrained by domestic pressures, but divorced or separated women have more need to supplement their income.

It is striking in the ISITO household survey data, as noted above, that members of households which appear to be more integrated into wider social networks are more likely to engage in secondary employment, a finding which is consistent with the impression derived from the ISITO qualitative interviews that most secondary employment is situational, with offers of work being provided by friends and relatives. It is also very striking that an individual is much more likely to be involved in secondary employment if another household member also has supplementary employment – there does not appear to be a household division of labour in this respect. It rather appears that if the household members are oriented to increasing their income then all pull together. This suggests that subjective factors may play an important role in motivating secondary employment.

**Subjective factors**

A wide range of economic and socio-demographic variables are only weak predictors of the likelihood of an individual engaging in secondary employment (the pseudo-R-squared for the regressions typically ranging from 0.06 to a high of 0.20). It would seem that the objective socio-demographic factors captured in the regressions do not provide very strong incentives or constraints inducing or impeding people from engagement in secondary employment. This might lead us to surmise that much of the explanation for engagement in secondary employment comes down to situational and subjective factors. From our qualitative, work-history, interviews and our observation within enterprises it seems clear that the dividing line between those involved and those not involved in secondary employment is not determined entirely by objective and socio-demographic characteristics, but also by such social-psychological factors as the individual's activism, enterprise, mobility and initiative and by their inclusion in networks of connections and social information. Some people are more enterprising and energetic than others, and it is these people who are most likely to overcome the barriers and take on additional work to increase their incomes and widen their experience. In all the data sets there is quite a strong relationship between the likelihood of having additional employment and various indicators of a positive mood and self-image. Broadly speaking, those who are in a good mood are twice as likely to have a second job as those who are in a bad mood, although, of course, it may be that it is having a second job, or at least the income that it brings in, that puts them in a good mood. Those with second jobs are also more confident in their abilities: on both the VTsIOM and the RLMS data those with second jobs are far more likely to be confident that they could get another job in their own profession if they lost their primary job and in the RLMS survey those with second jobs are much more confident that they have the qualities valued in the contemporary economy.

## INCOME FROM SECONDARY EMPLOYMENT

Secondary employment performs a variety of functions for the individual undertaking it. For the vast majority of people, the main explicit motivation for seeking additional employment is to supplement their income. Thus, in July 1997 VTsIOM asked those who either had or wanted to have additional employment what were their motives. Almost three-quarters cited the inadequacy of their main income as a reason for seeking additional work and one in 11 said they needed money to make a large purchase. Taking on additional work may also be a way of trying out a new kind of work, with a view to changing jobs. Thus, one in 12 said they wanted to find more interesting work and, in similar vein, one in 20 saw supplementary work as a way of making useful contacts. One in 20 also said that they wanted something to occupy their spare time. On the other hand, in March and September 1996 respondents were asked whether they would continue with their supplementary job if they could earn a decent wage in their main job, and more than half said that they would, suggesting that there are more than direct pecuniary motives for engaging in secondary employment.

In the Supplement to the October 1997 Labour Force Survey in Komi and Kemerovo, 82 percent of those with supplementary employment said that they had done the work because they wanted to earn more, 13 percent because they were not able to work full-time in their main job (the implication being that this was a result of lay-offs or short-time working), 3 percent as insurance in case they lost their main job and 2 percent because it was their hobby. The overt motivation of those respondents to the Institute of Population survey who were working in more than one job was equally clear: 88 percent said that they did more than one job in order to earn more money, one-third in order to get themselves into a more stable situation, 17 percent because they liked it and 4 percent because their enterprise was at a standstill (ISEPN RAN, 1998).[35]

Although only a minority of the population have regular secondary employment, as much as half the population may be involved in secondary employment at some time of another. Moreover, we have seen that many people earn as much or more from their secondary employment as they do from their primary jobs. To appreciate the economic significance of secondary employment we have to look at its implications for the household budget. How much does it add to the household income, and to what extent does it provide a means by which the most impoverished households are able to make ends meet?

Secondary employment makes a substantial contribution to the money income of many of the households which have such a source of income. In the ISITO work history survey of industrial employees, one-third of respondents reported that their households had earnings

---

[35]    When asked why they liked or disliked having more than one job, 88 percent said they liked it because it gave them more money and 38 percent because it gave them more stability, but 61 percent said that they liked it because it gave them better contacts, 39 percent better opportunities and 33 percent more freedom from control. The reasons for disliking having several jobs are predictable: 85 percent noted the heavy workload, 62 percent the lack of free time and 8 percent the prevention of career development (ISEPN RAN, 1998, p. 126).

from secondary employment and estimated that such earnings contributed on average 23 percent to the household budget. Four percent of all respondents ranked this as their household's most important source of income, 20 percent ranked it second and 6 percent ranked it third (usually after primary wages and social benefits). For three-quarters of these households, supplementary earnings amounted to less than a quarter of household income, but for 10 percent of households it amounted to half or more of their household income. In the ISITO household survey, 60 percent of the heads of the one-third of households which had secondary earnings considered those earnings to be important for the security of the household.

The contribution of secondary earnings to household income revealed by our three main data sources is shown in Table 2.18 (ISITO),[36] Table 2.19 (RLMS) and Table 2.20 (VTsIOM). The data in each of these surveys is consistent in showing that secondary employment makes a significant and often substantial contribution to the household incomes of those lucky enough to have such a source of income.[37] In all three surveys, the median secondary earnings for those households which had such income were the equivalent of about two-thirds of the official subsistence minimum for one adult at the time of the survey, falling to a little under half the subsistence minimum in the RLMS data following the 1998 crisis.

Although fewer households reported that they had secondary employment, income from secondary employment makes about the same contribution to the household budget in the RLMS data as it does in the other datasets. This might be partly a result of non-payment and the fact that the RLMS data relates to the previous month, while the

---

[36] Those households in the ISITO survey in which the head acknowledged a supplementary income but no individuals declared any secondary income or employment (see above, p. 25) reported a higher household income, relative to the reported individual incomes of household members, than others, indicating that supplementary income was allowed for in the reported household income. Examination of the data suggests that unreported secondary income has a bigger impact on the analysis of the composition of household income than on its reported totals and it does not affect the conclusions regarding the determinants of secondary employment.

[37] This leaves aside the question of the extent to which secondary incomes are available to the household budget. Culturally, there is a fairly well-established understanding in Russia that secondary earnings are at the disposal of the individual, a phenomenon which is common in other countries (Pahl, 1980, p. 320). This practice would appear to be confirmed by the fact that, in the ISITO data, in households with declared secondary earnings, but not in those without secondary employment, the declared individual incomes of household members are significantly higher (by almost 20 percent) than the household income reported by the head of household. This would imply that only about a third of individual secondary earnings are at the disposal of the household.

ISITO data relates to the average income (over the past three months), so that many more RLMS than ISITO households reported little or no money income (non-payment affects secondary income much less, since people have little reason to work in second jobs if they are not paid).

The proportion of household income derived from secondary employment is also very similar in all three datasets, with little relationship between household primary income and the absolute level of secondary earnings. The highest income deciles earn proportionately less but absolutely more and the households with no other source of money income earn almost as much as the more prosperous households from secondary employment. Secondary employment makes a very substantial contribution to the household income of the poorest households whose members are fortunate or enterprising enough to have such employment.

*Table 2.18: Percentage of household income contributed by supplementary earnings by household income ranking (ISITO household survey data).*

| Ranking by household income per head net of secondary earnings by city | Mean percentage of household income (all households) | Percentage of households with reported secondary income | Mean percentage of household money income (only households with secondary income) | Median secondary income of households with such income (roubles) |
|---|---|---|---|---|
| First decile | 22 | 40 | 55 | 365 |
| Second decile | 7 | 23 | 30 | 300 |
| Second quintile | 4 | 18 | 24 | 300 |
| Third quintile | 3 | 17 | 20 | 300 |
| Fourth quintile | 3 | 18 | 19 | 300 |
| Ninth decile | 3 | 18 | 17 | 500 |
| Tenth decile | 4 | 22 | 17 | 500 |
| Total | 6 | 21 | 28 | 300 |
| N | 3723 | 3723 | 788 | 788 |

*Note: The first decile includes 29 households whose sole income was from secondary employment. The dollar exchange rate at the time of the survey was 6.13. Household income excludes loans and gifts.*

*Table 2.19: Percentage of household money income contributed by supplementary earnings, by household income ranking (RLMS 1994–2000).*

| Ranking by household money income per head net of secondary earnings by region | Mean percentage of household money income (all households) | Percentage of households with reported secondary income | Mean percentage of household money income (only households with secondary income) | Median secondary income of households with such income ($) |
|---|---|---|---|---|
| No income | | 17 | | 39 |
| First decile | 14 | 24 | 59 | 31 |
| Second decile | 7 | 19 | 37 | 28 |
| Second quintile | 5 | 15 | 30 | 28 |
| Third quintile | 3 | 12 | 25 | 29 |
| Fourth quintile | 2 | 11 | 21 | 34 |
| Ninth decile | 2 | 13 | 19 | 38 |
| Tenth decile | 2 | 12 | 16 | 42 |
| Total | 6 | 15 | 38 | 32 |
| N | 18 548 | 18 548 | 2 703 | 2 703 |

*Note: Money income excludes loans and gifts. Nine percent of households reported no (or negative) money income, other than that from secondary employment, varying from 5 percent in 1994 and 2000 to 17 percent in 1996 (those with negative money income had made a net cash loss on domestic production). Distributions do not differ significantly from year to year, except that the proportion of those with no income engaged in secondary employment fell from 24 percent in 1994 to 10 percent in 1996 and increased to 32 percent in 2000 (this partly reflects changes in the extent of non-payment of wages and benefits, since those with no income as a result of non-payment are much less likely to have secondary employment). The median secondary income of all households is the mean of the medians in each round. The median increased from $25 in 1994 to $58 in 1996, then fell to $17 in 1998 and $22 in 2000, reflecting the collapse of the rouble in August 1998.*

The fact that the lowest income households are the most likely to have secondary employment, and that their earnings from secondary employment are almost as substantial as those of the more prosperous households, would seem strongly to support the view that secondary employment is a very important component of the household survival strategies of the lowest income households. However, the data has to be interpreted cautiously. Many of these households have low (or no)

money income net of secondary earnings because household members
have decided to concentrate their efforts on what they report as
secondary employment. Some of these people have kept their formal
registration as employees of declining enterprises, but in fact their real
jobs are in much better paid unregistered employment, or they put their
efforts into more lucrative entrepreneurial activity. Others who are
working in unregistered employment report that they have no primary
job, because they have no registered place of work.

*Table 2.20　Percentage of household money income contributed by
supplementary earnings, by household income ranking
(VTsIOM March 1993–May 1998, weighted data).*

| Ranking by household money income per head net of secondary earnings by region and month | Mean percentage of household money income (all households) | Percentage of households with reported secondary income | Mean percentage of household money income (only households with secondary income) | Median secondary income of households with such income (thousand roubles) |
|---|---|---|---|---|
| No income | | 45 | | 386 |
| First decile | 9 | 17 | 52 | 218 |
| Second decile | 5 | 15 | 35 | 192 |
| Second quintile | 4 | 12 | 29 | 216 |
| Third quintile | 3 | 11 | 27 | 253 |
| Fourth quintile | 3 | 12 | 24 | 299 |
| Ninth decile | 3 | 13 | 24 | 389 |
| Tenth decile | 3 | 15 | 22 | 558 |
| Total | 5 | 13 | 36 | 267 |
| N | 102 167 | 104 451 | 13 758 | 15 447 |

*Note: Data before January 1994 and after January 1997 relates only to the
secondary earnings of the respondent (between those dates the respondent
accounted for all secondary earnings in 87 percent of households with secondary
earnings). Income is indexed to January 1996 prices, at which time the subsistence
minimum for working adults was 388 600 roubles and the dollar exchange rate
was 5 560; 1 210 households reported a total money income less than or equal to
that reported from secondary employment.*

Agricultural workers were notorious even in the Soviet period for
putting all their effort into their private plots and, in the RLMS data,
agricultural workers were twice as likely to have no net money

income, accounting for 17 percent of those with primary employment in households with no net money income. In the ISITO data, 90 percent of those in households with no net income who had supplementary employment were self-employed or worked unregistered in very small private businesses in the lucrative branches of trade, finance and repairs. In the RLMS survey, 38 percent of the second jobs of those from households with no other income were in occupations in transport, trade and catering, the predominant spheres of unregistered employment.

Although the lowest income households are the most likely to have secondary earnings, and secondary earnings make up the highest proportion of their household budgets, secondary employment makes only a marginal contribution to the relief of poverty. Since many low income households earn very little from their secondary employment, reported secondary employment only reduces the incidence of poverty (defined in relation to the official subsistence minimum) by about two percentage points in both the ISITO and the RLMS survey data (allowing about 5 percent of the households which would otherwise be in poverty to rise above the poverty line). If, in the ISITO data, we add to the reported household income of every household which appears to have undeclared secondary employment a sum equal to that earned by those who declare such employment, the effect is to increase the mean household income by about 10 percent uniformly across all the income groups, reducing the incidence of poverty by about six percentage points: a significant, but not substantial contribution to the survival prospects of the Russian household (Clarke, 2001).

To investigate the hypothesis that secondary employment can be considered to be an element of a household survival strategy, we have to look more closely at the relationship between individual and household income and the decision to undertake secondary employment.

## SECONDARY EMPLOYMENT AS AN ELEMENT OF A HOUSEHOLD SURVIVAL STRATEGY

The majority of people say that they take on secondary employment in order to increase their incomes, and secondary employment can make a substantial contribution to the household budgets of those who undertake it. However, the data considered in the previous section suggests that there is little variation in either the incidence of secondary employment or the amount earned according to the level of household income net of secondary earnings. It would seem *prima facie* more plausible to argue that secondary employment is a means by which those who have the initiative, incentive and opportunity to do so supplement their basic income regardless of their material situation, than that it can be seen as a particular response to a crisis of household subsistence. In this section we will look more closely at the data to ask to what extent individuals and households undertake secondary employment in response to financial and other difficulties.

Secondary employment was the traditional way in which households increased their incomes in the Soviet period and the traditional forms of secondary employment persist today, supplemented by new forms of casual, part-time and self-employment opened up by the growth of small businesses and the new market economy. But the opportunities for secondary employment are restricted by the limited demand for such employees on the part of employers, by the limited possibilities of self-employment and by the constraints imposed by the demands of a primary job or domestic responsibilities. Access to supplementary employment tends to depend on having the appropriate personal connections, since most hiring is on the initiative of the employer who seeks an employee through such connections. Thus, about half the population say that they are unable to undertake secondary employment for one reason or another, while three times as many people would like to have additional employment as in fact have it.

Those who already work long hours in their main job or have heavy domestic responsibilities do not have the time and energy to engage in secondary employment, while those who do not have the required professional or personal skills or, even more important, the connections necessary to get such work are largely excluded from the secondary labour market. The better-off earn much more from supplementary employment than do the poor, but such employment makes a greater relative contribution to the household income of the poorest households because their incomes without such an addition are so low. For those without specific and appropriate skills and connections, supplementary employment entails working long additional hours for a fairly meagre reward. Those least favoured in the primary labour market also tend to be those least successful in the secondary labour market, being less likely to have secondary employment and earning less when they do have it. Thus the evidence tends to indicate that informal employment provides a larger and more diversified source of household income for those households which are able to take advantage of their opportunities rather than a means by which the disadvantaged can compensate for the collapse of their money incomes.

This conclusion is supported by the fact that there does not appear to have been a dramatic growth in secondary employment since the Soviet period, and there is no evidence that its incidence increased as the economy moved deeper into crisis. The incidence of secondary employment is not particularly high by international standards, particularly when we take into account the fact that much of the work characterised as secondary employment in Russia is a substitute for the overtime working and part-time and casual primary employment that is common in other countries.

The August 1998 crisis had a very uneven impact and it hit some households particularly hard, but it seems to have had little impact on the incidence of secondary employment. According to the RLMS data, there was a significant increase in the incidence of individual economic activity in 2000 compared with the mid-1990s, but changes in individual circumstances seem to have had little impact on the incidence of secondary employment. Those who had suffered most in the crisis, comparing their situation in 1998 with that in 1996, seem to have been more likely to have changed jobs but not more likely to have taken on supplementary employment in 2000, while the only significant impact of a relative decline in household money income was a reduction in spending, particularly on food. The Goskomstat Labour Force Survey data suggests a marked increase in the incidence of secondary employment in 1999 over 1998, with a subsequent decline in 2000 (though changes in methodology mean that the data is not strictly comparable). This increase was concentrated on secondary self-employment and in the traditional branches of the economy, suggesting that it was a demand-side response to temporary labour shortages as production increased.

If secondary employment were an important element of the survival strategies of those in most distress, we would expect those suffering from the non-payment of wages and benefits, lay-offs and short-time working to be more likely than others to undertake secondary employment. However, we have seen that, apart from long-term lay-offs which leave the victim with the time to find and do additional work, such misfortunes have no significant impact on the probability of undertaking secondary employment (except that RLMS respondents who had not been paid their wages were more likely to have engaged in individual economic activity).

If the primary motive for undertaking secondary employment were to make up for a shortfall in household income, then we would expect those with lower household incomes per head to be more likely to have second jobs. In fact, those with lower household incomes are significantly less likely to have secondary employment, but this is to be expected because secondary employment significantly increases household income, so the relevant measure is the household income net of all secondary earnings.

Tables 2.24 to 2.28 (at the end of the chapter) report the results of a series of regressions exploring the probability of undertaking secondary employment and of undertaking regular as opposed to occasional secondary employment. In the VTsIOM data there is a significant negative relationship between household income per head, net of secondary earnings, and the probability of engaging in secondary employment, and particularly with having a regular second job, but the relationship to household income is not monotonic. In the other data sets there is no significant functional relationship with household income, but in general, as we have seen in the last section, the groups with the lowest monetary incomes are significantly more likely than average to have secondary employment, while those in higher income groups are generally more likely to have secondary employment than those with middle incomes.[38] However, as noted in the last section, many households have a low household income, net of secondary earnings, because their members have chosen to concentrate their efforts on lucrative secondary employment and either do not work in a primary job, or retain their registration in a low-paying job

---

[38]    In order to allow for temporal and regional variations, the variable used in the VTsIOM analysis is the income from primary employment (or household income per head, net of secondary earnings) relative to the average reported in the relevant survey in the same region (11 geographical regions) and the same type of population centre (ten types, ranging from national capitals to villages). In the analysis of the RLMS data the wage (household income per head, net of secondary earnings) is last month's wage (income) relative to the mean in the survey site in that round of the survey and in the ISITO data it is the average wage (income) relative to the mean of each city. In the latter two surveys household income is the aggregate of reported individual incomes, which tends to be a littler higher than that reported by the head of household. The reported results are not affected by the choice of income measure. Since neither logarithmic nor quadratic nor cubic income functions fit the data very well, income is included in the regressions presented here in the form of dummy variables representing income deciles.

which makes few, if any, demands on them in order to maintain their work record and pension rights. Thus, the direction of causality is by no means clear. Some households will have low or no monetary income net of secondary employment because they have decided to concentrate their household resources on the latter, which is an entirely rational strategy when we remember that hourly earnings from secondary employment tend to be considerably higher than earnings from primary jobs. To identify the direction of causality we need to relate the decision to undertake secondary employment to the household income prior to that decision.

In principle the RLMS data, which is a panel survey, enables us to explore the dynamics of household decision-making by relating the engagement in secondary employment to the circumstances of the household in previous rounds of the survey. Unfortunately, attempts to use the RLMS panel data to investigate changes over time were completely inconclusive, with a variety of objective and subjective measures of individual and household income in previous rounds having absolutely no relation to the decision to undertake secondary employment. This does not mean that there is no relationship, since most of the RLMS data on income and employment relates only to the month prior to the survey, so the comparison of two months one or two years apart may be a poor indicator of changing circumstances, since there are substantial fluctuations in earnings month by month at both the individual and the aggregate levels. For example, the average money wage reported by those interviewed by RLMS in December 2000 was more than double that of those interviewed in September and that reported in January 1999 (though only eight respondents) was almost three times that reported in November 1998!

So far we have looked at the relationship between household income and the decision to undertake secondary employment. However, it may be that people make their secondary employment decisions not so much on the basis of the circumstances of the household, but on the basis of their own personal circumstances, particularly if, as is still the common custom in Russia, the individual has some claim on secondary earnings for his or her personal spending. In this case we would expect the decision to undertake additional employment to be more sensitive to the primary wage received by the individual than to the income of the household as a whole. However, we would expect the level of the primary wage to affect the incentives to undertake primary employment in two contrary directions. On the one hand, those who earn less in their first job are more likely to need to take a second job to supplement their income. On the other hand, we might expect those who earn more in their primary jobs also to be able to earn higher wages in a second job and so to have more incentive to take on such a job. In general, it seems to be the former tendency that prevails. Although in the VTsIOM data the individual wage is not significant in determining the probability of engaging in secondary employment, in the RLMS data there is a significant inverse logarithmic relation between the wage earned in the primary job and the probability of having a second job or engaging in individual economic activity. The relationship is weaker in the ISITO data, only being significant in relation to occasional secondary employment (and of having worked in a second job in the previous month). This data suggests that necessity is a stronger factor than opportunity in determining the probability of engaging in secondary employment.

There is no evidence that a fall in wages makes people more inclined to undertake secondary employment. In the VTsIOM data, those who said that their primary wage had increased relative to prices were slightly more likely to have secondary employment than those whose real wage had fallen (although we only have this data for January 1997 and January 1998). In the RLMS data there is no significant relationship between change in primary wage income between rounds and the probability of having secondary employment.

The fact that the individual wage appears to be a more significant determinant of the probability of engaging in secondary employment than is the household income might suggest that secondary employment decisions are part of individual rather than household earning strategies. This supposition is supported by examination of the relation between the secondary employment decisions of individuals within households. In a household strategy it makes sense for the highest earner to put in the extra working hours needed to raise the household income, but in fact, in the ISITO household survey data, in couple-headed households the lower-earner is slightly more likely than the higher earner to take on a second job, as can be seen in Table 2.21, suggesting that low-earners seek to supplement their income regardless of the situation of other household members.

This conclusion is reinforced by the fact that the income and employment situation of other household members has no impact on the decision to undertake secondary employment if the relevant variables are inserted into the regressions, except that an individual is much more likely to undertake secondary employment if other household members also have second jobs, perhaps because access to secondary employment depends on social connections which are likely to be shared by household members. This suggests that employment decisions are not made as part of a household employment strategy, which would imply that there would be a household division of labour, with the highest earner being fully committed to the labour market. Employment decisions seem to be taken more or less independently by household members, perhaps with a 'demonstration effect' by which the successful experience of one household member in the secondary labour market induces others to follow, so that household members tend to sink or swim together.

*Table 2.21: Who has secondary employment? (couple-based households in which both partners are working).*

| Percentage | All households | Non-pensioner households |
|---|---|---|
| Neither | 67 | 64 |
| Both | 5 | 5 |
| Low earner | 15 | 16 |
| High earner | 13 | 14 |
| N | 1 786 | 1 559 |

*Source: ISITO household survey.*

If low wages provide an incentive to engage in secondary employment, we would expect those earning less than their potential in their main job to be more likely to take on additional work, both because of their relatively lower wages and because they would be expected to earn relatively more in their second jobs. However, the extent to which the actual earnings in the primary job diverge from the earnings predicted by a standard wage regression has no impact on the probability that an individual would have a second job in any of the three data sets, although in the ISITO household survey those who said that their enterprise paid lower wages than comparable enterprises were significantly more likely to have had second jobs.

We would expect the decision to take on a second job to be influenced not only by the level of wages in the primary job, but also by the earnings that could be expected from supplementary employment, but this is difficult to test because we do not know how much those who do not have a second job would earn, or would expect to earn, if they did have a job, although there is a significant correlation between earnings in primary and secondary employment.[39] We can predict people's likely secondary earnings with a wage regression, but earnings depend on so many contingent factors that the standard errors of such wage regressions are very high, so the predicted wage provides a poor indicator of the wage that an individual could in fact expect to earn.[40] In none of the three data sets is there a significant relationship between the probability of engaging in secondary employment and the secondary wage predicted in a separate wage regression.

We have so far been looking at the impact of objective income indicators on the secondary employment decision. However, the motivating factor in taking up additional employment is likely to be not so much the absolute level of current individual or household income as the extent to which people are satisfied with that income. We can explore the relationship between secondary employment and the respondent's assessment of changes in and degree of satisfaction with their level of wages and household income, although it is again difficult to disentangle cause and effect. In the VTsIOM data, those who said that they were more or less dissatisfied with their wage in their main job were not more likely to have a second job than those who were more or less satisfied. On the other hand, those who said that their household income had increased relative to prices and those who evaluated the material position of their household as being more prosperous were significantly *more* likely to have secondary employment than those whose income had fallen or who were less satisfied with their economic situation, although in each case the increase in income and the favourable evaluation may have been a result of the income brought in by secondary employment. The same applies to the strong positive relationship between both the head of household's assessment of the material position of the family and the individual's satisfaction with his or her income and household members' engagement in secondary employment in the ISITO data.

---

[39]   The Pearson coefficient for the correlation between primary and secondary earnings in the RLMS data is 0.35, in the VTsIOM data is 0.33 and in the ISITO data is 0.42, although the correlation between hourly earnings in first and second jobs is lower at 0.26 in the RLMS data and 0.25 in the ISITO data.

[40]   The R squared in a standard regression of the secondary wage on age, sex and education, including quadratic terms for the latter two variables, controlling for region and type of population centre, in the three data sets is between 0.09 and 0.19.

The same caveat applies to the finding in the ISITO household survey data that those who said that their family had experienced financial difficulties in the past two years were no more likely than those who had faced no such difficulties to be involved in secondary employment and to the very significant positive relationship in the RLMS data between the probability of engaging in secondary employment and both the assessment of the degree of positive change in the household's economic situation over the past five years (only asked in 1998 and 2000) and the subjective ranking of the level of household prosperity. Indeed, those who have secondary employment rank significantly more highly on a whole range of measures of well-being, but we cannot draw any clear conclusions from this: it may be that those who are more optimistic and more contented are more likely to take the initiative to find additional work, or it may be that having additional work fosters their sense of well-being.

RLMS and VTsIOM on occasion ask respondents what they consider to be the income that a household needs to live normally, and if we compare this with the household income (net of secondary earnings) reported by the respondent we have an alternative indicator of the degree of satisfaction or dissatisfaction with the level of household income. In the RLMS data, those with a lower household income, net of their secondary earnings, in relation to that regarded as necessary to lead a normal life were marginally, but not to a statistically significant degree ($p>0.075$), more likely to engage in additional income earning activities. There is no statistically significant relationship in the VTsIOM data. Thus, the analysis of indicators of dissatisfaction with the current levels of individual or household income does not support the hypothesis that there is a positive relationship between such dissatisfaction and the likelihood of being involved in secondary employment.

Reviewing the evidence as a whole, we can conclude that there is no unambiguous relationship between either subjective or objective measures of individual or household income and the likelihood of engaging in secondary employment. Those with lower household incomes are less likely to have secondary employment, but their low household income is a result of the fact that they have no secondary earnings. Those with lower household incomes net of secondary earnings are more likely to have secondary employment, but this might be because they have reduced their other sources of income by concentrating their efforts on their secondary employment. Those who are more satisfied with their income are more likely to have secondary employment, but their satisfaction is as likely to be a result as a cause of the decision to take a second job. There is slightly more evidence that secondary employment is undertaken to compensate for a low individual wage in primary employment, though the relationship is only significant in the RLMS data.

A final point that needs to be considered is the relationship between primary and secondary employment decisions. In the analysis so far, we have implicitly assumed that the individual makes a decision about taking a second job in the context of their wage in a given primary job. However, from the economist's point of view it is by no means clear that it is ever rational to take a second job. If the individual earns more in the first job than he or she can earn in a second job, then it makes more sense to work longer hours in the first job, rather than to take on a second job elsewhere. Indeed, in the Labour Force Survey data, a small majority of those seeking additional work would like to work longer hours rather than have a second job, but this may not be possible, either because of hours inflexibility or because additional hours are not paid: in the ISITO household survey only 6 percent of respondents were paid for working overtime at a higher rate, 40 percent were not paid anything for working overtime, and one-third of respondents never worked overtime at all. From this perspective, secondary employment arises because of the inflexibility of hours and payment systems as people have to take a second job because it is impossible to earn more by working longer hours at their first job.

If, as is most often the case, the individual earns more at the second job than at the first job, the question arises of why people do not change jobs rather than continue with a low-paid primary job. The answer to this is most likely to be found in the fact that most secondary employment is casual and occasional and does not provide the stability and security that many people look for in a primary job, and that much of it is unregistered, so that it does not provide a record of labour service to contribute to a pension or entitlement to such statutory benefits as holiday pay and sick leave.

We can conclude that secondary employment provides a significant source of secondary income for many Russian families, but 'secondary employment' does not provide the answer to the riddle of how Russian households survive in conditions of declining income and employment. The survey data consistently shows that only a small proportion of the population has a regular source of additional income from supplementary employment. The evidence from the ISITO survey would seem to indicate that there is a significant degree of concealment of secondary earnings and employment from researchers. However, even if we allow for a high level of non-response to questions on informal employment, the evidence still suggests that the majority of the population has no such source of income, and only a minority is able to count on a regular and substantial addition to the household income from this source.

Secondary employment has both positive and negative social consequences. On the one hand, it provides a partial resolution of the financial problems of those households which have members active in the secondary labour market – the ISITO survey indicates that secondary employment contributes on average over a quarter of the household budget to about a fifth of households, the VTsIOM and RLMS data suggest that it contributes an even larger proportion of income, but of fewer households. On the other hand, it can provide a substantial source of additional income for those with high professional skills, many of whom may have low-paid primary jobs in declining enterprises or in the public sector. Secondary employment may also widen a person's perception of their possibilities and abilities and soften their adaptation to new economic and employment relations, although we found little evidence that secondary employment plays a significant role in encouraging labour mobility: indeed, by enabling people to remain in what would otherwise be untenable jobs it may inhibit such mobility. However, in ISITO case studies of new private enterprises we found that it was very common for the founders of such enterprises initially to have established their new activity as a form of supplementary employment.

At the same time, one cannot ignore the negative consequences of secondary employment. For the worker it involves having to work extremely long hours, often in poor conditions involving a degradation of professional skills, under insecure and unstable terms without any of the social protection and social benefits that still attach to most formal employment.[41]

From the perspective of hard-pressed employers, facilitating or even encouraging secondary employment enables them to hold on to the

---

[41] In the 2000 round of RLMS, around 90 percent of primary jobs provided the holiday pay, sick and maternity leave required by law, while fewer than half of second jobs provided these benefits. Primary jobs were between two and three times as likely to provide other benefits such as medical treatment, sanatoria, child care, loans and subsidies for food, transport and education as were second jobs.

core of the labour force in anticipation of future recovery. On the other hand, the ability provided to employers to retain a labour force while paying low or no wages is hardly in the best interests of their employees and may act as a barrier to economic restructuring. Secondary employment provides a flexible labour force for small businesses in the new private sector, but it also fosters the growth of the informal economy, which reinforces the deregulation and criminalisation of economic activity, while the ready supply of casual, insecure and unprotected labour that it provides facilitates the survival of companies which base their competitive strength on cutting labour costs and avoiding taxation rather than through investment and efficient work practices. From the perspective of the state, informal employment entails a loss of tax and social insurance revenues, but at the same time it provides a safety valve by enabling the more energetic and enterprising to provide for themselves in difficult economic conditions, diverting them from potentially more dangerous collective mobilisation (the energies of many leaders of the workers' movement which emerged in the late 1980s were indeed diverted into channels of 'commercial' activity).

*Table 2.22: OLS regressions – dependent variables: log of earnings in main job and log hourly earnings in second job (relative to mean for region, type of population centre and month; VTsIOM data, March 1993 to May 1998).*

| | Log of earnings in main job | | | Log of hourly earnings in second job | | |
|---|---|---|---|---|---|---|
| | B | Std error | Variable mean | B | Std error | Variable mean |
| (Constant) | −1.65*** | 0.04 | −0.38 | 1.58*** | 0.13 | 1.79 |
| Education (primary or less is reference) | | | | | | |
| Incomplete secondary | 0.10*** | 0.02 | 0.09 | 0.11 | 0.08 | 0.09 |
| Secondary | 0.13*** | 0.02 | 0.17 | 0.14 | 0.07 | 0.17 |
| Vocational | 0.18*** | 0.02 | 0.11 | 0.14 | 0.08 | 0.11 |
| Technical | 0.22*** | 0.02 | 0.31 | 0.25*** | 0.07 | 0.25 |
| Incomplete higher | 0.29*** | 0.03 | 0.03 | 0.32*** | 0.08 | 0.06 |
| Higher education | 0.38*** | 0.02 | 0.27 | 0.50*** | 0.07 | 0.29 |
| Male | 0.31*** | 0.01 | 0.45 | 0.35*** | 0.04 | 0.52 |
| Husband | 0.06*** | 0.01 | 0.36 | 0.04 | 0.03 | 0.36 |
| Wife | 0.003 | 0.01 | 0.35 | 0.06* | 0.03 | 0.26 |
| Age | 0.03*** | 0.00 | 39.06 | 0.00 | 0.01 | 38.37 |
| Age squared/100 | −0.04*** | 0.00 | 16.50 | −0.02** | 0.01 | 16.60 |
| Primary employment status (waged or salaried employee is reference) | | | | | | |
| Full-time student | | | | −0.31*** | 0.05 | 0.07 |
| Pensioner | | | | −0.35*** | 0.05 | 0.11 |
| Housekeeper | | | | 0.01 | 0.06 | 0.04 |
| Unemployed | | | | −0.11** | 0.04 | 0.08 |
| Employed on contract | 0.07*** | 0.01 | 0.08 | 0.15*** | 0.04 | 0.07 |
| Self-employed | 0.38*** | 0.03 | 0.02 | 0.29** | 0.09 | 0.01 |
| Entrepreneur | 0.60*** | 0.02 | 0.03 | 0.81*** | 0.06 | 0.03 |
| Wage paid in full and on time | 0.17*** | 0.01 | 0.52 | | | |
| Branch of primary job (trade and services is reference) | | | | | | |
| Industry, etc. | 0.04*** | 0.01 | 0.40 | −0.05 | 0.04 | 0.37 |
| Agriculture | −0.30*** | 0.01 | 0.10 | −0.20** | 0.06 | 0.09 |
| Public services | −0.22*** | 0.01 | 0.23 | −0.24*** | 0.05 | 0.28 |
| Public administration | 0.04*** | 0.02 | 0.05 | 0.01 | 0.08 | 0.03 |
| State security | 0.14*** | 0.02 | 0.04 | −0.21* | 0.09 | 0.03 |

*Table 2.22 (Continued)*

| Sector of primary job (state enterprise is reference) | | | | | |
|---|---|---|---|---|---|
| State company | 0.06** | 0.01 | 0.18 | −0.02 | 0.04 | 0.15 |
| Co-operative, etc. | 0.01 | 0.01 | 0.09 | 0.05 | 0.05 | 0.09 |
| Non-state company | 0.20*** | 0.01 | 0.05 | 0.15* | 0.06 | 0.07 |
| Private company | 0.24*** | 0.01 | 0.08 | 0.11* | 0.05 | 0.11 |
| Individual labour activity | 0.27*** | 0.03 | 0.02 | 0.24* | 0.10 | 0.03 |
| Socio-economic status in primary job (unskilled worker is reference) | | | | | |
| Managers | 0.49*** | 0.02 | 0.08 | 0.48*** | 0.08 | 0.08 |
| Professionals | 0.31*** | 0.01 | 0.26 | 0.32*** | 0.06 | 0.33 |
| Junior specialists | 0.19*** | 0.01 | 0.08 | 0.18* | 0.08 | 0.07 |
| Administrative and commercial | 0.34*** | 0.02 | 0.07 | 0.37*** | 0.08 | 0.07 |
| Clerical; sales and service staff | 0.11*** | 0.01 | 0.12 | 0.18** | 0.07 | 0.09 |
| Skilled workers | 0.28*** | 0.01 | 0.29 | 0.26*** | 0.06 | 0.29 |
| N | 54 970 | | | 11 911 | | |
| R Squared | 0.287 | | | 0.115 | | |
| Standard error of regression | 0.672 | | | 1.11 | | |

Significance of coefficients: ***$p<.001$ ; **$p<.01$; * $p<.05$

*Notes: Dummy variables were also included for the region, type of population centre and year. Coefficients for features of the primary job in the secondary wage regression are for a separate regression run for those with such a job.*

*Table 2.23: OLS regression – dependent variable: log of hours worked last month in supplementary job (VTsIOM data, March 1993-May 1998).*

|  | Those in work | | | Those not in work | | |
|---|---|---|---|---|---|---|
|  | B | Std error | Variable mean | B | Std error | Variable mean |
| (Constant) | 3.06*** | 0.13 | 3.79 | 3.60*** | 0.14 | 4.11 |
| Occupational status (waged or salaried employee is reference) | | | | | | |
| Full-time student |  |  |  | 0.09 | 0.11 | 0.20 |
| Pensioner |  |  |  | 0.20 | 0.11 | 0.38 |
| Housekeeper |  |  |  | 0.08 | 0.11 | 0.11 |
| Unemployed |  |  |  | 0.22* | 0.10 | 0.24 |
| Employed on contract | 0.10** | 0.03 | 0.10 |  |  |  |
| Entrepreneur | 0.17** | 0.06 | 0.04 |  |  |  |
| Self-employed | 0.11 | 0.09 | 0.02 |  |  |  |
| Education (primary or less is reference) | | | | | | |
| Incomplete secondary | 0.23* | 0.11 | 0.07 | –0.01 | 0.07 | 0.15 |
| Secondary | 0.26* | 0.11 | 0.14 | 0.01 | 0.07 | 0.23 |
| Vocational | 0.25* | 0.11 | 0.12 | –0.08 | 0.07 | 0.09 |
| Technical | 0.26* | 0.11 | 0.28 | 0.10 | 0.06 | 0.22 |
| Incomplete higher | 0.27* | 0.12 | 0.04 | 0.01 | 0.08 | 0.09 |
| Higher education | 0.23* | 0.11 | 0.36 | –0.04 | 0.07 | 0.17 |
| Male | 0.11** | 0.04 | 0.54 | 0.14*** | 0.04 | 0.43 |
| Husband | 0.09* | 0.04 | 0.43 | 0.11* | 0.05 | 0.22 |
| Wife | –0.05 | 0.03 | 0.26 | –0.01 | 0.04 | 0.27 |
| Household size | 0.02* | 0.01 | 3.26 | 0.01 | 0.01 | 2.93 |
| Age group (reference is 25–39) | | | | | | |
| Aged under 24 | –0.02 | 0.03 | 0.12 | –0.07 | 0.05 | 0.30 |
| Aged 40–49 | 0.00 | 0.02 | 0.28 | 0.03 | 0.05 | 0.09 |
| Aged over 50 | –0.05 | 0.03 | 0.11 | 0.02 | 0.07 | 0.07 |
| Pension age–75 | 0.03 | 0.05 | 0.04 | 0.01 | 0.07 | 0.33 |
| Over 75 | –0.59 | 0.40 | 0.00 | –0.22 | 0.17 | 0.01 |
| Wage paid in full and on time | 0.02 | 0.02 | 0.49 |  |  |  |

*Table 2.23 (continued)*

| Branch of primary job (trade and services is reference) | | | | | |
|---|---|---|---|---|---|
| Industry, etc. | 0.05 | 0.03 | 0.37 | | |
| Agriculture | −0.01 | 0.05 | 0.09 | | |
| Public Services | 0.00 | 0.04 | 0.29 | | |
| Public administration | 0.01 | 0.06 | 0.03 | | |
| State security | 0.15* | 0.07 | 0.03 | | |
| Sector of primary job (collective etc. is reference) | | | | | |
| State company | −0.01 | 0.03 | 0.15 | | |
| Co-operative, etc. | −0.05 | 0.04 | 0.10 | | |
| Non-state company | −0.04 | 0.04 | 0.07 | | |
| Private company | −0.01 | 0.04 | 0.11 | | |
| Individual labour activity | 0.00 | 0.08 | 0.03 | | |
| Socio-economic status in primary job (unskilled worker is reference) | | | | | |
| Managers | −0.06 | 0.05 | 0.08 | | |
| Professionals | −0.05 | 0.05 | 0.33 | | |
| Junior specialists | −0.06 | 0.05 | 0.07 | | |
| Administrative and commercial | 0.01 | 0.05 | 0.07 | | |
| Clerical, sales and service staff | −0.05 | 0.05 | 0.09 | | |
| Skilled workers | −0.05 | 0.04 | 0.28 | | |
| Log of primary wage | 0.02 | 0.02 | −0.33 | | |
| Log of secondary earnings | −0.30** | 0.01 | −0.52 | −0.33*** | 0.01 | −0.94 |
| Log of household income per head | 0.01 | 0.01 | −0.36 | 0.02** | 0.00 | −0.81 |
| N | 6448 | | | 3416 | | |
| R squared | 0.18 | | | 0.24 | | |
| Standard error | 0.79 | | | 0.77 | | |

Significance of coefficients: ***p<.001 ; **p<.01; * p<.05

*Note: Secondary earnings, primary wage and household income per head are relative to the mean for the region, month and type of population centre. Dummies for region, type of population centre and year were also included in the regression.*

*Table 2.24: Multinomial logistic regression – probability of having permanent, regular or occasional secondary employment; those with a primary job (ISITO household survey).*

| | Permanent | | Regular | | From time to time | |
|---|---|---|---|---|---|---|
| | Odds ratio | Std error | Odds ratio | Std error | Odds ratio | Std error |
| Male | 0.48 | 0.21 | 0.72 | 0.39 | 2.20** | 0.59 |
| Married man | 2.47* | 1.04 | 1.27 | 0.64 | 0.94 | 0.21 |
| Married woman* | 0.54** | 0.13 | 0.40** | 0.14 | 0.99 | 0.20 |
| Education (reference is secondary or less) | | | | | | |
| Middle special | 1.15 | 0.25 | 1.77 | 0.60 | 1.15 | 0.17 |
| Incomplete higher | 1.58 | 0.77 | 3.57* | 1.77 | 1.36 | 0.44 |
| Higher education** | 2.59** | 0.80 | 1.63 | 0.73 | 1.38 | 0.30 |
| Postgraduate | 15.27*** | 10.09 | 2.99 | 3.58 | 1.79 | 2.05 |
| City (Kemerovo is reference) | | | | | | |
| Samara | 1.30 | 0.31 | 1.09 | 0.34 | 1.23 | 0.21 |
| Lyubertsy | 1.28 | 0.35 | 1.59 | 0.51 | 0.82 | 0.18 |
| Syktyvkar | 0.62 | 0.16 | 1.02 | 0.35 | 1.40 | 0.24 |
| Occupational status in primary job (skilled worker is reference) | | | | | | |
| Manager | 0.25* | 0.14 | 1.16 | 0.59 | 1.16 | 0.31 |
| Professional | 0.70 | 0.23 | 1.23 | 0.50 | 1.14 | 0.28 |
| Junior specialist | 0.87 | 0.30 | 0.71 | 0.33 | 1.05 | 0.24 |
| Clerical and sales | 0.74 | 0.28 | 0.85 | 0.39 | 0.55* | 0.16 |
| Service personnel | 0.74 | 0.29 | 0.71 | 0.33 | 0.83 | 0.21 |
| Unskilled worker | 0.87 | 0.26 | 0.84 | 0.33 | 0.73 | 0.14 |
| Branch of employment (industry is reference) | | | | | | |
| Construction | 1.59 | 0.54 | 1.73 | 1.04 | 1.26 | 0.30 |
| Transport | 0.25* | 0.14 | 2.20 | 1.19 | 1.26 | 0.28 |
| Trade | 1.08 | 0.33 | 3.98** | 1.75 | 0.90 | 0.19 |
| Services | 0.77 | 0.48 | 6.23** | 3.62 | 0.73 | 0.29 |
| Public administration | 1.05 | 0.35 | 3.44* | 1.74 | 1.01 | 0.23 |
| Education and health** | 2.00* | 0.62 | 4.89** | 2.36 | 1.41 | 0.30 |
| Wage delays and interruptions to employment (in past year) | | | | | | |
| Owed wages by employer | 0.94 | 0.19 | 0.96 | 0.24 | 1.24 | 0.17 |
| Paid partly in kind | 1.56 | 0.39 | 1.45 | 0.55 | 0.98 | 0.16 |
| Now on admin. leave | 2.26 | 1.45 | 0.00*** | 0.00 | 2.10 | 0.89 |
| Ad. leave in past year* | 1.17 | 0.34 | 1.52 | 0.62 | 1.39 | 0.25 |

*Table 2.24 (continued)*

| | | | | | | |
|---|---|---|---|---|---|---|
| Short-time working | 1.00 | 0.00 | 1.00 | 0.00 | 1.00 | 0.00 |
| Sector (state enterprise or organisation is reference) | | | | | | |
| Privatised | 0.71 | 0.18 | 1.20 | 0.42 | 1.05 | 0.17 |
| New private | 0.45* | 0.15 | 0.80 | 0.32 | 1.50* | 0.30 |
| Income decile (fifth decile is reference) | | | | | | |
| First decile | 2.14 | 0.92 | 1.06 | 0.62 | 0.98 | 0.33 |
| Second decile* | 1.29 | 0.50 | 1.67 | 0.77 | 1.70* | 0.44 |
| Third decile | 1.21 | 0.41 | 0.91 | 0.46 | 1.07 | 0.30 |
| Fourth decile | 1.32 | 0.46 | 0.67 | 0.36 | 1.33 | 0.36 |
| Sixth decile | 0.61 | 0.22 | 0.50 | 0.25 | 0.77 | 0.21 |
| Seventh decile | 0.46* | 0.18 | 0.72 | 0.35 | 1.05 | 0.27 |
| Eighth decile | 1.00 | 0.33 | 0.72 | 0.33 | 1.08 | 0.28 |
| Ninth decile | 0.57 | 0.22 | 0.62 | 0.31 | 0.89 | 0.24 |
| Tenth decile | 0.63 | 0.24 | 0.74 | 0.37 | 1.04 | 0.29 |
| Log of wage* | 0.94 | 0.13 | 0.81 | 0.15 | 0.78* | 0.08 |
| Age group (25–39 is reference) | | | | | | |
| Under 24 | 1.00 | 0.32 | 1.61 | 0.61 | 1.45 | 0.29 |
| 40 to pension age | 1.03 | 0.20 | 1.16 | 0.31 | 0.95 | 0.12 |
| Pension age*** | 0.33* | 0.13 | 0.52 | 0.30 | 0.43** | 0.13 |
| Number in household | 0.80* | 0.07 | 1.05 | 0.13 | 0.93 | 0.07 |
| Other(s) have second jobs*** | 2.13*** | 0.46 | 2.24** | 0.59 | 1.90*** | 0.30 |
| Proportion working | 0.96 | 0.46 | 2.80 | 1.94 | 0.39** | 0.13 |
| Household has children | 1.14 | 0.26 | 1.56 | 0.49 | 0.95 | 0.14 |
| Network*** | 1.72*** | 0.22 | 1.08 | 0.18 | 1.38*** | 0.13 |
| New private network* | 1.12 | 0.12 | 1.33* | 0.17 | 1.10 | 0.09 |
| Gift relations with others*** | 1.09 | 0.21 | 1.54 | 0.39 | 1.86*** | 0.26 |
| N | 3 578 | | | | | |
| Chi square | 15 514 | | | | | |
| Pseudo R squared | 0.10 | | | | | |

Significance of coefficients: ***p<.001 ; **p<.01; * p<.05. Indicators in the first column relate to the significance of the variable in relation to the presence or absence of any form of secondary employment.

*Notes: Estimates of standard errors allow for clustering in households.*

*All variables are dummies, except for number in household (mean 3.3), proportion of household members working (mean 0.6), network (the number of network links identified per adult household member, mean 0.7), new private network (the proportion of nominated links who work in the new private sector, mean 0.3) and log of primary wage in relation to the city mean (mean –0.4).*

*Table 2.25: Multinomial logistic regression – probability of having permanent, regular or occasional secondary employment; those without a primary job (ISITO Household Survey).*

| | Permanent | | Regular | | From time to time | |
|---|---|---|---|---|---|---|
| | Odds ratio | Std error | Odds ratio | Std error | Odds ratio | Std error |
| Male*** | 2.51 | 1.24 | 2.48 | 1.22 | 2.86*** | 0.65 |
| Married man* | 0.82 | 0.35 | 0.59 | 0.28 | 0.62* | 0.13 |
| Married woman* | 1.06 | 0.45 | 1.14 | 0.50 | 0.73 | 0.14 |
| **Education (reference is secondary or less)** | | | | | | |
| Middle special | 1.20 | 0.36 | 1.09 | 0.32 | 1.24 | 0.18 |
| Incomplete higher | 2.43 | 1.64 | 1.80 | 1.01 | 0.78 | 0.31 |
| Higher education | 2.54** | 0.86 | 0.95 | 0.37 | 0.99 | 0.20 |
| Postgraduate | 22.35** | 25.57 | 0.00*** | 0.00 | 0.00*** | 0.00 |
| **City (Kemerovo is reference)** | | | | | | |
| Samara | 0.85 | 0.27 | 3.50** | 1.30 | 1.12 | 0.17 |
| Lyubertsy | 0.42 | 0.20 | 2.14 | 0.93 | 0.85 | 0.17 |
| Syktyvkar | 1.16 | 0.40 | 2.31 | 1.07 | 1.03 | 0.19 |
| **Income decile (fifth decile is reference)** | | | | | | |
| First decile* | 2.68 | 1.89 | 1.45 | 0.74 | 1.85* | 0.51 |
| Second decile | 2.13 | 1.49 | 1.27 | 0.67 | 1.13 | 0.32 |
| Third decile | 1.55 | 1.16 | 1.70 | 0.85 | 0.75 | 0.22 |
| Fourth decile | 3.06 | 2.08 | 0.76 | 0.51 | 0.93 | 0.28 |
| Sixth decile | 2.16 | 1.61 | 0.87 | 0.53 | 0.84 | 0.28 |
| Seventh decile | 0.31 | 0.38 | 0.67 | 0.51 | 0.65 | 0.23 |
| Eighth decile | 1.29 | 0.97 | 0.45 | 0.32 | 0.53 | 0.20 |
| Ninth decile | 0.75 | 0.71 | 0.46 | 0.38 | 0.53 | 0.21 |
| Tenth decile | 1.37 | 1.08 | 0.42 | 0.32 | 0.85 | 0.30 |
| **Age group (25–39 is reference)** | | | | | | |
| Under 24 | 0.91 | 0.38 | 0.50 | 0.22 | 1.09 | 0.20 |
| 40 to 49 | 1.10 | 0.38 | 0.76 | 0.26 | 0.86 | 0.16 |
| Over 50 | 0.84 | 0.46 | 0.42 | 0.25 | 0.80 | 0.19 |
| Pensioner** | 0.35 | 0.20 | 0.26 | 0.20 | 0.20*** | 0.06 |
| Number in household | 1.02 | 0.11 | 0.92 | 0.12 | 1.04 | 0.06 |
| Other(s) have second jobs** | 1.70 | 0.58 | 2.04* | 0.69 | 1.47* | 0.26 |

*Table 2.25 (continued)*

| | | | | | | |
|---|---|---|---|---|---|---|
| Proportion of household members working** | 0.22* | 0.14 | 0.74 | 0.44 | 0.46* | 0.15 |
| Household has children** | 0.93 | 0.32 | 0.54 | 0.20 | 0.70* | 0.12 |
| Network** | 1.49 | 0.39 | 1.45 | 0.36 | 1.41** | 0.18 |
| New private network | 1.43* | 0.23 | 1.18 | 0.19 | 0.99 | 0.10 |
| Engaged in gift relations with others | 0.79 | 0.23 | 1.51 | 0.44 | 1.30 | 0.18 |
| N | 3460 | | | | | |
| Chi squared | 14121 | | | | | |
| Pseudo R squared | 0.17 | | | | | |

Significance of coefficients: ***p<.001 ; **p<.01; * p<.05. Indicators in the first column relate to the significance of the variable in relation to the presence or absence of any form of secondary employment.

*Notes: Estimates of standard errors allow for clustering in households*
*All variables are dummies, except for number in household (mean 2.9), proportion of household members working (mean 0.3), network (the number of network links identified per adult household member, mean 0.4) and new private network (the proportion of nominated links who work in the new private sector, mean 0.2).*

*Table 2.26: Logistic regression – probability of having a second job and individual economic activity (RLMS pooled data 1994–2000).*

| | Workers: second job | | Workers: IEA | | Not-Working: IEA | |
|---|---|---|---|---|---|---|
| | Odds ratio | Std error | Odds ratio | Std error | Odds ratio | Std error |
| Age*** | 1.12*** | 0.03 | 1.06* | 0.02 | 1.14*** | 0.02 |
| Age squared/100*** | 0.86*** | 0.03 | 0.90*** | 0.03 | 0.83*** | 0.02 |
| Male** | 1.25 | 0.24 | 2.32*** | 0.38 | 1.18 | 0.13 |
| Married man | 0.82 | 0.14 | 0.97 | 0.12 | 1.29* | 0.14 |
| Married woman*** | 0.68** | 0.10 | 0.87 | 0.12 | 0.61*** | 0.06 |
| Number in household*** | 0.91* | 0.04 | 0.82*** | 0.03 | 0.89*** | 0.02 |
| Household has children | 0.97 | 0.11 | 1.27* | 0.12 | 1.03 | 0.09 |
| Proportion of non-working pensioners in household | 0.69 | 0.21 | 0.93 | 0.24 | 0.66** | 0.10 |
| Other household member(s) have second jobs*** | 1.65*** | 0.16 | 1.83*** | 0.16 | 2.44*** | 0.18 |
| Log of wage | 0.83** | 0.05 | 0.78*** | 0.04 | | |
| Income deciles (fifth decile is reference) | | | | | | |
| No net money income | 0.92 | 0.19 | 0.62** | 0.11 | 1.37** | 0.16 |
| First decile*** | 1.08 | 0.19 | 1.20 | 0.16 | 1.39** | 0.17 |
| Second decile | 1.05 | 0.18 | 0.90 | 0.13 | 1.17 | 0.15 |
| Third decile* | 1.21 | 0.19 | 0.98 | 0.13 | 1.38* | 0.18 |
| Fourth decile | 0.95 | 0.16 | 0.95 | 0.13 | 1.21 | 0.16 |
| Sixth decile | 0.92 | 0.16 | 0.89 | 0.13 | 1.10 | 0.15 |
| Seventh decile | 0.78 | 0.13 | 0.75 | 0.11 | 1.20 | 0.17 |
| Eight decile** | 0.65* | 0.11 | 0.80 | 0.11 | 1.08 | 0.17 |
| Ninth decile* | 0.72* | 0.11 | 0.78 | 0.10 | 1.31 | 0.21 |
| Tenth decile** | 0.84 | 0.13 | 0.70** | 0.09 | 0.87 | 0.15 |
| Urban *** | 2.11*** | 0.31 | 1.39** | 0.14 | 1.20* | 0.09 |
| Labour force status (reference is working at the time of the survey) | | | | | | |
| Maternity leave or horseperson** | 0.93 | 0.97 | | | 0.31* | 0.15 |
| Paid leave | 1.39 | 0.67 | 1.40 | 0.51 | | |
| Unpaid leave** | 0.92 | 0.91 | 1.58 | 0.94 | | |
| Student | | | | | 0.50*** | 0.07 |

*Table 2.26 (Continued)*

| | | | | | | |
|---|---|---|---|---|---|---|
| Invalid*** | | | | | 0.31*** | 0.06 |
| Unemployed*** | | | | | 1.55*** | 0.13 |
| **Employment Status (reference is skilled worker)** | | | | | | |
| Manager | 1.09 | 0.30 | 0.62 | 0.15 | | |
| Professional** | 1.63* | 0.31 | 1.15 | 0.18 | | |
| Non-manual | 0.85 | 0.16 | 0.97 | 0.14 | | |
| Unskilled worker | 0.97 | 0.20 | 0.65** | 0.11 | | |
| Log of hours worked in main job*** | 0.70*** | 0.05 | 0.86* | 0.05 | | |
| Wages not paid** | 1.09 | 0.11 | 1.28** | 0.10 | | |
| Some wage paid in kind** | 1.17 | 0.15 | 1.38** | 0.14 | | |
| Has been on administrative leave | 0.88 | 0.14 | 1.37** | 0.16 | | |
| **Employer in primary job (reference is state or mixed enterprise)** | | | | | | |
| Private enterprise* | 1.06 | 0.10 | 1.14 | 0.09 | | |
| High school grade (0 to 12)* | 1.06 | 0.04 | 1.03 | 0.03 | 1.05* | 0.02 |
| **Education (reference is secondary or Less)** | | | | | | |
| Professional course*** | 1.28* | 0.13 | 1.42*** | 0.11 | 1.24** | 0.09 |
| Technical-vocational (incomplete secondary) | 1.08 | 0.18 | 1.22 | 0.14 | 0.96 | 0.11 |
| Post-secondary technical* | 1.20 | 0.16 | 1.42*** | 0.13 | 1.00 | 0.09 |
| Professional-technical*** | 1.29* | 0.14 | 1.25* | 0.11 | 1.09 | 0.09 |
| Higher education*** | 1.64 | 0.23 | 1.13 | 0.13 | 0.99 | 0.12 |
| Postgraduate*** | 3.64 | 1.02 | 1.47 | 0.49 | 2.66 | 1.38 |
| **Year of survey (1994 is reference)** | | | | | | |
| 1995 | 0.96 | 0.13 | 0.84 | 0.09 | 1.28** | 0.12 |
| 1996* | 0.92 | 0.13 | 0.81 | 0.09 | 0.97 | 0.09 |
| 1998 | 0.94 | 0.13 | 0.75* | 0.09 | 1.12 | 0.10 |
| 2000** | 1.18 | 0.15 | 0.89 | 0.09 | 1.69*** | 0.15 |
| N | 18 138 | | 18 130 | | 17 752 | |
| Chi squared | 398*** | | 542*** | | 1 218*** | |
| Pseudo R squared | 0.08 | | 0.08 | | 0.20 | |

Significance of coefficients: ***$p<.001$ ; **$p<.01$; * $p<.05$

*Notes: The regression also included seven regional dummy variables and 21 dummy variables for the industry of primary employment in the regressions for those in work (this data is not yet available for the 2000 round). The incidence of secondary employment, particularly in individual economic activity, was significantly higher in Moscow and St Petersburg, but otherwise there was little regional variation. The incidence of second jobs was significantly higher for those working in their first jobs in education and science. Those working in housing and utilities and, especially, personal services were significantly more likely to engage in individual labour activity, those working in transport less likely to do so.*

*Estimates of standard errors allow for clustering in the pooled data. Standard errors of household-level variables will be underestimates because no allowance is made for clustering in households. Significance levels in the first column relate to any form of secondary employment. There is no significant variation in the coefficients from year to year.*

*The coefficient reported for the log of the previous month's wage (relative to the mean for the round and polling site) is from a separate regression, since many respondents had received no wage the previous month. Income deciles are defined in relation to the region and year of survey and relate to the household money income per head net of all secondary earnings (see note to Table 2.19). The inclusion of the dummy variable for zero income does not affect the significance for the coefficient on the non-payment of wages. All variables are dummies, except for age (mean 39 for workers, 52 for non-workers), age squared (mean 1685 for workers, 3123 for non-workers), number in household (mean for workers 3.4, for non-workers 3.0), proportion of pensioners in the household (mean for workers 0.07, for non-workers 0.45), log of working hours (mean 5.0) and log of primary wage (mean −0.31). Education dummies are not mutually exclusive, except that postgraduate is coded 0 for higher education.*

*Table 2.27: Multinomial logistic regression – probability of having secondary employment and of having regular or occasional secondary employment; those with no primary employment (VTsIOM data. March 1993 – May 1998).*

|  | Yes | | Regular | | Occasional | |
|---|---|---|---|---|---|---|
|  | Odds ratio | Std error | Odds ratio | Std error | Odds ratio | Std error |
| Age group (reference is 24–39) | | | | | | |
| Under 24 | 1.03 | 0.06 | 1.14 | 0.20 | 0.93 | 0.09 |
| 40 to 49 | 0.94 | 0.06 | 0.71 | 0.14 | 0.91 | 0.09 |
| Over 50 | 0.63*** | 0.05 | 0.39*** | 0.10 | 0.50*** | 0.07 |
| Pension age–75 | 0.47*** | 0.03 | 0.45*** | 0.09 | 0.25*** | 0.03 |
| Over 75 | 0.10*** | 0.02 | 0.07*** | 0.04 | 0.06*** | 0.03 |
| Education (primary or less is reference) | | | | | | |
| Incomplete secondary | 1.30** | 0.10 | 2.27** | 0.58 | 1.24 | 0.21 |
| Secondary | 1.65*** | 0.13 | 2.01** | 0.53 | 1.49* | 0.25 |
| Vocational | 2.08*** | 0.19 | 2.56** | 0.76 | 2.26*** | 0.40 |
| Technical | 2.03*** | 0.16 | 3.19*** | 0.81 | 1.72** | 0.28 |
| Incomplete higher | 2.96*** | 0.28 | 4.56*** | 1.32 | 2.47*** | 0.47 |
| Higher education | 2.52*** | 0.20 | 4.06*** | 1.05 | 2.35*** | 0.39 |
| Male | 1.84*** | 0.09 | 1.39* | 0.19 | 2.02*** | 0.17 |
| Married man | 0.84** | 0.05 | 1.20 | 0.19 | 0.72** | 0.07 |
| Married woman | 0.82*** | 0.04 | 0.75* | 0.11 | 0.74** | 0.07 |
| Number in household | 0.94*** | 0.01 | 0.92* | 0.04 | 0.92*** | 0.02 |
| Reason for non-participation (reference is unemployed) | | | | | | |
| Student | 0.94 | 0.06 | 1.48* | 0.28 | 0.82 | 0.09 |
| Pensioner | 0.96 | 0.06 | 1.81** | 0.32 | 0.70** | 0.08 |
| House person | 0.59*** | 0.04 | 0.56* | 0.13 | 0.49*** | 0.06 |
| Income decile (fifth decile is reference) | | | | | | |
| First decile | 3.20*** | 0.21 | 3.91*** | 0.77 | 4.04*** | 0.50 |
| Second decile | 1.51*** | 0.11 | 1.77** | 0.38 | 1.40* | 0.19 |
| Third decile | 1.20* | 0.09 | 1.53* | 0.33 | 1.22 | 0.17 |
| Fourth decile | 1.14 | 0.09 | 1.07 | 0.24 | 1.22 | 0.18 |
| Sixth decile | 0.90 | 0.07 | 1.16 | 0.25 | 1.03 | 0.15 |
| Seventh decile | 0.93 | 0.08 | 1.02 | 0.24 | 1.29 | 0.19 |
| Eighth decile | 0.93 | 0.08 | 1.31 | 0.30 | 1.00 | 0.16 |
| Ninth decile | 0.90 | 0.08 | 1.24 | 0.29 | 0.84 | 0.14 |
| Tenth decile | 1.20* | 0.10 | 1.29 | 0.32 | 1.18 | 0.19 |

*Table 2.27 (continued)*

| Type of population centre (reference is Moscow and St Petersburg) | | | | | | |
|---|---|---|---|---|---|---|
| Oblast centre | 0.85* | 0.06 | 0.57** | 0.11 | 0.91 | 0.11 |
| Other city | 0.77*** | 0.04 | 0.58*** | 0.08 | 0.80* | 0.07 |
| Town | 0.79** | 0.06 | 0.76 | 0.14 | 0.69** | 0.09 |
| Rural | 0.69*** | 0.03 | 0.48*** | 0.07 | 0.63*** | 0.05 |
| Year of survey (1995 is reference) | | | | | | |
| 1993 | 0.73*** | 0.05 | | | | |
| 1994 | 1.05 | 0.06 | 1.25 | 0.19 | 1.41** | 0.17 |
| 1996 | 0.78** | 0.06 | 0.74* | 0.10 | 1.02 | 0.10 |
| 1997 | 0.59*** | 0.05 | 0.54** | 0.09 | 0.75** | 0.08 |
| 1998 | 0.39*** | 0.04 | 0.28** | 0.10 | 0.71* | 0.12 |
| Region (North European region is reference) | | | | | | |
| North-West Region | 1.08 | 0.09 | 0.59 | 0.19 | 0.90 | 0.17 |
| Central Region | 1.02 | 0.07 | 0.81 | 0.17 | 0.84 | 0.12 |
| Volgo-Vyatsky Region | 0.99 | 0.10 | 0.85 | 0.24 | 1.29 | 0.24 |
| Black Earth Region | 0.64*** | 0.07 | 0.55 | 0.18 | 0.52** | 0.11 |
| Volga Region | 1.16 | 0.09 | 1.13 | 0.27 | 1.36* | 0.21 |
| North Caucasus | 1.34*** | 0.11 | 1.16 | 0.28 | 1.65** | 0.26 |
| Ural | 1.02 | 0.08 | 1.02 | 0.24 | 1.00 | 0.16 |
| West Siberia | 1.29** | 0.11 | 0.70 | 0.18 | 1.06 | 0.18 |
| East Siberia | 0.99 | 0.10 | 0.92 | 0.27 | 0.85 | 0.16 |
| Far East | 0.98 | 0.10 | 0.85 | 0.25 | 1.02 | 0.19 |
| Simple question | 0.77*** | 0.04 | | | | |
| N | 39 686 | | 15 386 | | | |
| Chi squared | 3 086*** | | 1 958*** | | | |
| Pseudo R squared | 0.11 | | 0.14 | | | |

Significance of coefficients: ***p<.001 ; **p<.01; * p<.05

*Notes: All variables are dummies, except for number in household (mean 2.7). 'Simple question' distinguishes those who were simply asked whether or not they had additional employment from those who were asked whether they had regular, occasional or no additional employment.*

*Table 2.28: Multinomial logistic regression – probability of having secondary employment and of having regular or occasional secondary employment; those with primary employment (VTsIOM data, March 1993 – May 1998).*

| | Yes | | Regular | | Occasional | |
|---|---|---|---|---|---|---|
| | Odds ratio | Std error | Odds ratio | Std error | Odds ratio | Std error |
| Male | 1.65*** | 0.08 | 1.42** | 0.18 | 1.77*** | 0.16 |
| Married man | 0.93 | 0.04 | 0.82 | 0.10 | 0.99 | 0.08 |
| Married woman | 0.77*** | 0.03 | 0.76** | 0.07 | 0.76*** | 0.06 |
| Number in household | 0.94*** | 0.01 | 0.99 | 0.03 | 0.93*** | 0.02 |
| **Age group (reference is 24–39)** | | | | | | |
| Under 24 | 1.05 | 0.04 | 0.93 | 0.11 | 1.12 | 0.09 |
| 40 to 49 | 0.89*** | 0.03 | 0.96 | 0.07 | 0.83** | 0.05 |
| Over 50 | 0.73*** | 0.03 | 0.77* | 0.09 | 0.69*** | 0.06 |
| Pension age | 0.55*** | 0.04 | 0.65** | 0.10 | 0.43*** | 0.06 |
| Over 75 | 0.70 | 0.35 | 0.85 | 0.93 | 0.49 | 0.52 |
| **Education (primary or less is reference)** | | | | | | |
| Incomplete secondary | 1.19 | 0.16 | 1.34 | 0.56 | 0.94 | 0.22 |
| Secondary | 1.27 | 0.16 | 1.68 | 0.67 | 1.04 | 0.24 |
| Vocational | 1.50** | 0.20 | 1.36 | 0.55 | 1.27 | 0.29 |
| Technical | 1.47** | 0.19 | 1.74 | 0.69 | 1.24 | 0.28 |
| Incomplete higher | 1.88*** | 0.27 | 2.48* | 1.04 | 1.25 | 0.32 |
| Higher education | 2.04*** | 0.26 | 2.59* | 1.03 | 1.61* | 0.37 |
| **Branch (trade is reference)** | | | | | | |
| Industry | 0.86*** | 0.03 | 0.98 | 0.10 | 1.04 | 0.08 |
| Agriculture | 0.76*** | 0.04 | 0.73 | 0.13 | 0.74** | 0.08 |
| Public services | 1.27*** | 0.05 | 1.67*** | 0.19 | 1.33** | 0.11 |
| Public administration | 0.61*** | 0.05 | 0.77 | 0.15 | 0.83 | 0.12 |
| Security forces | 0.62*** | 0.05 | 0.53** | 0.12 | 0.67** | 0.10 |
| **Sector (state enterprise is reference)** | | | | | | |
| State company | 0.94 | 0.04 | 0.85 | 0.09 | 1.00 | 0.07 |
| Co-operative etc. | 1.27*** | 0.06 | 0.98 | 0.15 | 1.49*** | 0.14 |
| Non-state company | 1.30*** | 0.07 | 1.05 | 0.14 | 1.44*** | 0.13 |
| Private company | 1.20*** | 0.06 | 0.85 | 0.11 | 1.40*** | 0.12 |
| Individual labour activity | 1.11 | 0.11 | 1.01 | 0.25 | 1.03 | 0.18 |

*Table 2.28 (Continued)*

| | | | | | | |
|---|---|---|---|---|---|---|
| Occupational status (Unskilled worker is reference) | | | | | | |
| Managers | 1.07 | 0.07 | 0.96 | 0.19 | 0.84 | 0.11 |
| Professionals | 1.44*** | 0.08 | 1.56** | 0.23 | 1.13 | 0.12 |
| Non-manual | 1.05 | 0.06 | 1.10 | 0.16 | 0.98 | 0.10 |
| Skilled worker | 1.25*** | 0.06 | 1.19 | 0.17 | 1.36** | 0.13 |
| Income decile (Fifth decile is reference) | | | | | | |
| First decile | 2.43*** | 0.14 | 3.13*** | 0.46 | 2.59*** | 0.27 |
| Second decile | 1.40*** | 0.08 | 1.46* | 0.23 | 1.47*** | 0.16 |
| Third decile | 1.16* | 0.07 | 1.41* | 0.22 | 1.18 | 0.13 |
| Fourth decile | 1.18** | 0.07 | 1.59** | 0.24 | 1.06 | 0.12 |
| Sixth decile | 0.96 | 0.06 | 1.07 | 0.17 | 1.05 | 0.12 |
| Seventh decile | 0.93 | 0.05 | 1.12 | 0.17 | 1.01 | 0.11 |
| Eighth decile | 0.90 | 0.05 | 0.87 | 0.14 | 0.88 | 0.10 |
| Ninth decile | 0.87* | 0.05 | 0.96 | 0.15 | 0.86 | 0.09 |
| Tenth decile | 0.91 | 0.05 | 1.13 | 0.17 | 0.84 | 0.09 |
| Log primary wage# | 1.04 | 0.23 | 1.07 | 0.06 | 1.01 | 0.05 |
| Last wage paid in full and on time | 1.00 | 0.03 | 1.14 | 0.08 | 0.91 | 0.05 |
| Employment Status (Reference is waged employee) | | | | | | |
| Self-employed | 1.00 | 0.11 | 0.68 | 0.24 | 1.29 | 0.25 |
| Work on contract | 1.32*** | 0.06 | 1.24* | 0.12 | 1.38*** | 0.10 |
| Entrepreneur | 1.07 | 0.08 | 1.36 | 0.27 | 1.12 | 0.16 |
| Type of population centre (reference is Moscow and St Petersburg) | | | | | | |
| Oblast centre | 0.91* | 0.05 | 1.10 | 0.14 | 0.86 | 0.08 |
| Other city | 0.72*** | 0.03 | 0.70*** | 0.07 | 0.68*** | 0.05 |
| Town | 0.78*** | 0.05 | 0.63** | 0.09 | 0.74** | 0.07 |
| Rural | 0.68*** | 0.03 | 0.52*** | 0.06 | 0.58*** | 0.04 |
| Year of survey (1995 is reference) | | | | | | |
| 1993 | 0.62*** | 0.03 | | | | |
| 1994 | 0.84*** | 0.04 | 1.14 | 0.16 | 0.97 | 0.10 |
| 1996 | 0.94 | 0.05 | 1.20 | 0.16 | 1.02 | 0.09 |
| 1997 | 0.77*** | 0.05 | 0.95 | 0.13 | 0.86 | 0.08 |
| 1998 | 0.66*** | 0.05 | 0.86 | 0.16 | 0.71* | 0.10 |
| Region (North European region is reference) | | | | | | |
| North-West region | 1.25** | 0.08 | 1.18 | 0.22 | 1.07 | 0.16 |
| Central region | 1.16** | 0.06 | 1.00 | 0.14 | 0.93 | 0.10 |
| Volgo-Vyatsky region | 0.64*** | 0.05 | 0.64* | 0.14 | 0.57*** | 0.09 |

*Table 2.28 (Continued)*

| | | | | | | |
|---|---|---|---|---|---|---|
| Black Earth region | 0.65*** | 0.05 | 0.33*** | 0.09 | 0.52*** | 0.09 |
| Volga region | 1.10 | 0.06 | 0.95 | 0.16 | 1.15 | 0.14 |
| North Caucasus | 1.29*** | 0.08 | 0.87 | 0.15 | 1.47** | 0.18 |
| Ural | 0.95 | 0.05 | 0.81 | 0.13 | 0.91 | 0.11 |
| West Siberia | 1.01 | 0.06 | 0.83 | 0.14 | 0.81 | 0.12 |
| East Siberia | 1.02 | 0.07 | 0.76 | 0.14 | 0.87 | 0.13 |
| Far East | 0.95 | 0.07 | 0.98 | 0.19 | 0.87 | 0.13 |
| Simple question | 0.75*** | 0.03 | | | | |
| N | 57 150 | | 18 526 | | | |
| Chi square | 3 033*** | | 1 400*** | | | |
| Pseudo R squared | 0.06 | | 0.06 | | | |

Significance of coefficients: ***$p<.001$ ; **$p<.01$; * $p<.05$

*Notes: The first column combines responses to a simple question, asking whether the respondent does or does not have additional employment, with those to a question offering the opportunity to distinguish between regular and occasional secondary employment. As the dummy for the simple question indicates, the former question provides a significantly lower incidence of secondary employment.*

*All variables are dummies, except for number in household (mean 3.3) and log of primary wage (mean –0.4).*

*#The coefficient of log wage (relative to the mean in that location that month) is from a separate regression, which excludes those who received no wage the previous month.*

# 3. The Russian Dacha and the Myth of the Urban Peasant

## THE RUSSIAN CRISIS AND THE RISE OF SELF-SUFFICIENCY

The impression that has been cultivated by the Russian and international mass media is that Russians have returned to their peasant roots in a repudiation not only of their Soviet past but of the history of the entire twentieth century. This impression is easily confirmed by looking at news-stands and bookstalls, which are covered with magazines and books providing every kind of instruction and advice on the cultivation of your rural plot, or by switching on the radio or television, which are similarly replete with experts and consultants on small-scale farming, or visiting a shopping centre, which will almost always have a specialist shop that supplies 'Everything for the dacha', or trying to leave any large city on a Friday evening in summer by bus, train or car, all of which are jammed with urban dwellers on the way to their garden plots. This impression is so powerful that the phenomenon has been subjected to barely any investigation by social scientists. The authors of one of the very few serious publications on the subject reproduce without question the typical view that 'the majority of the population now produces its own food supply to a considerable extent' (Seeth et al., 1998, p. 1611). There is no doubt that, as in the past, this is true of the rural population and even of many of the inhabitants of small towns, but is it really the case that urban dwellers, who comprise the vast majority of the Russian population, have become urban peasants?

In this chapter I want to subject the myth of the urban peasant to a critical analysis. I will start by reviewing the data on the use of domestic agricultural plots and on the scale of self-provisioning with agricultural produce by urban residents. We then test the hypotheses that the use of land by urban residents is the response to a deficit of money income or, more generally, is the result of decisions about the allocation of household resources between domestic production and income-earning activities. Having rejected these hypotheses we narrow the focus to the specific question of self-provisioning with food, looking at the acquisition of food from others and at production for the household's own needs to ask whether the previous hypotheses can explain such production. Finally, we put forward and test an alternative explanation for the pervasive practice of domestic production of agricultural produce by urban residents in Russia.

The principal data source that will be used in this chapter is the ISITO Household Survey conducted in April and May 1998 in Samara, Kemerovo, Syktyvkar and Lyubertsy. While we lose the rather dubious benefit of being able to generalise to the level of Russia as a whole, we gain in being able to analyse the data in finer detail, making allowance for substantial regional variations. The questionnaires included blocks about the use of dacha and the domestic production of food at both individual and household level.[1] Other data sources are used to complement this survey data. First, the published distributions from the Goskomstat Household Budget Survey. Second, the data of the 1994 Goskomstat microcensus, a 5 percent sample of the whole population based on the 1989 census returns, which included questions on land holding, income sources and household composition. Third, the data of the Russian Longitudinal Monitoring Survey, a panel survey which has been conducted with an all-Russian sample in two waves since 1992 and which includes a block of questions on domestic agricultural production.

## HOW EXTENSIVE IS THE USE OF LAND BY URBAN HOUSEHOLDS IN RUSSIA?

According to the 1994 microcensus, 58.3 percent of all households had a plot of land, with larger households being more likely to have a plot (the range being from 48 percent of single-person households to 72 percent of households with five or more people). Twenty-two percent had a plot adjoining their home (*priusadebnyi uchastok*), 16.9 percent an allotment or a plot attached to a dacha (*sadovyi ili dachnyi*

---

[1]    We follow Russian practice in using the evocative term 'dacha' to refer to all the various ways in which urban residents have the use of land for leisure or for subsistence production.

*uchastok*), 9.5 percent a vegetable garden (*ogorod*), 7.7 percent a plot and a vegetable garden adjoining their home (*priusadebnyi uchastok i ogorod*) and 2.2 percent some other kind of combined plot of land (Goskomstat, 1997).[2] However, this includes both urban and rural residents, virtually all of the latter having plots.

*Table 3.1:*   *Percentage of population of urban census districts in each region with each type of plot and median size of plots (sotki).*

| | Priusadebnyi uchastok | | Sadovyi or dachnyi uchastok | | Ogorod | | All plots | | |
|---|---|---|---|---|---|---|---|---|---|
| | % | Median | % | Median | % | Median | % | Mean | Median |
| Moscow City | 4.0 | 10 | 15.9 | 6 | 1.5 | 6 | 21.4 | 8.1 | 6 |
| St Petersburg | 3.9 | 10 | 18.4 | 6 | 4.6 | 4 | 26.6 | 7.7 | 6 |
| Northern region | 7.0 | 6 | 18.5 | 6 | 13.0 | 3 | 36.5 | 6.8 | 6 |
| North West region | 17.6 | 9 | 23.5 | 6 | 15.9 | 5 | 53.9 | 8.4 | 6 |
| Central Region | 17.7 | 6 | 22.6 | 6 | 12.2 | 5 | 48.9 | 7.1 | 6 |
| Volgo Vyatsk | 16.6 | 6 | 28.5 | 6 | 11.1 | 5 | 51.9 | 6.8 | 6 |
| Black Earth | 27.1 | 5 | 24.7 | 6 | 11.9 | 8 | 56.3 | 8.5 | 6 |
| Volga Region | 15.8 | 4 | 28.6 | 6 | 8.6 | 5 | 49.3 | 6.0 | 6 |
| North Caucasus* | 24.8 | 5 | 21.0 | 6 | 8.5 | 5 | 50.2 | 6.0 | 6 |
| Urals | 14.2 | 5 | 28.5 | 6 | 12.4 | 5 | 50.8 | 6.4 | 6 |
| Western Siberia | 16.5 | 4 | 25.7 | 6 | 12.8 | 5 | 49.8 | 6.6 | 6 |
| Eastern Siberia | 14.9 | 4 | 29.0 | 6 | 15.7 | 5 | 53.6 | 7.0 | 6 |
| Far East | 8.3 | 6 | 27.1 | 6 | 14.3 | 5 | 46.5 | 7.4 | 6 |
| Kaliningrad | 15.0 | 3 | 25.0 | 6 | 20.1 | 6 | 54.4 | 6.1 | 6 |

*Notes:*
* *Data not available for Chechen Republic. Central and Northwestern regions exclude Moscow and St Petersburg cities respectively.*
*Source: Author's calculations from 1994 microcensus data.*

Table 3.1 shows that even among the urban population, the overall level of dacha ownership right across Russia is very high, although the

---

[2]   These were the categories to which respondents were invited to assign their plots. In principle the *priusadebnyi uchastok* would be the larger plot typical of rural inhabitants engaged in personal subsidiary agriculture, the *sadovyi uchastok* a plot allocated by an enterprise or organisation, a *dachnyi uchastok* a plot attached to a dacha and an *ogorod* usually a smaller plot specifically for growing vegetables. In fact it is not clear from the microcensus data that there are any such clear distinctions – the median size of each type of plot held by urban dwellers in each region is more or less the same, although the *ogorod* is sometimes marginally smaller. Note that the urban population is the population of urban census districts, many of which include inhabitants of outlying rural districts.

distribution of the different forms of holding differs quite a lot between regions. The proportion of the urban population with a plot of land ranges from a low of 36 percent in the sub-Arctic Northern Region to a high of 56 percent in the Black Earth region. Land use in large cities is significantly less than this, but even in Moscow and St Petersburg, according to the microcensus data, in 1994, 21 percent and 27 percent respectively had plots of land.

Basic details of landholding of the households in the ISITO sample are shown in Table 3.2.[3] Half the households questioned said that they had used some land during 1997. More than half owned the land they used, about a quarter used the land of relatives and friends and most of the remainder used land allocated by their enterprise or organisation. The practice of using land distributed by enterprises was more common in Kemerovo, while relatively more people in Lyubertsy used the land of relatives. Very few people rented the land that they used (the totals sum to more than 100 because some households used more than one plot of land). Most of the holdings are very small. Forty percent of households used land of the traditional size for allotments of five to six sotki (one sotka is one hundredth of a hectare). Fewer than 4 percent of the households in any of the cities used over 20 sotki. Fewer than 1 percent of households in the ISITO sample used as much land in total as the average size of personal agricultural holding reported by Goskomstat's agricultural production data (36 sotki), covering both urban and rural holdings. Well under 10 percent in any of the ISITO four cities had as much as the 15 sotki which Seeth et al., 1998 (p. 1612) cite as the average size of the dachas of urban residents in their sample of three cities in Western Russia (Pskov, Rostov and Orel), although this is far larger than the microcensus figure for the urban population of these oblasts (nine, six and eight sotki respectively).

The percentage of the urban population having plots in each region in the RLMS 1996 data is similar for most regions to the microcensus data, except for Moscow and St Petersburg (where RLMS reports 46 percent with plots), North Caucasus (62 percent) the Urals (58 percent) and Western Siberia (59 percent). These divergences are probably explicable by the features of the specific sites selected by RLMS in each region.

---

[3]   Eighty-three out of 4 023 households (of whom 45 were in Kemerovo) said that they did not use land, but later said that they grew some of their own produce. It is most likely that almost all of these people were using land allocated by their enterprises or organisations to grow potatoes. They are not included in the analysis.

*Table 3.2: Land holding in four large cities.*

| Percentage of households | Samara | Kemerovo | Lyubertsy | Syktyvkar | Total |
|---|---|---|---|---|---|
| Using land | 50 | 67 | 33 | 57 | 52 |
| of whom: | | | | | |
| Own land | 63 | 60 | 54 | 65 | 61 |
| Rent land | 5 | 7 | 5 | 6 | 6 |
| Use land distributed by enterprise | 11 | 23 | 15 | 8 | 15 |
| Use land of friends or relatives | 23 | 22 | 28 | 22 | 23 |
| Mean size of land used (sotki) | 7.8 | 7.9 | 7.8 | 8.1 | 7.8 |
| Median size (sotki) | 6 | 6 | 6 | 6 | 6 |

*Source: ISITO Household survey.*

*Table 3.3:  Percentage of urban and rural households using land,
(RLMS surveys 1992–2000).*

| | Urban Households | Rural Households |
|---|---|---|
| July–October 1992 | 47.7 | 88.2 |
| December 1992–March 1993 | 48.9 | 89.7 |
| October 1994 | 55.6 | 94.9 |
| October 1995 | 54.6 | 95.0 |
| October 1996 | 55.1 | 94.1 |
| October 1998–January 1999 | 53.6 | 92.9 |
| September–December 2000 | 51.2 | 90.7 |

*Source: RLMS survey, 1992–2000. The data from the first phase (1992–93) is not strictly comparable with that from the second phase (1994–2000) since the sampling frame, methodology and questions differed. In the first phase the relevant question related to growing anything on the household's land, in the second phase to using any land. Questions about the use of land were not asked in the third and fourth rounds of the first phase of RLMS.*

The RLMS data gives us some indication of the dynamics of land use, suggesting that the use of the dacha has seen a small decline, particularly since the August 1998 crisis (Table 3.3), a tendency whose significance is confirmed by the regression results in Table 3.9. The median size of plot of urban households was six sotki and of rural households was 15 sotki. Sixty percent of urban plots were up to six sotki in size, and only 4 percent were over 20 sotki, whereas a third of rural plots were over 20 sotki. Only a few plots, mostly in rural districts, were larger than a hectare in size.

## HOW MUCH OF RUSSIA'S FOOD IS HOME-GROWN?

Outside Moscow and St Petersburg, the majority of urban households use plots of land. But what do they do on these plots? Is it true that 'the majority of the population now produces its own food supply to a considerable extent'?

Those who believe that self-sufficiency is becoming the rule rather than the exception in Russia can find powerful support from the widely quoted official statistics, according to which well over half of the total amount of food by value produced in Russia is produced on the garden plots of the population, having increased rapidly from just over a quarter in 1990. According to Goskomstat's agricultural production data, the share of domestic plots in the total value of agricultural output has developed as shown in Table 3.4.

In 2000, according to the official statistics, over 90 percent of all potato production, more than three-quarters of all fruit and vegetables, more than half of all meat, half the milk, over half the wool and almost a third of the eggs produced came from household plots (Table 3.5). These figures are quite remarkable: even if the rural population were entirely self-sufficient, they would imply that the urban population is producing a very substantial proportion of its own food: it would appear that Russia has indeed become a nation of urban peasants.

These figures are very misleading because Goskomstat's category of domestic production combines household subsistence production with almost all smallholding agriculture.[4] The figures in Table 3.5 distinguish between 'personal subsidiary agriculture', which is the traditional form of rural agricultural holding, and the much smaller 'collective and individual orchards and vegetable plots', many of which are held by urban residents. The latter plots were originally formed in the 1960s and 1970s as agricultural co-operatives, often on

---

[4]     The methods of data collection and estimation are described in Goskomstat, 1996a, pp. 584-596. Data on production from subsidiary plots is gathered as part of the regular household budget survey and their livestock holdings are estimated by projections from livestock census data.

the outskirts of towns and cities and sometimes with the aim of developing methods of smallholding production, individuals paying rent and communal service charges for the use of the land. In the 1980s they became increasingly a means by which enterprises and organisations made plots of land available to their employees, acquiring land from the local authority or renting fields from a local *kolkhoz*, and dividing the land into small plots. 'In practice, these plots are "individual", with the land belonging to communes, public enterprises or organisations' (OECD-CEET, 1991, p. 37). This category has increased from 18.5 million families using 1.29 million hectares in 1988.

*Table 3.4:    Percentage of agricultural production by value by category of producer at current prices.*

|      | Agricultural enterprises | Domestic agriculture | Farmers' plots |
| --- | --- | --- | --- |
| 1970 | 69 | 31 |   |
| 1980 | 71 | 29 |   |
| 1990 | 74 | 26 |   |
| 1991 | 69 | 31 |   |
| 1992 | 67 | 32 | 1 |
| 1993 | 57 | 40 | 3 |
| 1994 | 55 | 44 | 2 |
| 1995 | 50 | 48 | 2 |
| 1996 | 49 | 49 | 2 |
| 1997 | 47 | 51 | 2 |
| 1998 | 39 | 59 | 2 |
| 1999 | 42 | 57 | 2 |
| 2000 | 43 | 54 | 3 |

*Sources: Goskomstat, 1999e; Goskomstat, 2001.*

'Personal subsidiary agriculture' (LPKh) was already supplying a substantial proportion of farm produce by the late Soviet period. This agriculture was based on the small plots of land (legally limited to half a hectare per family until the end of the Soviet period) originally allocated to the peasants in the thirties to enable them to avoid starvation, but in the Brezhnev period it developed into a 'partnership' between the private and public sectors in which the public sector paid the costs while the private sector increasingly reaped the rewards – a

*Table 3.5   Number of producers, land under cultivation and production of various products on personal plots*

| | 1980/ 1976–80 | 1991 | 1992 | 1993 | 1994 | 1995 | 1996 | 1997 | 1998 | 1999 | 2000 % of total production |
|---|---|---|---|---|---|---|---|---|---|---|---|
| Private plots (million hectares) of which | 3.5 | 6.0 | 8.5 | 8.8 | 9.3 | 9.9 | 9.9 | 10.2 | 10.5 | 11.9 | |
| *Personal subsidiary agriculture (LPKh)* | | | | | | | | | | | |
| Number of families (thousand) | | 17 100 | 19 288 | 16 553 | 16 582 | 16 295 | 16 250 | 16 374 | 15 993 | 15 500 | |
| Area of private plots (thousand hectares) | 3 000 | 4 590 | 6 826 | 5 825 | 6 062 | 5 810 | 5 805 | 5 923 | 6 433 | 6 137 | |
| *'Collective' and individual orchards and vegetable plots* | | | | | | | | | | | |
| Number of families (thousand) | | 19 000 | 21 418 | 22 546 | 22 353 | 22 407 | 22 114 | 21 624 | 19 620 | 19 243 | |
| Area of collective plots (thousand hectares) | 500 | 1 440 | 1 684 | 1 821 | 1 830 | 1 845 | 1 843 | 1 809 | 1 707 | 1 699 | |
| *Production on all forms of personal plots* | | | | | | | | | | | |
| Potatoes (million tonnes) | 25.3 | 24.8 | 29.9 | 31.1 | 29.8 | 35.9 | 34.9 | 33.8 | 28.7 | 28.8 | 92 |
| Vegetables (million tonnes) | 3.0 | 4.8 | 5.5 | 6.3 | 6.4 | 8.3 | 8.2 | 8.5 | 8.4 | 9.5 | 78 |
| Fruit and berries (million tonnes) | 1.1 | 1.4 | 2.0 | 1.9 | 1.6 | 1.7 | 2.5 | 5.3 | 2.1 | 1.8 | 86 |
| Meat (million tonnes slaughtered) | 2.1 | 2.9 | 2.9 | 3.0 | 2.9 | 2.8 | 2.8 | 2.7 | 2.7 | 2.6 | 57 |
| Milk (million tonnes) | 12.9 | 13.5 | 14.8 | 16.1 | 16.3 | 16.3 | 16.3 | 16.1 | 16.0 | 15.8 | 50 |
| Eggs (billion eggs) | 10.8 | 10.4 | 11.2 | 10.9 | 10.8 | 10.2 | 9.9 | 9.9 | 9.9 | 9.9 | 29 |
| Wool (thousand tonnes) | 41 | 57.7 | 57.5 | 56.0 | 45.3 | 39.8 | 35.4 | 31.2 | 26.3 | 22.9 | 57* |

* 1999

*Source: Goskomstat, 1998d, 2000a, 2001*

form of privatisation that was later generalised to the economy as a whole! For example, although the peasants were given ownership of the individual animals, livestock was almost all raised on the land, fed with the fodder and maintained with the resources of the state and collective farms (OECD-CEET, 1991, p. 39 estimates the extent of the reliance on public pasture and fodder). Of course, in the Soviet period the peasants were not free to sell this produce: the peasants were required to make deliveries of produce to the state or collective farm as their payment for the use of public assets, and were permitted to sell only the surplus that they were able to produce above those compulsory deliveries. Moreover, they were only permitted to sell such produce in person, on the '*kolkhoz* markets' that grew up in every town. It was strictly illegal to sell through any kind of private intermediary, although this restriction was increasingly flouted through the 1980s and this trade was an important basis for the development of commercial activity in the Gorbachev era. By 1989 about 90 percent of the 30 million rural households had such plots, compared with 24 percent of those in urban areas, 'mainly in small towns and the outskirts of cities' (OECD-CEET, 1991, p. 37). This production on domestic plots has nothing to do with subsistence agriculture but was a device introduced in the Soviet period in an attempt to increase the exploitation of the rural population.

The apparent massive increase in domestic production indicated by the figures since 1990 is also very misleading. There has been a sharp decline in agricultural production as a result of the reduction of subsidies, falling incomes and growing import competition: the total volume of agricultural production fell by 44 percent between 1990 and 1998, before recovering slightly. Thus, the growing proportion of food produced on domestic plots is more a result of the decline in production on former state and collective farms, the value of which at constant prices fell by almost two-thirds between 1990 and 1998, than of the growth of domestic production, which grew by 20.7 percent in volume between 1990 and 1993, but since then slowly declined to 12.3 percent above the 1990 level in 1998. Production increased by almost 10 percent between 1998 and 2000, but the increase was greater on the former state and collective farms than on individual plots (Goskomstat, 2001). Moreover, the increase in the proportion of foodstuffs produced by the peasantry was not a result of any increase in productivity on peasant plots but of their spontaneous privatisation of state and collectively owned rural assets. Thus, there was a very substantial increase in the area of land allocated to private plots, from 3.9 million hectares in 1990 to 5.6 million hectares in 1991 and 8.5 million hectares in 1992 (Goskomstat, 1999e) and a substantial 'spontaneous' privatisation of livestock by the peasantry (OECD-CEET, 1991, p. 42). The number of family plots and the area under their cultivation has actually fallen since 1992, although almost all of the fall took place between 1992 and 1993 (Table 3.5).

These peasant plots have little to do with subsistence agriculture but they also have little to do with the commercialisation of agriculture because, while the peasants are now legally free to sell their produce, they are still required to deliver produce in exchange for their land and for the use of the means of production of the local farm which is the basis of their production. It is their use of publicly owned assets that enables these peasant producers to perform the apparently remarkable feat of producing half the meat, wool and milk produced by the whole agricultural sector on less than 5 percent of the total area devoted to pasture and fodder (their share of the production of potatoes, fruit and vegetables, by contrast, is only a little more than their reported share of the land, including collectively owned orchards, under the relevant type of cultivation, indicating that they are not much more productive than state and collective farms). The new commercial farms, meanwhile, have twice as much land at their disposal as are found in family plots, but produce only 2 percent of total agricultural production, apparently less than one-twentieth as productive as their peasant competitors.[5] It should not be surprising that commercial farming has made so little progress in Russia. The barrier to such progress does not so much lie, as many western commentators presume, in the resistance of the directors of state and collective farms so much as in the fact that peasant farmers continue to have free access to the land and most of the productive resources of larger farms. It is these millions of peasant producers, not merely the handful of directors of state and collective farms, who are resisting the full privatisation of land that would deprive them of their livelihoods.

An alternative official data set is the Household Budget Survey, which throws a rather different light on the phenomenon (Ministry of Labour and Social Development and Goskomstat Rossii, 1997; Goskomstat, 1999b, c, d). Although it still includes smallholders as

[5]  In 2000 there were still only 261100 commercial farmers who had registered themselves as small farming enterprises, cultivating an average of 55 hectares each, and their number has been falling since 1996.

domestic producers, the 1996 data allows us to compare consumption and purchases at the level of the household, rather than comparing aggregate production and consumption data, and so to get a better indication of how much food people produce for themselves. According to this data, Russian households in 1996 grew 73 percent of their potatoes, 59 percent of their vegetables, 43 percent of their fruit, a quarter of their meat and milk products and 15 percent of their eggs, all by volume. This total is averaged across the urban and the rural population. Goskomstat does not publish a complete rural-urban breakdown of the data, but from the published data we can calculate that, although the urban population consumes only about two-thirds as many potatoes and vegetables as does the rural population, it spends well over three times as much on buying such products.[6] The data also shows that in the large cities of Moscow and Saint Petersburg people grew less than 20 percent of their potatoes, less than 10 percent of their vegetables, very little fruit and virtually none of their meat, eggs or dairy products. It would seem that, while self-sufficiency may well be a feature of rural existence in Russia, and those in smaller towns and cities may produce a significant proportion of their food for themselves, the dependence of city dwellers on their garden plots is much less than is generally imagined.

The conclusion that domestic production in large cities is dominated

---

[6]  Most estimates of the proportion of food that is home-produced are based on production data, not consumption data, which will tend to lead to substantial overestimates, particularly to the extent that some of the product will eventually be sold, given away or will spoil. L. Ovcharova and I.I. Korchagina calculated on the basis of unpublished Goskomstat budget survey data for 1996 that domestic production accounted for 43 percent of total food consumption by value: urban households grew 23 percent of their own food by value and rural households 75 percent (Ovcharova, 1997), but this estimate seems to derive from production data. A direct calculation from the published budget survey data on consumption and expenditure (which gives money expenditure and the quantities purchased and consumed for the main food groups) suggests that in the last quarter of 1996 across all households 24 percent of food by value was home-grown, while in St Petersburg 3 percent and in Moscow 4 percent was .home grown. This is still well above the RLMS estimate that 14 percent of food by value was home grown in the last quarter of 1996 (Mroz and Popkin, 1997). According to the RLMS data, urban households grew 11 percent and rural households 47 percent of their food by value in 1998 and urban households grew 9 percent and rural households 49 percent of their food by value in 2000. From 1997 the Goskomstat budget survey data has been collected on a new basis. In 1997 home production accounted for 18 percent, in 1998 for 16 percent and in 1999 for 15 percent of food consumption by value, while in urban households it accounted for 11 percent in 1997, and just under 8 percent in 1998 and 1999, with gifts from others accounting for a further 3–4 percent. In Moscow and Saint Petersburg domestic production of food was insignificant, although gifts from others accounted for a tiny part of consumption (Goskomstat, 1999c, 2000b).

*Table 3.6:   Percentage of households buying some or all of their food
              needs and average percentage produced themselves
              (ISITO household survey data, April–May 1998).*

| Percentage | Samara | Kemerovo | Lyubertsy | Syktyvkar | Total |
|---|---|---|---|---|---|
| Buy all potatoes | 58 | 17 | 67 | 28 | 43 |
| Buy some potatoes | 14 | 11 | 15 | 20 | 14 |
| Buy no potatoes | 29 | 72 | 18 | 53 | 42 |
| Home produced | 23 | 65 | 17 | 50 | 38 |
| Given by others | 12 | 13 | 7 | 14 | 12 |
| Buy all vegetables | 42 | 23 | 65 | 46 | 43 |
| Buy some vegetables | 31 | 27 | 25 | 36 | 30 |
| Buy no vegetables | 27 | 50 | 10 | 19 | 28 |
| Home produced | 35 | 54 | 16 | 30 | 35 |
| Given by others | 9 | 12 | 5 | 7 | 9 |
| Buy all fruit | 51 | 84 | 77 | 96 | 73 |
| Buy some fruit | 38 | 14 | 20 | 3 | 22 |
| Buy no fruit | 11 | 2 | 3 | 1 | 5 |
| Home produced | 26 | 7 | 8 | 1 | 13 |
| Given by others | 5 | 2 | 2 | 1 | 3 |
| Buy all dairy products | 94 | 92 | 98 | 94 | 94 |
| Buy some dairy products | 5 | 5 | 2 | 4 | 4 |
| Buy no dairy products | 1 | 3 | 0 | 2 | 2 |
| Home produced | 0 | 1 | 0 | 2 | 1 |
| Given by others | 2 | 4 | 1 | 2 | 2 |
| Buy all meat | 92 | 85 | 97 | 91 | 91 |
| Buy some meat | 6 | 9 | 3 | 6 | 6 |
| Buy no meat | 2 | 6 | 1 | 3 | 3 |
| Home produced | 1 | 2 | 0 | 2 | 1 |
| Given by others | 4 | 8 | 2 | 4 | 4 |

by the production of potatoes and vegetables is confirmed by the
ISITO survey data. In the ISITO household questionnaire we asked
the head of household to estimate what proportion of their needs for
potatoes, vegetables, fruit, dairy products and meat they met through
buying, what proportion through their own production and what
proportion was given to them by others (such donations often being in

exchange for work done on the plot of a friend or relative). It turned out that the majority of households in each case either bought all or none of the relevant product, with most of the rest buying around half their needs of that product.[7] As in the Goskomstat and RLMS data for the big cities,[8] domestic food production was concentrated on potatoes and vegetables, with a significant proportion of fruit being grown in Samara, but very little meat or dairy produce of any kind was home produced (Table 3.6).[9] Not one household met of all its basic food needs from its dacha: far from being the land of self-sufficiency, self-sufficiency is another western concept that appears not to have penetrated far into Russia!

The fact that the ownership of land and the self-provisioning of the household is by no means universal, and that they vary considerably from one city and one region to another, raises the questions of why some people use land and others do not and of why some people use their land to grow their own food and others do not. Is the dacha a means by which households with a low money income meet their basic subsistence needs? Is it an element in a particular type of household survival strategy? Is it a cultural hangover from the peasant past? These questions will be addressed in the rest of this chapter.

## DECIDING TO USE A DACHA

The large-scale use of subsistence plots by city residents is not a legacy of Russia's peasant past, but was a phenomenon of the last years of the Soviet system.[10] The private plots of peasants had always played an important role in supplying the towns with food, but it was only under Brezhnev that this role received some encouragement,

---

[7] It is difficult to compute comparable figures from the RLMS data since this does not include consumption data. At the time of the surveys, more than 80 percent of urban households growing potatoes reported that they had produced or retained at least 90 percent of the average Russian consumption per head of potatoes.

[8] In the RLMS data, 3 percent of urban households produced some meat, 3 percent poultry, 1 percent milk and 4 percent eggs. According to the Goskomstat agricultural production data, two-thirds of the area under cultivation in private plots is planted with potatoes, and one-eighth is planted with vegetables.

[9] The ordering of the ISITO regions in the Goskomstat budget survey data, which refers to the whole oblast, is similar to that found in the ISITO survey. According to the budget survey, in 1996 18 percent of potatoes were home grown in Moscow city (71 percent in Moscow oblast), 57 percent in Samara, 77 percent in the Komi Republic and 95 percent in Kemerovo oblast.

[10] The analysis of the use of dachas here draws on and develops preliminary analysis in Varshavskaya and Karelina, 1998 and Alasheev et al., 1999.

although the government was still very ambivalent about stimulating private enterprise which might divert rural workers' energies from their principal task of feeding the cities and building socialism. Those living in towns who had plots of land attached to their homes or who retained family homes in the countryside had always had access to land on which they could grow vegetables for their families. There was a large-scale distribution of land to enable urban residents to survive during the war and post-war famines,[11] but it was only under Brezhnev that the strict regulations restricting the use of the dacha began to be relaxed. Under perestroika, and especially with the deepening crisis at the end of the 1980s, there was a further mass distribution of land to urban households, and a growing number of enterprises began to rent fields on which their employees could grow potatoes, even providing transport and adapting the rhythm of industrial production to the demands of potato cultivation.

Half the ISITO dachniki had started using their land in the last ten years. Although many people have a dacha because they have always had one, according to the RLMS data there appears to be a significant turnover among the urban dachniki, with 15 percent of urban land users ceasing to use land and about 17 percent of urban non-land-users taking up land use between each round (only about 2 percent of rural respondents give up their land use between rounds).[12] As we shall see, the use of a dacha to produce food involves quite a considerable expenditure of time, effort and, in many cases, money. It is therefore reasonable to regard the use of a dacha in any one year as the result of a decision taken in the light of the current status and situation of the household and its members.

The hypothesis that we wish to explore relates to the use of the dacha as an element in the survival strategy of the household. The most general formulation of the hypothesis is as follows:

**H1** The use of a dacha is a means by which households secure their food supplies in the face of a shortage of money.

In order to test this hypothesis we have to specify more precisely the range of opportunities and constraints facing the household which define the conditions under which it takes its decisions. However,

---

[11]  'By 1943 twelve million urbanites were growing vegetables, compared to five million in 1942' (Mitrofanov, 1989, pp. 331–2, cited Iarskaia-Smirnova and Romanov, 1999). The number had increased to 18.5 million by 1945 (Lovell, forthcoming).

[12]  There must be a suspicion that that some of this turnover reflects an inconsistency of response between rounds, because it is hardly time-dependent: the turnover is only slightly more over a two or three-year gap than over a one-year gap.

there is a prior issue, which is of both substantive and methodological relevance, which is that of who takes the decisions. The dacha is typically a collective undertaking which involves all the members of the household: in the ISITO sample, around 90 percent of the adult members of dachniki households worked on the dacha. Moreover, the dacha makes major demand on the time of all of those involved, with a certain minimum labour input required if anything is to be produced at all. This means that the decision to use a dacha has to be regarded as a discrete collective choice by which the members of the household have to commit a certain minimum of collective effort to use a dacha at all. Once the enabling decision has been taken, there are subsidiary choices to be made about how much labour to put in to the dacha above the minimum required to produce anything, and these may be individual choices about the marginal allocation of the labour-time of individual household members.

The dacha decision is constrained by the size of the disposable money income of the household which is determined, at least in part, by the employment decisions of individual household members. For the purposes of this analysis we will regard individual household members as making co-ordinated decisions about the deployment of their labour-time between income-earning employment and work on a plot of land with a view to maximising the welfare of the household as a whole. This may involve collective decision-making or it may be viewed as the outcome of an iterative process,[13] in which individual household members make their decisions about the extent of their involvement in income-earning employment, with the dacha decision being made within the context of a given household income constraint, the outcome of which feeds back into the employment decisions of individual household members.

We assume that the ISITO households are all in a situation in which they can choose to allocate the labour-time of household members between producing their own food and engaging in some income-earning activity to provide them with the money with which to buy their food. In the simplest model, we would expect those households

---

[13]   We assume that if the iterative solution does not converge on the collective one (for example, if a high wage-earner decides to give up paid work because of the burden of collectively imposed labour on the dacha, all household members then having to work much longer hours on the dacha in compensation) then the household will switch to collective decision-making mode. The decision-making process is likely to be an issue if there is a dislocation between those taking the decisions, those reaping the rewards and those doing the work. The ISITO survey data indicates that this is not particularly the case, but this is a matter that requires further investigation.

with a lower money income to be more likely to use a dacha because we can presume that the return to working the dacha will be relatively greater the lower is the money income, since such work is directed to meeting basic subsistence needs which everybody must satisfy. As a first approximation we would also expect the opportunity cost of engaging in subsistence agriculture to be lower for those households with a lower money income per head. This leads to

**H1.1** The probability of dacha use will be a decreasing function of household money income per head.

The money income of the household is not fixed. Some forms of money income accrue to particular household members as a right, independently of their employment status, the most important being pensions. Most retirement and old-age pensions are paid to those who qualify regardless of whether or not they have a wage income. In Russia the real value of the pension has been eroded and it has sometimes not been paid or been paid only with delays, but pensions have in general been the most reliable, and for many households the only, form of money income. Additional money income is acquired by the household through employment, either for a wage or, for a relatively small number of people, through self-employment. As we saw in the last chapter, the practice of multiple job-holding is not uncommon, with hourly earnings in second jobs typically being higher than in primary jobs.

From the economist's point of view, the decision to work a dacha is primarily a decision about the allocation of the labour-time of household members between alternative uses. In a simple model we presume that household members have a three-way choice in allocating their time, between leisure, waged employment and working a dacha, and that they will equate the returns from each at the margin. If we follow the economists in making the assumptions that leisure is a pleasure and work is a pain, that the marginal utility of leisure is a diminishing function of the amount of time devoted to it and that the marginal disutility of work is an increasing function of the time spent in work, then we would expect to find an inverse relationship between the amount of time spent in waged employment and the amount of time spent working the dacha.

**H1.2a** The higher the number of hours worked by those in paid employment, the less likely the household is to use a dacha.

**H1.3a** The higher the number of hours worked in secondary employment, the less likely the household is to use a dacha.

In fact working hours are relatively inflexible, particularly in Russia where part-time employment is not well-developed and overtime working is legally restricted, so that people's choice is often between whether or not to work, not for how many hours they will work. Moreover, few people are paid for overtime so that to work additional paid hours it is often necessary to take a second job. This leads to an alternative formulation of the hypotheses:

**H1.2b** The higher the proportion of household members in paid employment, the less likely the household is to use a dacha

**H1.3b** The higher the proportion of household members with second jobs, the less likely the household is to use a dacha

The opportunity cost of working the dacha will be higher for those who earn higher wages in their primary and their second jobs. If we presume that all individuals are equally productive in working the dacha, then we would expect households in which individuals earn higher wages in their primary or secondary jobs, or households in which employment income is a larger share of total household income, to be less likely to work a dacha. Thus we would expect:

**H1.2c** The higher the wage rate of individual household members and/or the proportion of wages in total household income, the less likely the household is to use a dacha.

**H1.3c** The higher the wage rate in secondary employment and/or the proportion of secondary earnings in total household income, the less likely the household is to use a dacha.

In the context of the Russian crisis many people find themselves in employment which generates only a reduced income or no income at all. We would expect those households which are deprived of money income by the non-payment of wages, by lay-offs or by short-time working to be more likely to have to acquire and work a dacha in order to meet their basic subsistence needs. The latter two would be expected to be more powerful than the first, since those subject to lay-offs and short-time working will have more free time than those still working but not being paid their wages. This leads to

**H1.4** The greater the wage debt,

**H1.5** the greater the degree of short-time working and

**H1.6**   the longer the lay-offs experienced by household members, the more likely the household will be to have a dacha.

The lower the wage that is available in paid employment, the more likely we would expect individuals to choose to work on the dacha rather than to work for a wage. At the margin, some individuals may have such limited wage-earning opportunities that they will devote all of their labour-time to the dacha. The corollary of the hypothesis that the more household members are employed the less likely is the household to work a dacha is the inverse, that the more household members who are not in paid employment the more likely is the household to work a dacha. We do not have any direct measure of the wage-earning opportunities of those who are not in employment, but it is reasonable to presume that the opportunities are less the lower is the level of education of household members. It is also reasonable to expect that pensioners, particularly those who are no longer working, have fewer opportunities of engaging in paid employment.[14] Children are proscribed by law from working in paid employment, but they can make a significant contribution to working the dacha. This leads to:

**H1.7**   The lower the level of education of adult household members, the more likely the household will be to have a dacha.

**H1.8**   The higher the number of pensioners in the household, the more likely the household will be to have a dacha.

**H1.9**   The more school-age children in the household, the more likely the household will be to have a dacha.

Self-provisioning with food is not simply a matter of desire, but also of capacity and opportunity. Although we would expect those with lower money incomes to be more inclined to produce their own food, to engage in domestic production households also need at least the minimum of resources (purchase or rent of a plot, travel expenses, tools, seeds, fertiliser, pesticides) required for cultivation. From this point of view households require a certain minimum level of household money income to be able to produce their own food at all. On this basis we may want to qualify H1.1 by:

**H1.10** Households in the lowest income groups will be less likely than those above a certain income threshold to use a dacha.

---

[14]   In the Russian context, the official retirement age is low but it is normal for pensioners to continue to work in paid employment to supplement their pension. Having left their job, however, it is nowadays very difficult for a retiree to get another one.

Since most urban residents have to travel considerable distances to reach their dachas, and have to transport their tools and their produce, we would expect those households with their own means of transport to be more likely to use a dacha.

**H1.11** Households which own private means of transport will be more likely to use a dacha.

We have noted that the decision to use a dacha is a discrete choice, in the sense that there is a certain threshold level of labour input below which it is impossible to produce anything and there are some economies of scale involved in agricultural production. For both of these reasons we would expect:

**H1.12** The larger the number of household members, the more likely the household will be to have a dacha.

On the other hand, since most people have to travel considerable distances to their dacha, the presence of young children or disabled adults may limit the possibility of dacha use by restricting the mobility of household members. Thus:

**H1.13** The larger the proportion of disabled household members, the less likely the household will be to work a dacha.

**H1.14** The larger the number of pre-school children in need of care, the less likely the household will be to work a dacha.

Finally, producers also need a certain amount of skill and expertise, as well as the physical capacity, to do the necessary work. The latter consideration would lead us to expect:

**H1.15** Households of rural origin will be more likely to use a dacha.

**H1.16** Households of old people will be less likely to use a dacha.

## TESTING THE HYPOTHESES

We have three different data sets on which we can test this set of hypotheses. First, the data of the ISITO household survey; second, the data of the 1994 microcensus; third, the RLMS data. We have run a large number of regressions with various specifications of the variables, the outcomes of which have generally been very consistent and the coefficients have turned out to be very stable. As will be seen, there is also a high degree of consistency, even down to the size of the coefficients, between the three data sets. The results reported here can therefore be considered to be very robust. We will first present the results of the analysis of all three data sets and then discuss their interpretation in relation to the hypotheses together.

## ISITO household survey data

A lot of different specifications of the independent variables were explored and those included in Table 3.7 are those which proved most powerful. Neither quadratic nor cubic nor log functions, nor total income as opposed to income per head, produced a significant functional relation to income. Income deciles provide marginally the best model as well as being the most interpretable, although the detailed pattern does not appear to be amenable to a meaningful interpretation. The average wage of the wage-earners had absolutely no impact. Professional group was not significant. The composition of household income is not significant, nor is the gender balance of the household in terms of either work or contributions to domestic labour. The education of the head of household is more significant as a scalar than as a set of dummy variables for different levels of educational attainment. The results reported here are robust: the coefficients are very stable across a wide range of formulations of the models.

Different indicators of the significance of primary and secondary employment have been tried (the proportion of household members with first and second jobs; the number of hours worked per head in first and second jobs; the proportion of household income contributed by primary and secondary wages). The coefficients on each are consistent, but none is significant. The variables reported here make the most significant contribution to the model.

*Table 3.7:   Logistic Regression – dependent variable: probability of having a dacha (ISITO household survey data, April–May 1998).*

| Variable | B | S.E. | Significance | Odds ratio |
|---|---|---|---|---|
| Household income per head – deciles by city (fifth decile is reference) | | | | |
| First | −0.52 | 0.16 | .0014 | 0.59 |
| Second | −0.30 | 0.16 | .0565 | 0.74 |
| Third | −0.10 | 0.16 | .5315 | 0.91 |
| Fourth | −0.20 | 0.16 | .2089 | 0.82 |
| Sixth | −0.10 | 0.16 | .5212 | 0.90 |
| Seventh | −0.21 | 0.16 | .1833 | 0.81 |
| Eighth | −0.17 | 0.16 | .2949 | 0.84 |
| Ninth | −0.27 | 0.17 | .1035 | 0.76 |
| Tenth | −0.43 | 0.17 | .0114 | 0.65 |
| Household composition (number in each age group) | | | | |
| Children under 7 | −0.04 | 0.12 | .7593 | 0.96 |
| Children 7–16 | 0.07 | 0.08 | .3339 | 1.08 |
| Adults 17–24 | 0.16 | 0.07 | .0234 | 1.17 |
| Adults 25–39 | 0.03 | 0.07 | .6959 | 1.03 |
| Adults 40 to pension age | 0.46 | 0.07 | .0000 | 1.58 |
| Pension age | 0.66 | 0.08 | .0000 | 1.93 |
| Education (secondary or less is reference): proportion of adults with | | | | |
| Vocational secondary | 0.20 | 0.11 | .0574 | 1.22 |
| Higher education | 0.35 | 0.12 | .0028 | 1.41 |
| Occupational Status (non-working adult is reference): proportion of adults | | | | |
| Working | 0.00 | 0.18 | .9898 | 1.00 |
| Registered unemployed | 0.29 | 0.35 | .3967 | 1.34 |
| Student | −1.72 | 1.36 | .2085 | 0.18 |
| Non-working pensioner | −0.35 | 0.22 | .1185 | 0.71 |
| Employment status (as percentage of those working) | | | | |
| Self-employed | −0.05 | 0.39 | .9064 | 0.96 |
| Have sec. employment | 0.21 | 0.14 | .1398 | 1.23 |
| On administrative leave | −0.57 | 0.45 | .2016 | 0.56 |
| Owed wages | 0.01 | 0.11 | .9576 | 1.01 |
| On leave in last year | 0.06 | 0.17 | .7239 | 1.06 |
| Short time working | 0.44 | 0.22 | .0419 | 1.55 |
| Average hours worked/day | 0.01 | 0.02 | .6739 | 1.01 |
| Male-headed household | −0.18 | 0.09 | .0439 | 0.83 |

*Table 3.7 (continued)*

| | | | | |
|---|---|---|---|---|
| Couple-headed household | 0.36 | 0.09 | .0001 | 1.44 |
| Proportion rural-born | 0.31 | 0.12 | .0083 | 1.36 |
| Has children requiring care | 0.03 | 0.11 | .7586 | 1.04 |
| Has adults requiring care | −0.33 | 0.12 | .0061 | 0.72 |
| Has a car | 1.23 | 0.10 | .0000 | 3.42 |
| City (reference is Lyubertsy) | | | | |
| Samara | 0.74 | 0.10 | .0000 | 2.09 |
| Kemerovo | 1.71 | 0.12 | .0000 | 5.53 |
| Syktyvkar | 1.29 | 0.12 | .0000 | 3.64 |
| Constant | −1.94 | 0.25 | .0000 | |
| N | 3 924 | | | |
| -2LL | 5 427 | | | |
| Model Chi square | 781 | | | |

## The 1994 microcensus data

The 1994 microcensus data allows us to test our findings on a much larger data set, a 5 percent sample of the whole Russian population (the Chechen Republic is excluded). Respondents were not asked about agricultural production, but they were asked about their possession of land. We have quite good indicators of the composition of the household because the microcensus asked about all of the income sources of each individual household member. This allows us to define how many members receive pensions, how many work, how many are full-time grant-supported students and so on. Unfortunately the data does not make it possible to distinguish particular cities, only separating the urban from the rural census districts of each oblast, except in the case of the cities of Moscow and St Petersburg which are distinct administrative units. However, it does allow us to look at the impact of income, household composition and employment status on the possession, if not on the use, of a dacha.

We cannot unambiguously identify the head of household in this data because the microcensus did not specifically identify the first respondent as the head of household, and in fact it seems arbitrary who is named first, since men and women are more or less equally in that position, whereas in the ISITO and other surveys women are far more likely to be identified as head of household.

Regressions have been run separately for all 89 administrative divisions for which data is available (no respondents possessed land in Taymir) as well as for the larger territorial units and for Russia as a whole using both regionally defined income deciles and a logarithmic function for the household income per head variable. The results of the regressions on the data set of 1.84 million households in urban census districts are summarised in Table 3.8. Regional dummies were included for all the regions and sub-regions in the dataset. Separate regressions were also run for each region and sub-region.

*Table 3.8:* *Logistic regression – dependent variable: probability of possessing a plot of land (All-Russia, urban population, 1994 microcensus data).*

| Variable | B | Standard Error | Odds Ratio |
|---|---|---|---|
| Number in household of | | | |
| Working adults | 0.33 | 0.01 | 1.39 |
| Non-working adults | 0.15 | 0.02 | 1.16 |
| Non-working pensioners | 0.26 | 0.02 | 1.30 |
| Under 8 | 0.12 | 0.01 | 1.12 |
| Under 16 | 0.37 | 0.01 | 1.45 |
| Non-working 16–19 | 0.39 | 0.01 | 1.48 |
| Proportion of adult household members with given income sources: | | | |
| Wage income | −0.09** | 0.04 | 0.91 |
| Entrepreneurial income | −0.28 | 0.05 | 0.76 |
| Employed by private individual | −0.32 | 0.06 | 0.72 |
| Stipend | −0.06** | 0.03 | 0.94 |
| Age or service pension | 0.37 | 0.03 | 1.45 |
| Invalidity benefit | −0.21 | 0.03 | 0.81 |
| Loss of breadwinner | 0.27 | 0.01 | 1.31 |
| Unemployment benefit | 0.29 | 0.06 | 1.33 |
| Private donations | −0.12 | 0.02 | 0.89 |
| Household income per head, deciles (reference is fifth decile) | | | |
| First | −0.08 | 0.02 | 0.92 |
| Second | −0.02* | 0.01 | 0.98 |
| Third | −0.01* | 0.01 | 0.99 |

*Table 3.8 (continued)*

| | | | |
|---|---|---|---|
| Fourth | 0.00* | 0.01 | 1.00 |
| Sixth | 0.02** | 0.01 | 1.02 |
| Seventh | 0.03*** | 0.01 | 1.03 |
| Eighth | 0.05 | 0.01 | 1.05 |
| Ninth | 0.08 | 0.02 | 1.08 |
| Tenth | 0.14 | 0.03 | 1.15 |
| **First named is** | | | |
| Under 25 | −0.69 | 0.02 | 0.50 |
| 40 to 59 | 0.48 | 0.01 | 1.62 |
| Over60 | 0.42 | 0.02 | 1.52 |
| Married | 0.64 | 0.02 | 1.90 |
| Country born | 0.21 | 0.02 | 1.24 |
| Lived here all life | 0.25 | 0.02 | 1.28 |
| **Educational level of first named (reference is primary)** | | | |
| Higher education | 0.16 | 0.04 | 1.17 |
| Special education | 0.04* | 0.02 | 1.04 |
| Secondary education | −0.17 | 0.02 | 0.84 |
| Less than primary | 0.23 | 0.02 | 1.26 |
| N | 1 840 048 | | |
| Model Chi square | 822 275.51 | | |
| Pseudo R squared | 0.1138 | | |

*Note: 88 Regional dummies were also included in the regression. Income deciles are computed for each region. Standard errors are adjusted for clustering on region. The first-named person was not specifically identified as the head of the household in the microcensus data.*
*All coefficients are significant at p<.001 except ***p<.01 ** p<.05 *p>.05*

**The RLMS data**

RLMS, like the ISITO questionnaire, asked about the use of land, as opposed to the microcensus which asked about possession. Table 3.9 shows the results of a regression using the 1994–2000 RLMS data. The coefficients do not differ significantly from one year to another and are consistent with those derived from the other datasets.

*Table 3.9:*   *Logistic Regression – dependent variable: probability of household using land in the last year (RLMS 1994–2000 pooled data, urban households).*

| Variable | Variable means | B | S.E. | Odds Ratio | Sig. |
|---|---|---|---|---|---|
| Household composition, number of | | | | | |
| Children under 7 | 0.21 | 0.10 | 0.07 | 1.10 | .176 |
| Children 7–18 | 0.47 | 0.20 | 0.05 | 1.22 | .000 |
| Adults 19–24 | 0.25 | 0.10 | 0.05 | 1.10 | .074 |
| Adults 25–39 | 0.61 | 0.29 | 0.05 | 1.33 | .000 |
| Adults 40 to pension age | 0.61 | 0.72 | 0.05 | 2.04 | .000 |
| Pension age | 0.57 | 0.84 | 0.06 | 2.32 | .000 |
| Proportion of adult household members | | | | | |
| Currently working | 0.54 | 0.22 | 0.11 | 1.24 | .046 |
| Disabled | 0.02 | –0.14 | 0.29 | 0.87 | .634 |
| Maternity leave | 0.05 | –0.40 | 0.20 | 0.67 | .043 |
| Paid leave | 0.01 | 0.00 | 0.33 | 1.00 | .999 |
| Unpaid leave | 0.00 | 0.28 | 0.41 | 1.32 | .498 |
| Unemployed | 0.07 | 0.00 | 0.15 | 1.00 | .981 |
| With higher education | 0.19 | 0.02 | 0.10 | 1.02 | .867 |
| Rural born | 0.37 | 0.22 | 0.09 | 1.24 | .012 |
| Proportion of employed household members | | | | | |
| Self-employed | 0.03 | –0.64 | 0.18 | 0.53 | .000 |
| Owed wages | 0.29 | 0.19 | 0.06 | 1.21 | .003 |
| Paid partly in kind | 0.04 | 0.51 | 0.16 | 1.66 | .001 |
| Had admin. leave | 0.06 | 0.47 | 0.11 | 1.60 | .000 |
| Have second jobs | 0.11 | 0.14 | 0.09 | 1.15 | .123 |
| Male headed household | 0.17 | –0.30 | 0.07 | 0.74 | .000 |
| Household has a car | 0.24 | 1.01 | 0.07 | 2.75 | .000 |
| Household money income per head, deciles (reference is fifth decile) | | | | | |
| First decile | 0.09 | –0.21 | 0.10 | 0.81 | .030 |
| Second decile | 0.07 | –0.15 | 0.10 | 0.86 | .136 |
| Third decile | 0.08 | –0.14 | 0.09 | 0.87 | .139 |
| Fourth decile | 0.09 | 0.03 | 0.09 | 1.03 | .754 |
| Sixth decile | 0.11 | –0.10 | 0.08 | 0.91 | .243 |

*Table 3.9 (continued)*

| | | | | | |
|---|---|---|---|---|---|
| Seventh decile | 0.11 | −0.07 | 0.09 | 0.94 | .442 |
| Eighth decile | 0.11 | −0.21 | 0.09 | 0.81 | .017 |
| Ninth decile | 0.11 | −0.16 | 0.09 | 0.85 | .079 |
| Tenth decile | 0.11 | −0.24 | 0.10 | 0.79 | .013 |
| Year of survey (1994 is reference) | | | | | |
| 1995 | 0.20 | −0.13 | 0.04 | 0.88 | .002 |
| 1996 | 0.20 | −0.12 | 0.05 | 0.89 | .011 |
| 1998 | 0.19 | −0.19 | 0.05 | 0.83 | .000 |
| 2000 | 0.20 | −0.26 | 0.05 | 0.77 | .000 |
| Constant | | −1.94 | 0.16 | | .000 |
| N | 12 493 | | | | |
| Model Chi square | 835.9 | | | | .000 |
| Pseudo R squared | 0.115 | | | | |

*Notes: The standard errors allow for clustering of data in panels. Since 92 percent of rural households have a dacha, their inclusion in the regression simply increases the standard errors. Income percentiles are calculated on the basis of the household money income per head reported the previous month within each of eight regions in each round. The self-employed are those who say that they do not work for an enterprise or organisation at which more than one person works.*

*In a separate regression including only those households with working members, the hours worked by household members in paid employment has no significant impact on the probability of land use.*

*Regional dummies were also included in the regression. The incidence of dacha use in Moscow and St Petersburg is substantially less and in the North and Northwest somewhat less than in other regions.*

## Testing the hypotheses

In all three data sets we find that the hypotheses relating to the opportunity to use a dacha are more or less strongly supported, the most important being the demographic composition of the household: the more adult members there are in the household, the more likely it is to possess a dacha (H1.12). A household based around a married couple is also substantially more likely to have a dacha. If the head of household is male, then the household is marginally less likely to have a dacha.

All three data sets show strongly that the more household members are pensioners, the more likely is the household to possess a dacha, which supports our hypothesis H1.8. The microcensus data also shows that having household members who are in receipt of benefits for loss of a breadwinner or of unemployment benefit also increases the probability of dacha ownership. It is likely that this is an indicator of the occupational status of household members, rather than of the existence of non-wage incomes, since households with members receiving a stipend are marginally and those with members receiving invalidity benefit are much less likely to have a dacha, the latter finding supporting our hypothesis H1.13. Households with members born or brought up in a rural district are significantly more likely to have a dacha, supporting hypothesis H1.15.[15] In the microcensus data, households of rural origin are as likely to possess land as are those in which the first-named person has lived in the same place all his or her life, suggesting that a rural origin compensates for the relative disadvantage of migrants in getting access to land – it is only those who were born in another urban district who are significantly less likely to have a dacha. Having an automobile is one of the strongest predictors of dacha ownership (H1.11).

The educational level of household members is a significant influence on the probability of having a dacha, but does not conform to our hypotheses. In the ISITO and microcensus data, those with higher levels of education are significantly *more* likely to have a dacha (in the RLMS data the coefficient is negative but not significant), which is contrary to our hypothesis H1.7 that those with higher levels of education would have better alternative opportunities of earning a living and so would be less drawn to working the land. We might speculate that this is to do with the greater flexibility and ability to learn of those with higher levels of education, qualities which are needed for what is in effect adopting a new profession, or it might reflect the cultural significance of the dacha, as a diversion from mental labour. In the microcensus data, those with the lowest levels of education were the most likely to own land, but this is probably a consequence of the fact that most of those who did not complete primary education are older people, and particularly those of rural origin, who are more likely to have a dacha.

The age pattern does not accord with our hypotheses H1.14 and H1.16, that having more young and old people in the household would

---

[15]  They are also significantly less likely to have a second job or engage in individual economic activity, suggesting that for these households working a dacha is an alternative to secondary employment. In general, for urban households there is no significant relationship in the ISITO or RLMS data between working a dacha and secondary employment.

reduce the likelihood of having a dacha since they would not be able to contribute their labour, while their care would demand the time of household members. In fact, the presence of young children does not have a significant impact on the probability of using land in the ISITO data, while it significantly increases the likelihood that the household will have land in the microcensus and RLMS data. In the ISITO household survey we asked specifically about childcare, but households in which children required care were no less likely to have a dacha than those which had no such responsibility. We also find in all our data sets that older households and those with more pensioners are much more likely to have a dacha than those headed by prime-age men or women, while younger households are less likely to do so. This may partly reflect the fact that many of the plots of land being used by households were distributed during the 1980s.[16] It looks from the data as though it is not until people reach their late 60s that their ability to maintain and work on a dacha is significantly reduced. All of this would seem to indicate that age is not much of an impediment to working a dacha although, as noted above, disability is more so.

All of the hypotheses considered so far are more or less uncontroversial, but they are all subsidiary to the central argument under consideration since none of them relate to the relationship between dacha use and household income and employment. Whatever may be people's reasons for wanting to have a dacha, it is obviously going to be a more realistic proposition if there are more household members, if there are more young and older people with free time and without other employment commitments, if the household has a rural origin, and so some experience of rural pursuits, or has been long-established in the town, and if the household has a car to transport its members, their tools and their produce.

When it comes to the critical set of variables, those relating to the impact of income and employment, the picture is much less clear. In the ISITO and RLMS surveys there is no significant functional relationship between income and dacha use, although the lowest and highest income deciles are the least likely to have land.[17] In both of

---

16   Several commentators have noted the association of dacha use with the older generation and the disdain of young people for working the land, something that is probably a generational difference rather than a reflection of transition since it was remarked on in the 1960s (Hervouet, 2001; Lovell, forthcoming).

17   Seeth, Chachnov and Surinov (1998, p. 1620) find that the lowest income quintile is the least likely to grow its own food. They conclude that the dacha is a means by which the middle and upper (though not the highest) income groups are able to increase their security.

these data sets the standard errors of the income coefficients are high, reinforcing the impression that there is no clear relationship between income and dacha use.

In the microcensus data, there is a tendency for income to be positively associated with dacha use, although the relationship is weak and it is not consistent across regions. Across urban Russia as a whole, with households assigned to deciles specific to each of the administrative units according to their income per head, we find that those in the bottom income deciles are the least likely to have a dacha, while those at the top of the income scale are significantly more likely than middle income groups to have a dacha, although even with this enormous dataset income has very little significant impact on the probability of dacha ownership, except at the very top of the scale. The relationship between income and dacha ownership is probably more complex than appears in the aggregate data, as is shown when we run separate regressions for the 89 republics, oblasts, krais and okrugs for which we have the microcensus data. Although we find that in the majority (53) of cases there is a significant positive relationship ($p<.01$) between the log of household income per head and the probability of owning a dacha (the best fitting functional relationship), in 11 cases there is a significant negative relationship. When we look at the distribution of land ownership by income deciles we find that where there is a significant difference between income deciles in any particular region, it is almost always only at the very top and/or the very bottom of the income distribution. In 30 of the 89 regions dacha possession among the bottom decile was significantly lower than among the middle income groups, although in five cases (Krasnodar, Amur, Chitinsk, Buryatia and Osetiya) it was significantly higher. In 25 cases dacha ownership was significantly higher in the top income decile, while in only eight cases was it significantly lower (Krasnodar, Krasnoyarsk, Amur, Belgorod, Tver, Dagestan, Tatarstan and Komi). The pattern that we have noted as weakly present in the data of the other two surveys, of dacha use apparently being less among both the rich and the poor, is very much the exception in the all-Russian and in the regional level data, found to be statistically significant in only two regions, Tatarstan and Tver. In the ISITO survey regions, the Samara microcensus data shows no significant income differences, while Kemerovo and Moscow city and oblast are three of the very few regions to reveal a reasonably monotonic relation between income and dacha use, with a logarithmic relationship being strongly significant in

Moscow and marginally significant in Kemerovo. Komi shows very low dacha use among high income households, but this is probably because the latter are primarily the oil, gas and coal industry workers in the Arctic north of the Republic where nothing can be grown.

All of this data certainly leads us to reject the fundamental hypothesis that the dacha functions primarily as a means by which the more impoverished households provide their own subsistence (H1.1).[18] This conclusion is reinforced when we take into account the effect of aggregation in the RLMS and microcensus data, which combines large cities with small towns, the former tending to have higher income and lower dacha ownership than the latter, so that the effect of aggregation would be to produce a picture of dacha use as a declining function of income. Even without taking this into account, it seems to be clear from the microcensus data that, if dacha ownership is a function of income, it is certainly not a decreasing function. The data may be consistent with the hypothesis (H1.10) that there is a certain income threshold below which households find it more difficult to support a dacha. It is conceivable that the observed relationship between income and dacha use is the result of the complex interaction of the two aspects of the relationship which derive from the fact that a dacha requires the investment of both time and money. The poor have the time but not the money, the rich have the money but not the time, and it is only the households in the middle who have both the time and the money. However, such a reformulation of the problem regards income only as a source of opportunity, not as a measure of opportunity cost, so it takes us no further towards explaining why people want to take the opportunity of owning and working on a dacha.

We can deal briefly with the question of more immediate financial difficulties: short-time working, the non-payment of wages and compulsory lay-offs, which are not recorded in the microcensus data. In the ISITO data the coefficients have the expected sign, and so are consistent with the hypotheses H1.4 to H1.6 that financial difficulties would be likely to encourage dacha use, but only in the case of short-time working is this factor significant and this is simply a result of the fact that short-time working and dacha use are more prevalent in Kemerovo and Syktyvkar. Once interaction terms are introduced into

[18]    In the microcensus data the receipt of private transfers from others has a strong negative association with dacha use, which is probably because those households without dachas would be expected to be more likely to receive private transfers of food from those who do have dachas (the microcensus question referred to 'all sources of means of subsistence', not just to income).

the regression the coefficient actually becomes negative and insignificant.

In the RLMS data, the more household members suffer from wage delays or have been paid partly in kind, the more likely is the household to use a dacha. However, this is most likely to be an indication of an association between high levels of dacha use and payment in kind at a local level, and these variables cease to be significant once we control for polling site, rather than merely for the large aggregate regions. As in the case of secondary employment, those who have experienced a spell of administrative leave have both the need for additional income and, unlike those who are working but have not received their wages, also have the time to spend seeking it. Thus, the more household members had experienced a spell of administrative leave, the more likely was the household to use a dacha, even controlling for polling site. The more household members who were currently unemployed, working less than their normal hours or on paid leave the more likely was the household to use land, though none of these factors is statistically significant.

The crucial set of hypotheses are those concerning the relationship between income and employment, since the central argument is that the basis of dacha ownership is the use of household resources to provide food through domestic production rather than using those same resources to earn money and buy food. The variables that we have considered so far all relate to the greater or lesser possibility of using land, without taking into account the alternative possibility of waged employment. The one conclusion that stands out very clearly from all of these data sets is that there is absolutely no evidence that working a dacha is regarded as an alternative to paid employment. The set of relevant hypotheses (H1.2a to H1.3c) either find no support or are directly contradicted by the data.

In both the RLMS and the ISITO household survey data, wages and working hours in main or second jobs (not shown here) are not significant determinants of the probability of having a dacha (H1.2a, 1.2c, 1.3a, 1.3c). Nor is the number of household members who are working nor the proportion of working members who have second jobs significant (H1.2b, H1.3b). Moreover, in every case the coefficient indicates that working for wages and working the dacha are if anything complements rather than alternatives: those households with relatively more working members and those which are more heavily involved in secondary employment are more likely to work a dacha, although the relationship is not sufficiently strong to be statistically significant.

The microcensus data provides no support for these hypotheses either. The more adult members of the household are working, the more likely is the household to have a dacha, only being marginally counteracted by the fact that the household is slightly less likely to possess land the more household members earn a wage rather than receiving a pension or unemployment benefit. At regional level, in six of the 13 aggregated regions, the more wage-earners there are in the household, the more likely it is to possess a dacha. However, in the North Caucasus, Moscow City and the Black Earth regions the reverse is the case, and the more wage-earners the less likely is the household to possess a dacha. In 25 of the 89 administrative divisions there is a significant positive relationship and in nine there is a significant negative relationship. The effect in either direction is small.

The only qualification to this conclusion is that over Russia as a whole, and in most regions taken individually, as well as in the RLMS (but not the ISITO) data, the more household members have incomes from entrepreneurial activity or from employment by a private individual, the less likely is the household to have a dacha, indicating that this kind of employment is an alternative to working a dacha, either because such work is very lucrative, or perhaps because of the time demands of working in the new private sector. It is interesting that in Moscow City the reverse is the case, those with entrepreneurial incomes being substantially more likely to have a dacha, indicating that in Moscow the dacha for some people has a different significance, as a status symbol for the rich.

Apart from this limited exception, we seem to be drawn to the inescapable conclusion that dacha ownership and waged employment are not alternatives, and so that the use of a dacha cannot be explained as the result of household decisions to produce food in response to economic difficulties or limited employment opportunities.

## WHY DO PEOPLE USE DACHAS?

We should not jump to such a conclusion prematurely. It may be that different households use dachas for different reasons, and that this diversity has been concealed beneath statistics that lump everybody together. Perhaps for the poor the dacha is a source of subsistence, while for the better off it is a place of rest and relaxation.

In the ISITO household survey we asked people what were the two most important reasons for using their dacha. We also asked those who did not have a dacha why they did not have one. The responses are summarised in Table 3.10.

*Table 3.10:  Reasons cited for having and for not having a dacha (ISITO Household survey, April-May 1998).*

|  | Samara | Kemerovo | Lyubertsy | Syktyvkar | Total |
|---|---|---|---|---|---|
| Most important reason for doing it (percent of dachniki) | | | | | |
| Hobby, leisure, we like to do it | 17 | 9 | 39 | 15 | 17 |
| Main source of subsistence | 28 | 52 | 14 | 35 | 36 |
| Additional produce for the table | 53 | 36 | 44 | 45 | 44 |
| Source of money income | 1 | 1 | 0 | 0 | 1 |
| Providing for a rainy day | 2 | 3 | 2 | 4 | 3 |
| Percentage of dachniki citing as one of two reasons for doing it | | | | | |
| Hobby, leisure, we like to do it | 48 | 31 | 68 | 39 | 43 |
| Main source of subsistence | 34 | 58 | 18 | 31 | 41 |
| Additional produce for the table | 79 | 68 | 76 | 71 | 73 |
| Source of money income | 4 | 2 | 2 | 2 | 3 |
| Providing for a rainy day | 18 | 23 | 16 | 18 | 19 |
| Why do you not use land for subsidiary agriculture? (All reasons cited) | | | | | |
| We don't need it | 6 | 11 | 6 | 10 | 8 |
| We do not want to do it | 17 | 11 | 11 | 13 | 14 |
| We do not have time to do it | 16 | 12 | 13 | 17 | 15 |
| We cannot for health reasons | 39 | 39 | 32 | 22 | 34 |
| We cannot get any land | 12 | 12 | 31 | 19 | 18 |
| We do not have the money to do it | 27 | 39 | 40 | 33 | 34 |

Very few households said that their dacha was important as a source of money income, and we found few households who sold any of the produce of their dacha, although there was a handful who had obviously become commercial smallholders, working fairly large plots of land on a commercial basis. Overall, 8 percent of those working a dacha sold some of the produce. In Samara and Kemerovo such 'commercial' operators earned an average of over 800 roubles ($130) a year from the sale of their produce. In Syktyvkar and Lyubertsy there were fewer commercial dacha holders, and the monetary contribution of the dacha to the household income was correspondingly much less. However, it would be wrong to see the dacha as making a significant contribution to the household money income of those who sell the produce: for well over half of these households the revenue from the sale of produce was not sufficient to cover their monetary outlay for the costs of that production. Thus, only 1 percent of all households had any net positive monetary income from subsidiary agriculture. We omit this group from further consideration because it is so small.

Half the urban households in the Russian Longitudinal Monitoring Survey grew some of their own food, but only 6 percent of those sold any of the produce in 1994–96 and 12 percent sold some of their produce in 1998 and 2000. For those who sold produce, the net income amounted to an average of 14 percent of the household's total money income (and 37 percent of the money income of rural households), but this is more an indication of low incomes than of high returns from subsidiary agriculture: the median monthly net income from sales for those households which sold some produce was only $4–5, falling to $2 in 1998, only a little more than one-tenth as much as households made from secondary employment (the median net income from sales by rural households ranged from $11 to $17). Goskomstat's budget survey found that in the fourth quarter of 1996, the last time that income data was gathered, sales of agricultural produce amounted to 2 percent of total household money income: 11.3 percent in the countryside, 0.1 percent in towns (Ministry of Labour and Social Development and Goskomstat Rossii, 1997). According to the Goskomstat Labour Force Survey in May 2000, 13 percent of the urban population aged 15–72 had worked to produce agricultural goods in the week prior to the survey, but only 9 percent of these intended to sell any part of the produce. Sixty-two percent of the rural population had worked on the land, but even here only 29 percent of these intended to sell any of the produce (Goskomstat, 2000d).

When we look at the mean household income of each group we find that there is a significant gradation of income in very much the direction that we would expect (Table 3.11). Those who say that they have a dacha as a leisure activity have a much higher mean income than those for whom the dacha is primarily a source of food, and those for whom the dacha is a supplementary source of food have a much higher mean income than those for whom it is the principal source of subsistence.[19] The subjective assessments of the importance of the dacha for the household subsistence for those who have a dacha accord quite closely with the reasons given for having a dacha: 91 percent of those who said that the dacha was their basic source of subsistence said that their domestic production was important in providing for the family, against 57 percent of those who said the dacha was primarily a hobby. Among those who do not have a dacha we find a similar sharp distinction in mean incomes, between those who choose not work a dacha: they did not want to, did not need to or did not have the time to do it, and those who are unable to work a dacha: they are in poor health, cannot get land or do not have enough money. This latter provides some foundation for the slight tendency indicated in the ISITO and RLMS data for dacha use to be concentrated among the middle income groups: the rich do not have the time to work a dacha, the poor do not have the money.

It seems clear that both those who have a dacha and those who do not are quite sharply differentiated from one another. As was suggested in hypothesis H1.10, the relatively lower level of dacha use among the lowest income households can be explained by the fact that they do not have the resources to work a dacha. The fact that dacha use does not fall off with income, in apparent contradiction of hypothesis H1.1, can be explained by the fact that higher income households keep their dachas for a different reason: not to produce food, but as a leisure activity. If we distinguish those dachniki for whom the dacha is a leisure activity from those for whom it is a way of producing their household's basic means of subsistence, we can run our regressions separately for each category (the results are not reproduced here).

[19]    Respondents could choose any number of reasons for not using a dacha, although most chose only one. Almost two-thirds of those who chose more than one reason made all their choices within the same group. The mean income of those who gave three reasons for not needing a dacha was twice the mean income of those who gave one reason for not being able to work a dacha and three times the mean income of those who gave three reasons for not being able to work it. The mean income of those who mixed their choices was almost exactly the mean of all those without a dacha.

*Table 3.11:   Mean household income per head by main reasons for having or not having a* dacha.

| | Percentage citing as main reason | Mean Household Income per head | Std. Error of Mean |
|---|---|---|---|
| Hobby, leisure, we like to do it | 17 | 830 | 30 |
| Additional produce for the table | 44 | 646 | 16 |
| Providing for a rainy day | 3 | 572 | 52 |
| Main source of subsistence | 36 | 519 | 14 |
| Total with a dacha | 100 | 629 | 10 |
| We don't need it | 8 | 996 | 71 |
| We do not want to do it | 14 | 852 | 51 |
| We do not have time to do it | 15 | 800 | 37 |
| We cannot get any land | 18 | 548 | 21 |
| We do not have the money to do it | 34 | 499 | 13 |
| We cannot for health reasons | 34 | 495 | 13 |
| Total without a dacha | 100 | 608 | 12 |

*Source: ISITO Household survey*

At first sight, separating the different types of dacha owner sets everything to rights. In particular, owning a dacha as a hobby is a strongly increasing function of income, while owning a dacha as a means of producing for the household's basic subsistence needs is a strongly decreasing function of income. Although most of the coefficients are not statistically significant, those households which use the dacha as a hobby tend to be smaller, younger and better educated than those which use the dacha as a basic source of subsistence. The one blot is the most important one: we might have expected the separation to have tidied up the relationship between employment and dacha ownership as well. We would expect those in employment to be more likely to use a dacha as a form of leisure both because these people are more likely to have the money to travel to and to maintain their dacha and because they are more likely to feel the need for a break after their working week. However, it turns out that there is no significant difference in the number of workers and the proportion engaged in secondary employment between those households which have a dacha as a hobby and those households which have it as their basic means of subsistence. Moreover, what people say does not necessarily correspond to what they do. Ninety-nine percent of subsistence producers say that they grow some of their own food, but so also do 93 percent of the hobbyists.[20]

*Table 3.12: Hours worked on the* dacha *and amount produced by hobbyists and subsistence producers ( ISITO Household survey).*

| Means (se mean) | Samara | Kemerovo | Lyubertsy | Syktyvkar | Total |
|---|---|---|---|---|---|
| Total hours worked | | | | | |
| By hobbyists | 654 (49) | 625 (49) | 443 (51) | 428 (68) | 560 (28) |
| By producers | 610 (47) | 686 (46) | 416 (95) | 462 (57) | 605 (29) |
| By all dachniki | 591 (29) | 641 (29) | 445 (39) | 437 (34) | 555 (16) |
| Percentage of potatoes produced | | | | | |
| Hobbyists | 38 (3) | 88 (2) | 43 (3) | 82 (3) | 57 (2) |
| Producers | 60 (3) | 93 (1) | 77 (6) | 91 (2) | 83 (1) |
| Percentage of vegetables produced | | | | | |
| Hobbyists | 65 (2) | 79 (2) | 44 (3) | 50 (3) | 60 (1) |
| Producers | 82 (2) | 81 (2) | 68 (5) | 60 (3) | 76 (1) |
| Percentage of fruit produced | | | | | |
| Hobbyists | 50 (2) | 7 (2) | 21 (2) | 2 (1) | 26 (1) |
| Producers | 55 (3) | 9 (1) | 24 (2) | 2 (1) | 24 (1) |
| Percentage of dachniki who produce nothing | | | | | |
| Hobbyists | 6 | 3 | 15 | 4 | 7 |
| Producers | 1 | 1 | 3 | 2 | 1 |
| All dachniki | 5 | 2 | 13 | 4 | 4 |

The fact that some people say that they work the land because they enjoy it does not mean that these people work any less hard on the land: there is no significant difference in the number of hours worked on the land by household members whatever they said was their motive for doing so (Table 3.12). Nor does it mean that the production of food is unimportant to them: those who said that the dacha was their main source of subsistence grew more than those who said that they

---

[20]    The numbers are too small for us to identify significant characteristics of those households which have a dacha but produce no food.

worked the dacha because they enjoyed it, but the difference is barely statistically significant in any of the crops in Syktyvkar and Kemerovo. In Samara and Lyubertsy hobbyists are relatively more likely to grow fruit than vegetables and potatoes so that, while they do produce substantially less potatoes and vegetables than subsistence producers, they grow just as much of their fruit. On the basis of this data, Lena Varshavskaya suggests that the motives people give may be as much a reflection of the image that the household seeks to uphold as of its actual motivation, with higher income and better educated households not wanting to identify themselves with subsistence production, while lower income and less educated households are more willing to elevate the traditional socialist values of labour over the post-Soviet values of leisure (Varshavskaya and Karelina, 1998). We clearly need to look more closely at what people actually do with their land.

## DACHAS AND THE DOMESTIC PRODUCTION OF FOOD

Most people with a dacha produce something, whatever they may say are their motives for having a dacha. However, it is not necessary to work your own plot of land to be able to live from home-produced food. According to the Goskomstat microcensus and budget survey data, in most regions the proportion of potatoes home-grown is substantially higher than the proportion of households having land, indicating that many people get their potatoes from friends and relatives. In the four cities covered by the ISITO survey, from 12 percent of households in Lyubertsy to almost 20 percent of households in Kemerovo did not have the use of their own dachas, but received produce from others (Table 3.13). Such donations are usually made in exchange for helping with production, particularly for help with planting, weeding or harvesting, or by providing a car to help with transport. Before turning to the domestic production of food, we should investigate whether acquiring food from others, whether as charitable gifts or in exchange for services rendered, provides an alternative survival strategy to market adaptation or domestic production.

The receipt of foodstuffs does not appear to be a purely casual affair. A significant proportion of the needs for fruit and vegetables of many households was met by donations from others and meat and dairy products were more often received as donations than produced on the household's own land. The fact that there is a strong correlation between the receipt of the various different products, particularly between potatoes and vegetables, on the one hand (R=0.71), and meat and dairy products, on the other (R=0.51), indicates that giving is systematic. The key question with regard to the receipt of foodstuffs is whether such donations represent a charitable gesture towards those in hardship, or an element in a network of reciprocity in which the recipient is perhaps expected to provide something in exchange. Our own and other ethnographic research inclines us towards the latter interpretation (Hervouet, 2001), and this is strongly supported by the data.

*Table 3.13: Methods of Provisioning ( ISITO Household Survey. April–May 1998).*

| Percent of households | Samara | Kemerovo | Lyubertsy | Syktyvkar | Total |
|---|---|---|---|---|---|
| Have a dacha | 50 | 67 | 33 | 57 | 52 |
| Receive some food from others | 16 | 19 | 12 | 18 | 16 |
| Buy all of their food | 34 | 14 | 55 | 25 | 31 |

When we run a series of regressions with the percentage of each product received as the dependent variable, we find that there is no significant relationship between household money income and the extent of receipts of food products, nor is there any tendency for lower income households to receive more than those who are better-off, indicating that in general such donations are not a form of social support for lower income households from their better-off friends and relatives.[21] This is confirmed by the fact that neither single-parent households, nor pensioner households nor those with dependent children or invalids receive any more of their food from others than the average household. On the other hand, the reciprocal character of the relationship is indicated by the fact that those most likely to receive foodstuffs are those best equipped to reciprocate: we find that households comprising a single person of working age are far more

---

[21] Income is not significant in any functional form. There is no significant difference in the likelihood of receiving food by any income decile against any other. Those in temporary difficulties, as a result of lay-off or non-payment of wages, are likely to receive more food from others, again indicating the reciprocal character of the assistance, since the expectation would be that they will be in a position to reciprocate. This data is discussed more fully in the next chapter.

likely than any other household type to be a recipient of all kinds of produce. More generally, the young are far more likely and the old far less likely to be recipients of food, the reverse of the case with regard to dacha use. The reciprocal character of the relationship is also indicated by the fact that those who told us that they worked on somebody else's dacha received more than twice as much food as others.[22] Thus the receipt of food appears to be a part of a wider network of reciprocal interaction between households, sometimes being provided in exchange for work done on the donor's dacha, sometimes as part of an exchange of different products between dacha owners (although dacha owners are significantly less likely to be recipients of foodstuffs), and on other occasions perhaps in exchange for other kinds of support, such as providing transport (although possession of a car does not make a household significantly more likely to be a recipient of foodstuffs).[23] Finally, it was clear when we asked people elsewhere in the questionnaire about giving and receiving help that for most people giving and receiving the products of the dacha is not considered as help but as an aspect of reciprocity and so these items tended not to be included in the respondents' lists of help given and received.

It seems clear that the receipt of food from others is not a matter of charity but of reciprocity, and so is something which people choose to involve themselves in as a part of wider decisions about the way in which they live their lives. Our ethnographic research and our own experience leads us to believe that it is extremely unlikely that anybody would seek to establish such reciprocal relationships specifically as a means of acquiring food, so it cannot be considered to be an aspect of a survival strategy in any narrowly economic sense. This is confirmed by the fact that there is no significant relationship between the proportion of income spent on food and the receipt of food from others – such receipts would appear to be a bonus rather

---

22  We only asked people in the individual questionnaire how much time they worked on 'their' dacha. Some people whose families did not have their own dacha nevertheless answered this question. The likelihood is that far more recipients received fruit and vegetables in return for working on somebody else's dacha. It is unlikely that products would be given in exchange for money, and indeed those who reported giving monetary help to others were no more likely to be recipients of food.

23  Given the very low level of urban domestic production of meat and dairy produce, we can guess that most of the donated meat and dairy produce has been given by rural residents or bought by the donors. Households with a rural origin receive on average twice as much meat and dairy produce as those with no such connections, but no more fruit and vegetables.

than a means of meeting essential subsistence needs. Thus, the acquisition of food is generally a by-product of involvement in reciprocal social relationships which provide other and more significant rewards. Nevertheless, it is yet another example of the extent to which social integration provides security against material hardship. Let us turn now to the production of foodstuffs, which is a decision which also has both social and economic dimensions that we have to try to unpack.[24]

What factors determine whether a household produces its own vegetables rather than buying them in the market? In particular, is domestic production an expression of a particular survival strategy, adopted by particular households in particular conditions? This is the question that we have already explored in relation to the ownership of a dacha, on the not unreasonable assumption that the reason why people in Russia acquire land is to grow their own food. However, looking specifically at the domestic production of food gives us a different angle on the question and in principle provides more analytical scope because we can investigate not only whether or not households produce their own food but also what and how much they produce.

In practice this scope is rather more limited than we might have hoped. On the one hand, as we have seen, very few urban households produce their own meat and dairy products and, in Kemerovo and Syktyvkar, even fruit. On the other hand, the tendency is for households to buy either all or none of their basic foodstuffs (18 percent of households produced all and 34 percent bought all of their

[24] The RLMS data includes very detailed questions on the production of food. However, for our purposes it is not very helpful because there are such large variations within and between regions: the regional dummies are about the only significant variables in the regressions. The fact that the ISITO data only relates to four cities reduces the intra-regional variation, while the regional dummies handle inter-regional variation. The fact that our findings on dacha use tend to conform closely to the microcensus and the RLMS data for the urban population as a whole gives us some confidence that our key findings would generalise to the urban population.

Sveta Yaroshenko, in her analysis of domestic production using this data, analytically links the decision between buying and producing potatoes and vegetables to two contrasting household survival strategies, one of which is oriented to maximising household money income in order to meet the subsistence needs of the household in money form, the other of which is oriented to minimising household money expenditure by engaging in or collaborating with others in domestic production, in order to free scarce monetary resources for other uses (Yaroshenko, 1999). However, this distinction proves to be untenable because there is little relation between money income and the production of food and, as we shall see later, by the fact that domestic food producers do not spend any less on the purchase of foodstuffs.

potatoes and vegetables), most of the remainder saying that they produced half their needs. This distribution of outcomes makes it inappropriate to examine the production of food by taking the percentage of each product grown as the dependent variable in an OLS regression. Instead we run a series of logistic regressions in which the dependent variable is the probability of growing at least 50 percent of the household's needs for the specific kind of product (although the results, shown in Table 3.14, do not turn out very different from the equivalent OLS regressions). These regressions were run for all households, the implication being that any household is able to acquire the land to grow food if it chooses to do so. In fact the RLMS data indicates that the turnover of dachniki is about 10–15 percent per annum, in which case this is probably a reasonable assumption. The only significant variables in a regression run only for those who have a dacha are the regional dummies, rural origin and automobile ownership.

The results of this exercise are to reinforce our earlier conclusions: the determinants of the likelihood of growing food on the dacha are almost identical to the determinants of ownership of a dacha in the first place. However, this is not a redundant finding because this conclusion applies to all those who have a dacha, whatever their declared motive for having it. The younger and better educated households and those who have higher incomes and better earning and employment opportunities, may say that they work the dacha as a hobby, but they nevertheless put in a lot of work and produce a lot of potatoes, vegetables and fruit.

It is not the poor who grow their own food: households with the lowest money incomes are significantly *less* likely than middle-income households to produce their own potatoes and vegetables, indicating that opportunity is more powerful than need in motivating self-sufficiency in basic foodstuffs. This is confirmed by subjective indicators: those who say that they do not have enough money even to buy food are also significantly *less* likely to grow their own potatoes, so domestic production does not provide a lifeline for the poor. Nor does domestic production have more than marginal significance for the relief of temporary hardship: the existence and extent of administrative leave, wage delays and short-time working all have no statistically significant impact on the probability of the household producing any of its own food (with the exception that those working short-time are marginally more likely to grow fruit).

Table 3.14: *Logistic regressions – probability of home-production of at least 50 percent of consumption of various products (ISITO household survey).*

| Variable | Potatoes | | | Vegetables | | | Fruit | | |
|---|---|---|---|---|---|---|---|---|---|
| | B | SE(B) | Exp(B) | B | SE(B) | Exp(B) | B | SE(B) | Exp(B) |
| No. of children under 7 | -0.14 | 0.11 | 0.87 | -0.06 | 0.10 | 0.94 | -0.35 | 0.15 | 0.70 * |
| Number of children 8–15 | 0.07 | 0.07 | 1.07 | 0.12 | 0.07 | 1.13 | -0.02 | 0.09 | 0.98 |
| Number of working age | 0.11 | 0.06 | 1.11 | 0.05 | 0.06 | 1.05 | 0.03 | 0.07 | 1.03 |
| Number of pension age | 0.25 | 0.09 | 1.29 ** | 0.39 | 0.09 | 1.47 ** | 0.19 | 0.10 | 1.22 |
| Number in work | 0.12 | 0.08 | 1.12 | 0.03 | 0.07 | 1.03 | -0.01 | 0.09 | 0.99 |
| Proportion of workers with second jobs | -0.06 | 0.16 | 0.94 | -0.18 | 0.16 | 0.83 | 0.01 | 0.19 | 1.01 |
| Is there a spouse? | 0.34 | 0.10 | 1.41 ** | 0.39 | 0.10 | 1.47 ** | 0.11 | 0.12 | 1.12 |
| Male-headed | -0.09 | 0.10 | 0.92 | -0.24 | 0.09 | 0.79 * | -0.06 | 0.13 | 0.94 |
| Household head under 25 | 0.13 | 0.18 | 1.14 | 0.24 | 0.18 | 1.28 | 0.16 | 0.26 | 1.17 |
| Household head 40–59 | 0.42 | 0.11 | 1.52 ** | 0.51 | 0.11 | 1.67 ** | 0.62 | 0.14 | 1.86 ** |
| Household head 60 and over | 0.45 | 0.17 | 1.56 ** | 0.33 | 0.16 | 1.39 | 0.45 | 0.20 | 1.57 * |
| Level of education of household head | 0.06 | 0.03 | 1.06 | 0.06 | 0.03 | 1.06 | 0.09 | 0.04 | 1.10 * |
| No. of rural-born household members | 0.34 | 0.07 | 1.40 ** | 0.17 | 0.06 | 1.19 ** | 0.11 | 0.08 | 1.11 |
| Household has a car or motorcycle | 0.90 | 0.10 | 2.47 ** | 1.06 | 0.09 | 2.89 ** | 0.72 | 0.11 | 2.06 ** |
| Av. hours worked per working member*100 | 0.07 | 0.06 | 1.07 | 0.03 | 0.05 | 1.03 | -0.09 | 0.07 | 0.91 |
| Average days admin. leave per working member*100 | 0.38 | 0.21 | 1.46 | 0.32 | 0.20 | 1.38 | -0.07 | 0.24 | 0.93 |

Table 3.14 (continued)

| | | | | | | | | | |
|---|---|---|---|---|---|---|---|---|---|
| Average amount in wages owed per working member (Roubles*10 000) | 0.42 | 0.22 | 1.52 | 0.18 | 0.20 | 1.20 | −0.06 | 0.29 | 0.94 |
| Average days on short-time per household member*100 | −0.08 | 0.15 | 0.92 | 0.09 | 0.15 | 1.09 | 0.33 | 0.15 | 1.39 * |
| Income quintiles (third quintile is reference) | | | | | | | | | |
| First | −0.29 | 0.13 | 0.75 * | −0.26 | 0.12 | 0.77 * | 0.15 | 0.15 | 1.16 |
| Second | −0.19 | 0.12 | 0.83 | −0.18 | 0.11 | 0.84 | −0.10 | 0.14 | 0.91 |
| Fourth | −0.38 | 0.12 | 0.68 ** | −0.30 | 0.12 | 0.74 * | −0.39 | 0.15 | 0.68 ** |
| Fifth | −0.28 | 0.13 | 0.76 * | −0.24 | 0.12 | 0.79 | −0.48 | 0.16 | 0.62 ** |
| Ratio of wage to total income | 0.03 | 0.18 | 1.03 | 0.10 | 0.18 | 1.10 | −0.17 | 0.22 | 0.84 |
| Proportion of income spent on food | 0.01 | 0.04 | 1.01 | −0.02 | 0.04 | 0.98 | −0.14 | 0.10 | 0.87 |
| Kemerovo | 2.06 | 0.11 | 7.83 ** | 0.92 | 0.10 | 2.51 ** | −1.21 | 0.12 | 0.30 ** |
| Syktyvkar | 1.45 | 0.11 | 4.26 ** | −0.08 | 0.10 | 0.93 | −2.87 | 0.24 | 0.06 ** |
| Lyubertsy | −0.38 | 0.12 | 0.68 ** | −1.12 | 0.12 | 0.33 ** | −1.34 | 0.13 | 0.26 ** |
| Constant | −2.62 ** | 0.22 | | −1.74 ** | 0.20 | | −1.34 ** | 0.26 | |
| N of households | 3782 | | | 3782 | | | 3781 | | |
| −2LL | 4080 | | | 4390 | | | 3030 | | |
| Model Chi square | 1010** | | | 685*** | | | 527** | | |

Note: * p<.05; ** p<.01
Level of education of the household head is measured on a scale of 1–6.

Those who are most likely to grow their own food are the households usually considered to be least at risk of poverty – a household with two working-age adults and no children. If the household also has co-resident pensioners, whose pensions are the most reliable source of money income in Russia, the household becomes even more likely to grow its own food. As in the case of dacha ownership, the most important resource that facilitates the domestic production of food is ownership of private transport, usually a car: those with a car or motorbike are on average twice as likely to grow their own food as those without. Moreover, car ownership has its biggest impact on low income families, low-income families with a car being well over twice as likely as those without a car to produce their own food.[25] It seems that, rather than being the last resort of those on the brink of starvation, domestic agricultural production provides an additional form of security for those who are already quite well placed to weather the storm.

As in the case of the ownership of a dacha, there is absolutely no indication in the data that domestic production is an alternative to earning money in order to meet basic consumption needs: neither the number of workers in the household, nor the average amount of time that they work nor the proportion of wages in total income, nor the proportion of household members who have second jobs is significant in determining the probability of the household producing its own food. Decisions about domestic food production would appear to be taken quite independently of decisions about paid employment.[26]

This conclusion is not modified if we run separate regressions for those who work a dacha as a hobby and those who work the dacha as the main source of subsistence. The coefficients on the income and employment variables are perverse, from the point of view of the

---

[25]  It may well be that there is an historical dimension to this, in that low-income families with a car are more likely to have been relatively more prosperous at some time in the past, and so better placed to acquire and work a dacha.

[26]  When it comes to the production of fruit, there is a significant tendency for the probability of home production to fall as income increases, and this is found across all the cities except for Syktyvkar, where very little fruit is grown, with the top 40 percent of income earners substantially less likely than all lower income groups to grow their own fruit. The same is found for the small number of meat and dairy producers. This is quite different from the pattern of production of potatoes and vegetables. It may be that this is a reflection of motivational differences, to the extent that those on lower incomes are more likely to be oriented to saving money and so to produce the relatively higher value foodstuffs. From a purely economic point of view we would expect the opposite, in the sense that higher income-earners would have a higher opportunity cost and so would require the returns from producing higher value foodstuffs to induce them to devote the time and effort to domestic production.

hypotheses that we have been exploring, although none of them are statistically significant, partly because we have only about 700 cases for each regression.[27]

## THE DYNAMICS OF DACHA USE

In principle we should be able to get some answers to our questions from looking at the dynamics of dacha use. If the use of dachas is a crisis phenomenon, then we would expect dacha use to follow the dynamics of the deepening crisis. Unfortunately there is very little data that can allow us to judge this question. The Goskomstat data (see Table 3.5) suggests that dacha use grew rapidly in the period of perestroika but peaked in 1993, although this data combines the very different phenomena of 'personal subsidiary agriculture' in the countryside and the use of plots by urban residents. In the ISITO survey regions there is strong anecdotal evidence that domestic agricultural production by urban residents is in decline in Moscow and Samara, while it is at least stable if not growing in Syktyvkar and Kemerovo. The RLMS panel data gives some idea of the dynamics of plot use. There appears to be quite a high turnover of dachniki in the RLMS sample, with about 15 percent of households acquiring a dacha and about 17 percent giving up between each round.[28] In the ISITO survey we only asked those who now have a dacha how long they have been using it, but the responses follow a more or less regular exponential pattern consistent with such a regular turnover, with no evidence of any significant expansion in dacha use. In the RLMS data there has been a small decline in the proportion of urban residents having plots since 1996. Comparing the size of plots from round to round, half remain unchanged, about a quarter got larger and about a quarter got smaller, the median increase being by 50 percent and the

---

27  For those who view the dacha as an economic activity, self-provision is an increasing function of income and of the number of workers in the household, the amount of secondary employment and hours worked. For those who view the dacha as a hobby, self-provision is a decreasing function of income (significant at the p<.05 level) and an insignificantly diminishing function of employment variables.

28  As noted above (note 12, page 126), there appears to be quite a high degree of inconsistency in responses between rounds, so it is difficult to know how much variation in responses is due to such inconsistencies. Half the households report a difference in area (often very substantial) in their possession from one round to the next and almost a quarter report a difference in form of tenure. The first phase data is not sufficiently reliable to be used for inter-temporal comparisons, and cannot be compared with the second phase data because the sample frame changed considerably.

median reduction by two-thirds, so the average size of plot remains unchanged. There has not been any significant change in the proportion of households growing each crop over the five rounds between 1994 and 2000, although there has been a slight shift from low-value potatoes towards higher value fruit since 1996. The proportion of households selling potatoes has remained low and stable, but the proportion selling fruit and vegetables has increased steadily since 1994, with a big increase in 1998, although it still only accounts for 3 percent of urban households in each case. It may be that the small decline in the proportion of urban households working a dacha and the increase in the proportion selling produce are both consequences of the economic crisis, as some are unable to afford to maintain their dacha, while a growing number of those with a dacha look to it as a source of supplementary income.

The typical new dachniki are almost the mirror image of the established dachniki: households headed by men under 25 with young children and fewer adult (and especially pensioner) household members are more likely to have started to use land recently. Income is completely insignificant in the regression, as are car ownership, hours worked, secondary employment, wage delays and payment in kind. In other words, starting to use a dacha seems to be a normal part of starting your own household, regardless of income and employment. There seems to be nothing distinctive about those who have stopped using land, except that older households, and especially those with pensioners, are less likely to have done so.

# THE COSTS AND BENEFITS OF DOMESTIC FOOD PRODUCTION

All the evidence that we have considered so far would seem to indicate that the availability of necessary resources, above all the time of household members, is the most important consideration in acquiring, retaining and working a dacha, but that opportunity costs are not taken into account in allocating labour time to the production of food. If the household is sufficiently large, has sufficient money and knowledge and household members have the inclination, then the household will acquire a dacha. Once the household has got a dacha it will almost always use the dacha to grow food, and it will usually grow a substantial proportion of its potatoes and vegetables and, where the climate is appropriate, a significant amount of fruit. The obvious implication of such a pattern of decision-making is that the time and effort put in to growing their own food is not regarded by those households which acquire a dacha as an unpleasant chore which must be compensated at the rate that the household member's labour would be compensated in the labour market. Perhaps working on the dacha is better viewed as a leisure activity, the Russian equivalent of jogging, which clears the mind, relaxes the body and stimulates the circulation every weekend through the summer. Unlike jogging, however, working the dacha has the beneficial side effect of producing a lot of food. The hard work that this demands makes it a particularly congenial form of leisure activity in a society which retains a very strong work ethic. Working a dacha with friends is also a very convenient form of socialising in circumstances in which many households cannot afford to provide the hospitality expected when they invite people into their own homes, and the exchange of dacha produce consolidates and extends the family's social networks.

Before finally rejecting the hypothesis that working the dacha can be regarded as a productive activity governed by the norms of economic rationality, we should look a bit more closely at the economic rationality of the domestic production of food. What is the order of magnitude of the costs and the benefits involved in this activity? As we will see, the costs in both money and labour time can be quite substantial, while the benefits, in terms of the value of useful product, appear very meagre.

Even in money terms, 'subsistence production' can be a costly activity. Over three-quarters of households who were using their own land, rather than that of other relatives, had to pay something for the use of the land. Although the mean payment was less than 200 roubles ($32) a year in the ISITO household survey, this is as much as a month's money income per head for the poorest households. Having paid for the land, there is the cost of tools, seeds, fertiliser and transport to be covered.[29] Twenty percent of those working dachas said that they had no money outlays at all, but of those who did, the mean monetary expenditure was 500 roubles ($82 at the time of the survey)

[29]   Between 69 percent and 72 percent of urban landholding households reported to RLMS over 1994 to 2000 that they paid an average of between $7 and $17 a year for the use of their land. Fewer than a quarter of urban landholders (the proportion declining steadily between 1994 and 2000) reported expenditure in the last 30 days on seeds, equipment and so on (the survey is in winter), spending an average of between $8 (1998) and $29 (2000).

per year. Moreover, this is almost certainly an underestimate: a diploma student of Lena Varshavskaya asked a sample of households first to estimate their total expenditure and then to enumerate it to achieve a more precise estimate, the result being an average of 20–30 percent higher than the original estimate.

Working a dacha does not only involve household members. Almost a quarter of the dachniki in the ISITO survey used land belonging to friends and relatives, while in one in four dachniki households a non-member of the household played at least one of the key roles in the process (making decisions about production, doing most of the work on the plot, processing the produce and, in rare cases, selling the produce). We asked the household head what proportion of the produce, if any, was given to friends or relatives. Over 60 percent of households gave away an average of 30 percent of the produce to others.[30] However, the exchange of food is more complicated than this: one quarter of the households with dachas also received some food from other people, while one in six households which did not work a dacha were nevertheless in a position to give food to others: overall at least 14 percent of households both gave and received food in the previous year.

On top of the monetary outlay, working a dacha can take up a considerable amount of time. Only one in ten adult members of households that had a dacha in the ISITO survey reported that they did not spend any time working on the land: the members of the average household that worked a dacha estimated that together they spent 860 hours per year working on their land.[31] Since the dacha season lasts for

[30] This is probably an underestimate because rather fewer of those who said that non-household members played a key role said that they gave away some of the produce. It is likely that the share in the product taken by non-household members who participate in production is often not considered as having been given to them but is viewed as the share due to them for their contribution. Only around a third of RLMS respondents reported having given some of their produce to friends or relatives, but these people reported giving away, on average, between a third (vegetables) and a half (fruit) of their harvest.

[31] Each individual household member was asked how many hours they worked on the dacha for how many months per year. The average across all households was 555 hours. However, this estimate excludes the contribution of those who did not complete an individual questionnaire: absentees and refusals, pensioners who had not worked since 1994 and those below working age, and those non-members of the household who contributed their labour. In some cases, where the household used land belonging to friends or relatives, individuals who worked on that land did not report it in the individual questionnaire, which referred to 'your dacha'. In over a quarter of households with dachas, none of the individual household members reported working on the plot, in 40 percent of cases because the household only comprised non-working pensioners who were not asked the detailed questions. If we leave these cases out of

an average of five or six months, this is the equivalent of working 19 eight-hour working days a month during the season.[32] At the individual level, there is no difference in the hours worked in paid employment or in secondary employment between those with a dacha and those without, further clear evidence that working on the dacha is not a substitute for paid employment.[33] Each employed household member who works on a dacha puts an average of an additional 82 hours of work per month into work on the land during the season, almost half as much as they work in their regular job. Non-working adults put in, on average, exactly the same amount of work, while non-working pensioners each put in an average of 120 hours a month. Moreover, 90 percent of those working dachas have to travel to reach their plot. The mean return travel time was around 90 minutes in Kemerovo and Syktyvkar, two hours in Samara and almost four hours in Lyubertsy.[34]

account, the average hours worked per year come to the 860 hours cited in the text. On the other hand, of course, the intensity of labour on the dacha might not be quite that of paid work (and drinking on the job is even more of a tradition in the former than in the latter). A small number of respondents lived for some time on the dacha and gave the total amount of time spent living on the dacha as their working time. Although such cases are too few to have a significant impact, they were recoded for the purpose of this analysis to give a maximum working time of 420 hours a month. The figures for Samara and Kemerovo above are substantially higher than the figures cited by Seeth et al. (1998, p. 1620) for residents of their oblast capitals, although the plots cultivated by their respondents were considerably larger than ours (a mean size of 22 sotki in Orel and Pskov, where people worked on average around 400 hours per year, though only 10 sotki in Rostov, where they worked an average of 326 hours per year).

[32]   Goskomstat's Labour Force Survey has asked about the expenditure of labour-time in subsidiary agriculture since 1998. In May 2000 the 20 percent of the adult population who had worked on the land in the previous week had worked an average of 21 hours: 14 percent of those producing for subsistence rather than sale had worked more than 31 hours on their dachas, one-third of whom also had regular jobs. This represented a massive 20 percent of the total labour input in the economy that week, or more than twice as much as the total hours worked in all forms of agricultural enterprises (Goskomstat, 2000d, pp. 133, 175, 177: no separate figures for urban and rural residents are provided). About half as many people work on the land out of the dacha season, and they put in rather fewer hours, so the labour input reported in the May and August rounds of the Labour Force Survey is about two and a half times as much as that reported in the November and February rounds.

[33]   Unfortunately the RLMS data is not of much use for the analysis of dacha activities since their survey is conducted outside the dacha season, while their questions relate to inputs of time and money in the previous week. Fewer than half of their respondents who worked dachas had done any work at all on the dacha in the previous week, those who had done so having worked an average of 12 hours. Nevertheless, as in the ISITO survey, there is no significant difference in the number of hours worked by men and women in their main or supplementary jobs between those with and those without dachas. Needless to say, women do far more domestic labour than men in both cases.

[34]   Many people travel to their dacha on a Friday night and return on Sunday evening or Monday morning throughout the season. Economic factors appear to play very little role in determining how much time people work on their plot. In a regression neither the size of the plot, nor the employment income of household members, nor their

Work on the dacha does not have the same significance for men and for women. Male dachniki work an average of almost 20 hours per month more in their paid work than do female dachniki who are in paid employment, and male dachniki with a second job work on average three hours longer at that than do women, while the women work an average of four hours per month more on the dacha than do the men. However, while the men do an additional 40 hours a month work around the home, the women spend an average of 90 hours a month on their domestic duties. Moreover, far from cutting back their domestic labour in order to devote more time to the dacha, women with a dacha do more domestic labour than those without, presumably because they are having to maintain two homes, while men with a dacha do less, the differences being small but statistically significant. As Lena Varshavskaya and Marina Karelina note, while the start of the dacha season marks the opening of a second labour front for men, for women it marks the opening of a third front (Varshavskaya and Karelina, 1998).

If working the dacha is to be regarded as work, rather than as a leisure activity, then we should cost the labour time of the dachniki at the opportunity cost, which we can estimate at the hourly rate that those engaged in secondary employment earn in their second jobs, or the hourly rate in their primary jobs of those who have no secondary employment (this presumes that the latter have no opportunity to engage in secondary employment, which generally pays at a substantially higher rate). We have this data for just over half our dachniki households, which gives us an average imputed labour cost per household of just over 6 000 roubles per household per annum ($1,000 at the then current exchange rate), without accounting for travel time. This is very nearly a third of the total money income of these households.

What do people get for this enormous labour input? We did not ask

secondary employment, nor the time taken to travel to the plot were significant determinants of the hours people reported working on their plots. The only significant determinants of the hours worked were the age of household members, those with an older head, with relatively fewer working members and with more pensioner members putting in more hours per head; the rural origin of household members, which was also associated with working longer hours on the plot; and the possession of a car, with car owners putting in longer hours. This contrasts with the finding reported by Seeth et al. (1998, p. 1620) that the time allocated to the household plot is sensitive to opportunities to earn money income, as indicated by the earnings of the lowest earner in the household, and to the time of travel. However, the latter analysis does not seem to have controlled for rural–urban differences within their sample, many of whom were rural commercial farmers.

the ISITO respondents to estimate the value or the volume of the output of their dachas, but we asked what proportion of their household's needs they satisfied.[35] We also have the data of the Goskomstat budget survey on household consumption and expenditure on various categories of food for urban households (Goskomstat, 1998d; Ministry of Labour and Social Development and Goskomstat Rossii, 1997). If we adjust these figures to current prices and apply them to the households in the ISITO survey we can derive a reasonably accurate estimate of the savings they make on producing their own foodstuffs. To this we must add the amount which some households received from the sale of their produce and deduct the amount that households (under-) reported that they spent on their dacha. The result is that the average net annual monetary equivalent of the return per head from working the dacha (without accounting for imputed labour costs) for those households which do so amounts to the princely sum of 138 roubles ($22), ranging from an average net loss of 37 roubles in Lyubertsy, to an annual net gain of 72 roubles in Syktyvkar, 180 roubles in Samara and 206 roubles in Kemerovo. The average return from a year's work on the dacha was the equivalent of the average earnings from one day in secondary employment.

Of course many of the ISITO dachniki may not have had the opportunity of undertaking additional paid employment. Another way of measuring the return to their labour would be to ask how successful is the use of the dacha as an element in the household's survival strategy? Does the domestic production of food enable households to survive without money? Or, more modestly, how much does it enable them to save out of the household budget? The most striking finding of all in our analysis of the data on domestic food production is that those who work a dacha spend exactly the same amount per head and

---

[35] The ISITO dachniki also gave away a proportion of the produce, but we can presume that this was either compensation for the labour input of others, or a pure surplus. The RLMS production data indicates that many households grow far more produce than they need for their own subsistence. RLMS asks people how much of each crop they grow, how much their family consumes, how much they give to others and how much they sell. On average over half the potatoes, 40 percent of the vegetables and a quarter of the fruit are not accounted for by respondents. The average reported consumption of home-grown potatoes by urban and rural households is about 60 percent of the Russian average per capita consumption, so it is very likely that respondents, who were interviewed in the autumn and winter, reported the fate of this year's harvest, in which case much of the fruit and vegetables would have been preserved for later consumption, gift or sale. Twenty percent of households consume or retain more than the Russian average consumption of potatoes, of whom 10 percent consume or retain more than twice the average consumption, so there is probably quite a lot of domestic overproduction of potatoes.

exactly the same proportion of their money income on food as those who do not (Table 3.15). This result applies overall and in each city separately and it applies however many other variables we control for. On this measure the gross return to working the dacha is nil: all that time and money is laid out without saving a kopeck on the household's food bills. This is not really so surprising, since spending on potatoes and vegetables is such a small proportion of the food budget.

*Table 3.15: Expenditure on food of households with and without a dacha.*

| City | Do you use any land? | Mean percentage of household income spent on food | Std error of mean | Mean household spending on food per head | Std error of mean |
|------|------|------|------|------|------|
| Samara | Yes | 0.67 | 0.05 | 313 | 7 |
| | No | 0.68 | 0.04 | 306 | 6 |
| Kemerovo | Yes | 0.68 | 0.05 | 314 | 7 |
| | No | 0.61 | 0.02 | 311 | 12 |
| Lyubertsy | Yes | 0.74 | 0.07 | 433 | 13 |
| | No | 0.70 | 0.02 | 406 | 10 |
| Syktyvkar | Yes | 0.69 | 0.03 | 377 | 10 |
| | No | 0.69 | 0.04 | 345 | 12 |
| Total | Yes | 0.69 | 0.02 | 342 | 4 |
| | No | 0.68 | 0.02 | 342 | 5 |

*Source: ISITO Household survey*

Other data confirms this finding for urban households. In the RLMS data, urban dacha owners spent a little more on food than non-dacha owners between 1994 and 1996, although the difference was only statistically significant in 1994, and spent almost exactly the same in 1998 and 2000. There was no significant difference in the proportion of money income spent on food, except in 2000, when households with a dacha did spend a significantly lower proportion of their money income on food, perhaps because such households were more likely to have reduced spending on food following the August 1998 crisis. Rural households spend less than half as much as urban households on food, but even in the countryside there is no significant difference in spending on food, either absolutely or as a percentage of money income, between dacha owners and the few non-owners, except in 1994, when dacha owners did spend a significantly lower proportion of their money income on food.

In the Goskomstat budget survey data we can only look at the oblast-level statistics, so we cannot separate out urban from rural residents, but even so, in a regression of the data for 75 oblasts there is no significant correlation between the proportion of potatoes home-grown in the oblast and spending on food as a proportion of total household expenditure, even when we control for the level of unemployment, the proportion of the population working in agriculture, the scale of non-payment of wages and the average real wage, the latter being the only variable in the regression that is at all significant, with the expected negative coefficient. If we introduce a series of regional dummies, the coefficient on the home growing of potatoes becomes larger and marginally significant ($p<.05$), but we would expect it to be so because on the basis of the RLMS data we expect such a relation to hold for the rural population of each oblast. It seems, therefore, that the RLMS and Goskomstat data are at least consistent with our finding that working a dacha does not lead to a reduction in food spending.

This should not really be so surprising, since the produce of the dacha is largely confined to the cheapest food products (and products whose relative price has been falling over the past few years): potatoes, beets, cabbage, carrots and onions, spending on which accounts for only a small part of the food bill for all but the poorest of families, and the poorest families cannot afford to work a dacha. However much of their vegetables they produce on their dacha, virtually all urban households have to buy all their bakery, meat and dairy products and, for the more prosperous, their processed and more exotic foods, in the market for money. According to the household budget survey data for Moscow and St Petersburg in 1996, potatoes and vegetables accounted for only about 8–9 percent by value of the total food consumption of the residents of big cities, or less than 4 percent of their total money spending. In the ISITO survey the average saving achieved by our dachniki amounts to 3 percent of their total household income, or 6 percent of their total household spending on food. This is about the same as the average household admits to spending on alcohol in the budget survey. Saving a few roubles by growing their own food gives the dachniki enough money to buy a box of chocolates or a few bottles of vodka and a bit of sausage for the weekend.

# THE MYTH OF THE URBAN PEASANT?

We have seen that there is no evidence that the domestic production of food has been chosen by households as a means of supplying themselves with the necessities of life as an alternative to acquiring those necessities by earning money and then purchasing them. Nor even that it is the last resort of those who have limited employment opportunities and do not have sufficient money income to buy their own food. The households with the lowest money incomes and in the greatest hardship are the least likely to grow their own food. Those with more working members, those who work longer hours in their main jobs, those who are engaged in secondary employment are certainly no less and if anything are more likely to engage in subsidiary agricultural activity. Those who engage in subsidiary agriculture do not work any shorter hours in their primary and secondary employment than those who do not. The monetary saving achieved through such engagement is miniscule, particularly when measured against the enormous labour input. Finally, those who grow their own basic foodstuffs spend no less on food and food products than those who do not. All of the evidence would indicate that working the dacha is primarily a leisure activity, that people do it as a form of relaxation to give them a break from their working lives and the pressures of urban life, and indeed almost half of all the ISITO dachniki cited this as one of the main reasons given for working their dacha. The fruit and vegetables that they produce are then merely a by-product, no more essential to their subsistence than is the product of the vegetable plot of any keen gardener. Many people say, in Russia as elsewhere, that they grow their own fruit and vegetables because that is the only way that they can get high quality produce, or be confident that it is ecologically pure (even though it is often produced on heavily polluted land).

However, that is not the end of the story. We still have to explain why this practice is so prevalent in Russia, why around half the urban population engages in it, despite the enormous costs and inconvenience involved, especially when the plots are often so far from home. So what is the significance of the dacha? Having debunked one myth, are we going to resurrect another? Is the dacha something deeply rooted in the psyche and culture of Russians, perhaps as a Jungian echo of their rural past, a symbolic celebration of the affinity between the Russian soul and the earth from which it was born, of the roots to which all Russians are drawn in periods of crisis? Working a dacha may have deep roots in the Russian psyche, but it is far from the bucolic idyll that many Westerners imagine: for the majority of the population of big cities it involves many hours crammed into buses or suburban trains, further hours of backbreaking work before the return journey, a substantial monetary outlay, beyond the reach of the poorer families, for a small and uncertain return. If it symbolises anything it symbolises the centuries of suffering that have been imposed on the Russian people and that have driven them back to the land not as the seat of their soul, but as the most basic guarantee of their survival. The dacha appears to make no economic sense at all, providing the most meagre of returns for an enormous amount of toil, but it is much more than a means of supplementing the family diet or of saving a few roubles. It is both a real and a symbolic source of security in a world in which nothing beyond one's immediate grasp is secure.

To bring out the real significance of subsistence agriculture we should return to the point that stands out most clearly from the ISITO data, that the most striking difference is between the different cities. Moreover, the variance in the amount of subsistence production is much greater than the variance in dacha use.[36] Subsistence production is highest not in those of the ISITO regions in which the climate is the most conducive to agricultural production, Samara and Moscow oblast, but in those regions which are the most hostile: the sub-Arctic North and Western Siberia.

How is this difference to be explained? Does the heart of Russian culture now lie not in the historic cities of Moscow and Samara, but in the Komi Republic and in Kemerovo oblast? Perhaps it does, with Komi still bearing the memories of its gulag past and Kemerovo of the forced resettlement of the 1930s, whose legacy remains today in the forced labour camps which still house a significant proportion of its population – to say nothing of the soul of Dostoevskii which still haunts Kemerovo's second city of Novokuznetsk. But perhaps there is a more mundane explanation.

The obvious explanation would refer to the depth of the economic crisis, although we have found only a very weak relation between

---

[36]  The same is true of the Goskomstat data: the mean proportion of the urban population having dachas across all regions is 50.6 percent, the standard deviation being 12.5, while the mean percentage of potatoes home-grown is 79.0 percent and the standard deviation is 21.7 (author's calculations from microcensus and household budget survey data).

subsistence agriculture and any of the indicators of crisis at the level of the individual household. Moreover, unemployment rates, wage levels and degrees of income inequality are not substantially different across the four ISITO cities, once we allow for relatively small differences in price levels.[37] Administrative leave and short-time working are about twice as common in Samara and Kemerovo, which have seen a collapse of their military-related industrial base, as in Syktyvkar and Lyubertsy, and yet the incidence of subsistence agriculture cross-cuts these pairs of cities.

It is not a matter of the existence of favourable conditions for agriculture since, as we have already noted, it is the regions with the most unfavourable climate which have the most highly developed domestic agricultural production (in fact, according to Goskomstat agricultural production data, yields per hectare in growing potatoes and vegetables are highest in the Komi Republic and Moscow oblast and lowest in Samara, with Kemerovo in the middle). Rather than being the paradox that it appears at first sight, however, this may be part of the key to the explanation, for these are the regions with less developed commercial agriculture, and so in which supplies of even the most basic foodstuffs have historically been precarious.[38] There have long been active and well-supplied *kolkhoz* markets in Central

---

[37] According to the October 1997 Labour Force Survey, unemployment rates were 13.9 percent for the Komi Republic, 8.8 percent in Moscow oblast, 9.9 percent in Samara oblast, and 11.2 percent in Kemerovo oblast (Goskomstat, 1998a). The Labour Force Survey samples for each city, which are in any case not representative, are not sufficient to conclude any more than that the unemployment rate in Kemerovo is significantly higher than in the other three cities, including Syktyvkar. In relation to Samara, the official subsistence minimum in Kemerovo in May 1998 was 1.12, Komi 1.21, Moscow oblast 1.04 (but Moscow city 1.53). Money wages, in relation to Samara, were Kemerovo 0.99, Komi 1.44, Moscow oblast 0.86, Moscow city 1.39. The prices of 25 basic goods were Kemerovo 1.03, Komi 1.19, Moscow oblast 1.06, Moscow city 1.19. The relation of the average wage to the regional subsistence minimum was 2.39 in Komi, 1.97 in Moscow city, 1.64 in Moscow oblast, 2.07 in Samara and 2.60 in Kemerovo (Goskomstat, 1998c).

[38] It was not only meat, fish and dairy produce that were in short supply, or often simply unobtainable, in Russia but there was also a general shortage of potatoes, as indicated by the relatively high prices in the *kolkhoz* markets – in 1988 potatoes in the markets cost more than three times their price in the state shops, a higher premium than on any food other than dairy products (OECD-CEET, 1991, p. 169). Shortages in state shops meant that by the late 1980s *kolkhoz* markets accounted for about one-quarter of the food purchases of urban residents, while by the end of the decade most food products were rationed in state shops. Production of potatoes fell substantially through the 1970s and 1980s to the extent that the Soviet Union became a potato importer. On the one hand, the labour intensive production methods meant that collective farms cut the area under cultivation in response to labour shortages. On the other hand, peasant producers concentrated their limited resources on livestock and the production of higher value crops (OECD-CEET, 1991, pp. 113–14 and *passim*).

Russia and in the Volga region, so that at least since the late 1950s people have been able to count on being able to buy their basic foodstuffs in the markets, even if the shops were bare. This was never the case in Siberia and in the Arctic, and in the late 1980s supplies were as unpredictable as ever. This was the time at which large amounts of uncultivated land were distributed to urban residents in precisely these regions so that they could assure their supplies of basic foodstuffs by growing their own.[39] Regional differences in the development of domestic agriculture may in part be a legacy of the past, but the legacy of the past lingers on not just in the supply of dachas, but also in the memory and in the daily experience of local residents. Thus, the desire to produce one's own vegetables is perhaps not so much a reflection of the poverty of the household but more of the limited development of the market for agricultural produce in the region in question.

The fear that people have today is what it has always been in the past, not so much that they will not individually have enough money to buy potatoes, although this is a fear that still haunts everyone, but that there will be no potatoes available to buy for any kind of money. The mass settlement of Kemerovo in the 1930s included a large number of 'kulaks' and refugees from famine-stricken Ukraine. When the deportees arrived, many of them lived for their first year literally off, on and sometimes under the land, sheltering from the cold in foxholes. Shortages and local famines remained a regular feature of life in the more remote regions through the 1940s and into the 1950s. It was the recurrence of shortages of basic goods that was one of the sparks that lit the fire of revolt in the late 1980s. We do not have to refer to folk memories to evoke these events, for they are still alive in the minds of those who lived through them, some of whom are still working the dachas they first created fifty or more years ago when a dacha really was a matter of survival.

[39] Since these were not agricultural regions there was ample land available for distribution, so it was much easier to get plots here than in Samara or in the Moscow region. This is reflected in the average time taken to commute to the plots, and in the much larger number of people in Lyubertsy who say that they do not work a dacha because they cannot get access to land. The official data in the Soviet period did not differentiate urban subsistence production from 'personal subsidiary agriculture', but during the 1980s there was a substantial fall in the production of both potatoes and fruit on the latter plots and a rapid increase in the output of 'collective gardens', much of which is accounted for by collectively owned land used by urban residents (*Sel'skokhozyaistvennoe proizvodstvo v lichnykh podsobnykh khozyaistvakh naseleniya*, Moscow, 1989, pp. 16–21, cited in OECD-CEET, 1991, p. 38).

Our hypothesis is that anxiety about the availability of food supplies relates not so much to the risk of shortages of supply as a result of the limited development of agricultural production, as to the risk of shortages resulting from failures in the system of distribution arising, on the one hand, as a result of the limited development of a market in agricultural produce and, on the other, as a result of the demonetisation of the regional economy, as expressed most particularly in the non-payment of wages. Thus, while Kemerovo and Samara have been hit equally by the recession, as indicated by the incidence of administrative leave and short-time working, it is Kemerovo and Syktyvkar that have been hit hardest by the phenomena of non-payment of wages and payment in kind: the average wage debt in Syktyvkar is more than twice and that in Kemerovo is four times that in Lyubertsy or Samara. In the ISITO survey, one in five had been paid in kind in Syktyvkar and one in three in Kemerovo, but fewer than one in twenty in Lyubertsy or Samara. Although these phenomena have no significant impact on the probability of the individual household growing its own food within each region, they are indicative of the degree of demonetisation of the regional economy that provides an incentive for all but those with the highest money incomes to grow their own food, rather than to risk relying on having to buy in a market in which they may not have the means with which to buy. The correlation coefficient between the log of the average total household wage debt and the percentage of potatoes home-produced in each of the four cities is 0.996.

Of course with only four cases the correlation could be spurious, but we can also test the hypothesis using the RLMS and Goskomstat data. In the RLMS data, we saw above that those with household members with unpaid wages, who had been paid in kind or had experienced a spell of administrative leave were significantly more likely to have a dacha. However, we find that there is an even stronger relationship between dacha use and the proportion of respondents at the polling site who had not been paid wages or had been paid in kind, though there is no significant relationship with the proportion who had been sent on administrative leave. When we control for the proportion of the population at each polling site having experienced these misfortunes, the coefficients of the household variables become smaller and cease to be statistically significant.

To test the hypothesis more rigorously we can turn to the Goskomstat data on the domestic production of potatoes derived from the old household budget survey (calculated from Ministry of Labour and Social Development and Goskomstat Rossii, 1997, Table N33). Unfortunately we do not have separate data for the urban population, but we can make some allowance for this by including the proportion of the urban population in the total population of the region as an independent variable (PCRURAL) (data for 1 January 1996 from Goskomstat, 1996e). There are several factors that we need to take into account in explaining regional variations in the domestic production of potatoes.[40]

First, transport bottlenecks and tendencies to regional autarchy make it likely that the level of production of potatoes within the region will be a significant factor in ensuring the security of supply. If anxiety about supplies is a matter of relatively low levels of production in the region, we would expect the population of those regions with lower levels of production per head of potatoes (POTPRDPC, from Goskomstat, 1996e) to be more likely to grow their own produce. We can also use the proportion of the workforce employed in agriculture as an indicator of the level of development of commercial agriculture in the region (AGPROP, Goskomstat, 1996c).

Second, we would expect people to be more confident that they will be able to buy potatoes the more highly developed is the system of retail trade in the region. We can capture this factor with the retail turnover per head of population, deflated by the regional price deflator to allow for wide differences in price levels between regions (RETAIL, Goskomstat, 1996e).

Third, it is not sufficient that potatoes are available in the market, people must be confident of having the money to buy those potatoes. This is not a matter of the level of wages, but of the likelihood that wages and social benefits will be paid at all. This factor is captured by the log of wage debt in the region, relative to the total wage bill (LOGUNPAY, data for January 1997 from Goskomstat, *Sotsial'no-ekonomicheskoe polozhenie Rossii*). In addition, we have a broader indicator of the extent to which the regional economy is monetised which is the log of the short-term credit extended in the oblast per head of population, deflated by the regional price deflator to allow for price variations (LOGCRED, from 1995 data in Goskomstat, 1996e).

We need to allow for the contrary hypothesis that we have explored

[40]   The indicators proposed below are the best that are available from nationally published data sources. They do not all relate to precisely the same point in time, but we are concerned only with the relations between different regions, not with the absolute levels, so this is not a problem.

earlier in this chapter, that domestic production of food is a response to economic hardship. The appropriate indicators at the regional level are the average level of wages relative to the regional subsistence minimum (REALWAGE, data for December 1996 from Goskomstat, *Sotsial'no-ekonomicheskoe polozhenie Rossii*), the level of earnings inequality, measured by the ratio of wages of the top to the bottom deciles (INEQUAL, data from Goskomstat, 1996b), and the level of ILO unemployment recorded by the labour force survey (UNEMPLOY, October 1995 data from Goskomstat, 1996c).

Finally, we need to include some control variables to allow for other relevant differences between regions. First, we would expect there to be a positive relationship between the fertility of the soil and the domestic production of potatoes. As an indicator of soil fertility we can take the production per hectare of potatoes (POTYIELD, published in Goskomstat, 1996e). Second, dietary patterns vary a lot across Russia so we would expect the domestic production of potatoes to be higher the higher the consumption per head in the region (POTCONS, from Ministry of Labour and Social Development and Goskomstat Rossii, 1997).

To facilitate interpretation of the data we have normalised all the independent variables, except for INEQUAL, in relation to the Russian average. The results of the OLS regression are presented in Table 3.16. The adjusted R squared for the regression is 0.68.

The results of the regression are certainly supportive of the arguments that have been put forward here. As we would expect, the level of the domestic production of potatoes is higher the relatively more people live in the countryside and it is higher in regions in which potato consumption is high and in which the land is well-adapted to potato growing. Just as we found in our analysis of the household-level data, it does not appear that households are more likely to grow their own potatoes in regions in which wages are lower or the degree of income inequality is higher. Moreover, it appears that people are less likely to grow their own potatoes in regions with higher levels of unemployment, which is the opposite of what one would expect if people were to turn to potato-growing as a means of household survival. It appears that the level of production of potatoes in the region has no significant impact on the proportion of potatoes that are home-grown, but there is a marginally significant tendency for the proportion of potatoes that are home-grown to decline as the proportion of the population employed in agriculture increases, which is consistent with our suggestion of an inverse relation between domestic production and the development of commercial agriculture.

*Table 3.16: OLS Regression – dependent variable, proportion of potatoes in oblast home grown (75 regions).*

|            | Coefficients | Std error | Sig. | Partial correlation coefficient |
|------------|-------------:|----------:|------|--------------------------------:|
| (Constant) | –0.01006     | 0.250     | .968 |                                 |
| PCRURAL    | 0.271        | 0.078     | .001 | 0.400                           |
| POTPRDPC   | 0.01228      | 0.039     | .753 | 0.040                           |
| AGPROP     | –0.138       | 0.055     | .015 | –0.300                          |
| RETAIL     | –0.04463     | 0.060     | .459 | –0.093                          |
| LOGUNPAY   | 0.445        | 0.171     | .012 | 0.311                           |
| LOGCRED    | –0.02779     | 0.011     | .011 | –0.315                          |
| REALWAGE   | –0.08910     | 0.083     | .288 | –0.134                          |
| INEQUAL    | 0.0006       | 0.004     | .875 | 0.020                           |
| UNEMPLOY   | –0.189       | 0.053     | .001 | –0.411                          |
| POTYIELD   | 0.167        | 0.085     | .054 | 0.241                           |
| POTCONS    | 0.355        | 0.084     | .000 | 0.472                           |

*Data sources and variable definitions: See text.*

The variables related to the demonetisation of the economy are statistically significant and their coefficients are in the expected direction: the higher the level of unpaid wages and the less extensive is the credit system the more are households likely to grow their own potatoes. There is also a negative, though not statistically significant, relation to the extent of the development of retail trade. Thus the data presented here is at least consistent with the argument that the most important factor underlying the domestic production of food is neither the poverty of the household nor of the region, nor is it an inadequate level of production of basic foodstuffs, it is the fear of market failure either on the side of the supplier, because of the inadequate development of commercial relations, or on the side of the buyer, because of the demonetisation of the household budget.

These results are suggestive, but should certainly not be regarded as definitive because the data is fairly crude, there are several outliers and there is a certain amount of collinearity between the independent variables in the regression. In particular, there is quite a high correlation between the relative size of the rural population and the proportion of the population working in agriculture, the reported level of unemployment and the extent of inequality and, negatively, with the level of wages and the scale of retail trade. There is also, not surprisingly, a fairly high correlation between the level and the productivity of potato production and the level of potato consumption. It is also noticeable that the non-payment of wages is quite strongly negatively correlated with the level of retail trade, which is not unexpected if we consider non-payment to be an aspect of the demonetisation of the economy, but there is no significant correlation between either of these variables and the level of credit, perhaps suggesting that our interpretation of the latter as an indicator of the level of monetisation of the regional economy is faulty.[41]

The collinearity means that the estimates are fairly sensitive to the inclusion or exclusion of particular cases, although LOGCRED and LOGUNPAY, the key variables from the point of view of our hypothesis, are those least affected and the size and significance of their coefficients is the most stable. Goskomstat data is not always of the highest quality, which makes it difficult to decide what to do about apparent outliers. Four regions report surprisingly low levels of domestic production of both potatoes and vegetables (Kalmykia, Murmansk, Volgograd and Rostov – the population of Kalmykia supposedly buy twice as many potatoes as they consume). The three North Caucasus Republics of Dagestan, Karachaevo-Cherkesskaya and North Osetiya-Alaniya report high levels of unemployment and low levels of domestic production of potatoes and vegetables. If these seven regions (all the cases with standardised residuals above 1.75) are excluded from the regression, LOGUNPAY and POTCONS remain statistically significant at the $p<.01$ level and LOGCRED and POTYIELD at the $p<.05$ level, with their coefficients not greatly changed. This is also the combination of variables that we end up with if we eliminate those variables whose coefficients are not significant, again with little change to their coefficients. Thus, it does seem that this data is consistent with the hypothesis that regional variations in the domestic production of food can be explained by the

---

[41]   If we run similar regressions with the proportion of vegetables that are home-grown as the dependent variable we get very similar results, with the coefficients being very similar, except that the coefficient of LOGUNPAY is smaller and statistically not significant, while that on LOGCRED is larger and more significant.

characteristics of the soil and consumption patterns, on the one hand, and by the demonetisation and limited development of the market economy, on the other.

## CONCLUSION

We have seen that subsistence production makes little or no contribution to the relief of poverty, partly because the poor do not have the resources to engage in subsistence production.[42] Does this mean that access to domestic agriculture should be widened, with a further distribution of land to those in need, perhaps providing credit to producers, subsidised transport to their plots and assistance with marketing? The clear implication of our analysis is that it does not, not least because its costs outweigh the returns. Domestic agriculture is an extraordinarily inefficient way of meeting the urban population's basic subsistence needs.[43] If people are short of food, it is much more efficient to give them the money to buy food and take steps to ensure that food supplies are maintained to local markets than to induce them to try to produce food for themselves.

Our analysis also shows just how regressive are the proposals currently being considered by the Russian government, on the initiative of the World Bank and its advisors, that people should

---

[42]   Seeth et al. (1998, p. 1618) conclude from their survey of the role of domestic agriculture in three oblasts in Western Russia that domestic agricultural production makes little contribution to the subsistence of the poor, finding no significant relationship in their data between possession of a plot and poverty indicators. They also imply that the primary significance of the dacha is its role in risk-avoidance, although they do not clearly distinguish between individual and collective risks. The real beneficiaries are the middle-income groups, particularly in the countryside. However, their assessment of the significance of domestic agriculture appears to be based on valuing its outputs at market prices, which leads them to conclude that rural incomes are much higher than those in the towns. This is unrealistic since subsistence producers do not sell the produce, while rural producers, who still tend to have to sell through middlemen, are unlikely to realise the market price. Moreover, the RLMS data suggests that domestic overproduction is not uncommon, so it is likely that a significant proportion of the produce goes to waste.

[43]   Seeth et al. (1998, p. 1623) recognise the enormous costs of domestic production, in absorbing large quantities of often highly educated labour, but propose that domestic agriculture should be given more support by policy makers. However, their sample is dominated by rural producers. The issues in the countryside are rather different from those of the urban peasant, but it could be argued that it has been the attempt to sustain an outdated peasant agriculture, on the basis of enormous implicit subsidies from the state and collective farms as well as the self-exploitation of the peasant household, that lies at the root of the failure of agricultural reform. This certainly has been a lesson that Western Europe has learned at enormous cost.

effectively be forced into domestic production by treating access to the land as a resource (or even as a potential resource) for those claiming social assistance. Even for those willing to live on potatoes and carrots and able to bear the initial costs of domestic production, domestic agriculture certainly cannot provide the money to pay for clothing, transport, electricity, water, heating, rent and service charges, education and medical treatment and all the other goods and services that can only be obtained for money.

Finally, 'subsistence' production not only contributes little to the subsistence of city dwellers, but it also makes a significant contribution to the crisis of commercial agriculture. One reason for the failure to develop the commercial production of basic food crops is that their price is so low as a result of domestic overproduction that, with the withdrawal of agricultural subsidies, in many regions it is not even worth the farms' paying for harvest labour.[44] This then sets up the vicious circle that fuels the demonetisation of agricultural production: since it is unprofitable to produce basic foodstuffs commercially in competition with the dachniki, these foods do not become regularly available in the local shops and markets, so providing a further stimulus for families to ensure their supplies by producing their own.

Of course, people should not be prevented from engaging in domestic agriculture, but the priority should be to break this vicious circle by introducing effective reforms into the system of agricultural production and distribution that can guarantee supplies of basic foodstuffs in the quantities and qualities demanded by the local population. Once people become confident of being able to buy what they need, they will make their own decisions about whether or not it is worth continuing to work the land, or whether they might rather convert their dacha into the pleasure dome of the western imagination. The significance of the dacha in the economic, social and cultural lives of contemporary Russian households is complex, but it provides neither the basis for the survival of the poorest households, nor a realistic alternative to participation in a monetised market economy.

---

[44] According to Goskomstat price data, the price of potatoes shot up in 1991, by more than twice as much as the consumer price index, but since then the increase in the price of potatoes has generally lagged behind inflation, so that by 1997 the relative price of potatoes had fallen by 25 percent compared to 1990. A small recovery in 1998–99 was followed by a sharp fall in 2000. Mroz and Popkin find, on the basis of the RLMS data, that the proportion of food by value that was home-produced had fallen between 1994 and 1996 primarily because of the decline in the relative prices of home-produced foodstuffs (Mroz and Popkin, 1997).

# 4. Social Networks and Private Transfers

Many commentators have noted the importance of social networks for supporting everyday life in Soviet and post-Soviet Russia.[1] Chronic shortages of goods and services and highly bureaucratised procedures in the Soviet period placed a premium on having friends in the right places who could provide information about and access to scarce resources, so that social networks provided 'compensatory redistribution networks of goods and services' (Srubar, 1991, cited Lonkila, 1997). These networks provided a socially stabilising but socially fragmenting safety valve as individual solidarity in the face of the regime was confined to small and usually tightly knit informal groups bound together by mutual exchange (Shlapentokh, 1989), while the exclusionary aspects of the formal regime were undermined by *blat* relations, which provided access to goods and services through informal connections (Ledeneva, 1998).

Many have related the widespread provision of mutual assistance between Soviet households to the conditions of survival under a totalitarian regime. However, this is perhaps an overly idealistic picture of the strength of relations of kinship and friendship (many people spied on and denounced friends and even relatives in the Soviet period). It is more plausible to argue that mutual expectations of assistance between friends and relatives could be sustained in the Soviet period primarily because full employment, relatively egalitarian income distribution and the wide coverage of universal welfare benefits limited the demands imposed by such expectations. The importance of such networks was recognised in popular sayings, such as '*Ti mne – ya tebe*' ('You give to me – I give to you') or '*Ne imei sto rublei, no imei sto druzei*' ('Don't have one hundred roubles, but have one hundred friends'), and was even embedded in the late Soviet constitution, which imposed an obligation on parents and children to

[1] This chapter builds on an earlier analysis of the ISITO data by Valery Yakubovich (Yakubovich, 1999). I am very grateful to Valery for his comments on an earlier draft of this chapter.

care for young children and elderly parents respectively (Yakubovich, 1999, p. 256). Despite the rapid growth of inequality since the collapse of the Soviet system, recent ethnographic studies, interview and survey research have found that such relations have persisted in their distinctive form through perestroika and the immediate post-Soviet period (Lonkila, 1997; Ledeneva, 1998, 1999a, 1999b; Rose, 1998, 1999a; Kosonen and Salmi, 1999).

Social networks are a very important resource for Russian households. Above and elsewhere we have shown the increased importance of informal connections in getting a job, particularly in the new private sector and especially in getting supplementary employment, in post-Soviet Russia (Clarke, 1999b). Thus we would expect those households with more extensive social networks to be less vulnerable to hardship – their members should be better placed to get primary and secondary employment and to secure access to social benefits. In the ISITO survey, individuals were asked a number of questions about significant others: with whom they spend most of their free time, with whom they discuss problems at work and through whom they might be able to get a job.[2] The average number of people nominated by each respondent in the household gives us a crude indicator of the extent of the household's social network. It turns out that the number of connections nominated by household members, particularly of non-relatives,[3] is a very significant variable in a regression with the household's income per head as the dependent variable. Those households in the top income decile nominated almost twice as many friends and 20 percent more relatives in total than those in the bottom decile.[4] Allowing for non-respondents, each household member nominated more than a third more contacts in the richest than in the poorest households.

---

[2]    Individuals were also asked who had had the decisive word when they last decided to change jobs and household heads were asked who made significant contributions to working the dacha and who was primarily responsible for the care of young children and the elderly or inform. These individuals were sometimes non-members of the household.

[3]    Although relatives may be more likely to provide support than friends, friends are likely to offer more diverse opportunities than are relatives (c.f. Granovetter, 1973).

[4]    Causality is likely to be reciprocal, since Russian traditions of hospitality make it more difficult to sustain social connections for those households who cannot afford to invite friends to their homes. Since some of the connections are work-related, households with more members in work or of working age will be likely to have more connections, but the results still hold even if we consider only social contacts.

*Table 4.1:* *Private transfers of money and goods (RLMS 1994–2000. Percentages of households giving and receiving help and loans and median value of the amounts given by donors and received by recipients from various sources; roubles indexed to June 1992 prices).*

|  |  | 1994 | 1995 | 1996 | 1998 | 2000 |
|---|---|---|---|---|---|---|
| | | Money or goods given | | | | |
| Total | Percent | 31 | 23 | 24 | 25 | 27 |
| | Roubles | 753 | 603 | 715 | 478 | 628 |
| Parents | Percent | 7 | 5 | 6 | 6 | 6 |
| | Roubles | 753 | 603 | 655 | 377 | 289 |
| Children | Percent | 12 | 10 | 10 | 11 | 12 |
| | Roubles | 753 | 904 | 935 | 503 | 567 |
| Others | Percent | 18 | 13 | 12 | 13 | 15 |
| | Roubles | 388 | 308 | 468 | 251 | 283 |
| | | Money or goods received | | | | |
| Total | Percent | 24 | 22 | 25 | 27 | 29 |
| | Roubles | 1 293 | 1 025 | 953 | 754 | 803 |
| Parents | Percent | 9 | 11 | 13 | 14 | 16 |
| | Roubles | 1 505 | 1 205 | 953 | 754 | 616 |
| Children | Percent | 4 | 4 | 5 | 6 | 6 |
| | Roubles | 753 | 573 | 482 | 503 | 425 |
| Other relatives | Percent | 6 | 5 | 6 | 6 | 8 |
| | Roubles | 753 | 603 | 479 | 503 | 289 |
| Friends | Percent | 4 | 3 | 3 | 3 | 4 |
| | Roubles | 452 | 603 | 476 | 388 | 322 |
| Of whom: | | | | | | |
| both gave and received | Percent | 9 | 6 | 7 | 8 | 8 |
| net amount received | Roubles | 646 | 295 | 238 | 339 | 205 |
| | | Loans | | | | |
| Lent | Percent | 17 | 14 | 14 | 11 | 13 |
| | Roubles | 646 | 603 | 482 | 377 | 425 |
| Borrowed | Percent | 20 | 20 | 21 | 20 | 17 |
| | Roubles | 1 204 | 1 205 | 953 | 531 | 709 |
| Of whom also lent | Percent | 3 | 2 | 2 | 2 | 2 |
| net borrowed | Roubles | 194 | 301 | 327 | 251 | 145 |
| N | | 3 973 | 3 769 | 3 750 | 3 622 | 3 777 |

Survey data supports ethnographic studies and more impressionistic evidence that Russian households rely heavily on the help of friends, and especially relatives, to cope with economic hardship. The New Russia Barometer Survey VII, administered by VTsIOM in spring 1998, found that respondents relied overwhelmingly on family and friends if they had a problem: one-third of respondents would definitely be able to borrow a week's wages from a friend in case of need, and a further one-third would probably be able to borrow as much (Rose, 1998). In the autumn of 1998, 20 percent of household heads told RLMS that they had turned to relatives to help them adjust to new living conditions, and 8 percent had turned to friends for help. In 2000, 23 percent of respondents had had to appeal more often to friends or relatives for monetary help. Around 30 percent of recipients in 1998 had found such support very helpful and about 60 percent had found it somewhat helpful. In the ISITO survey, in the spring of 1998, just over a third of those households which had experienced financial difficulty in the previous two years reported that they had coped with the support of relatives, while a quarter of household heads considered that the help of family and friends was an important source of household income, an equal number receiving such help but not considering it very important.[5] A considerably larger number of households give and receive the products of domestic agriculture, but do not report this as giving and receiving help.

The most important source of help is consistently found to be relatives, particularly parents. In the month prior to the RLMS surveys between 1994 and 2000, between 9 and 16 percent of households had received help from their parents, 4–6 percent from their children, 5–8 percent from other relatives and 3–4 percent from friends (Table 4.1). Parents also tended to give substantially more than other donors.

The ISITO survey contains rather more detailed information on the patterns of giving and receiving help. Each household head was asked to nominate up to three people whom household members had helped and three from whom they had received help in the previous year and in each case to identify the type of help given and received (money, foodstuffs, goods, loans). The distribution of help provided to others is shown in Table 4.2 and the distribution of help received from others in

---

[5]  A survey commissioned from VTsIOM by the World Bank in 1994 as part of its poverty assessment asked people on whom they would rely in case of need: 5 percent said government agencies, 42 percent said friends and family. The same survey showed that 37 percent were involved in the free exchange of favours and 27 percent regularly provided free help to friends and relatives (World Bank, 1995, p. 51).

Table 4.3. The predominance of transfers between parents and children stands out clearly in these tables, although the fact that each household nominated only three people will have exaggerated their overall dominance. Comparison of the two tables shows that the dominant direction of flow is from parents to their children.[6] It is also striking, though hardly surprising, that help is much more likely to be extended between friends in the form of a loan.

*Table 4.2*    *Percentage distribution of help provided to households (ISITO household survey; 4 023 households).*

| Help provided by | Money | Food | Goods | Loans | All help |
|---|---|---|---|---|---|
| Spouse | 0.5 | 0.4 | 0.5 | 0.0 | 0.3 |
| Parent | 52.6 | 47.9 | 42.5 | 33.2 | 40.9 |
| Of which: | | | | | |
|   Wife's parent | 35.2 | 31.2 | 28.5 | 21.3 | 26.5 |
|   Husband's parent | 17.4 | 16.8 | 14.0 | 11.9 | 14.4 |
| Child | 17.0 | 16.7 | 19.7 | 3.9 | 15.1 |
| Sibling | 10.4 | 11.1 | 11.5 | 11.7 | 11.3 |
| Grandparent | 2.4 | 1.5 | 0.5 | 1.7 | 1.7 |
| Grandchild | 0.7 | 0.6 | 0.6 | 0.0 | 0.5 |
| Other relatives | 8.6 | 11.3 | 10.6 | 11.6 | 12.0 |
| Not relatives | 7.8 | 10.4 | 14.2 | 38.0 | 18.1 |
| Total | 100 | 100 | 100 | 100 | 100 |
| N | 1 330 | 1579 | 871 | 666 | 2464 |

It is interesting to investigate the characteristics of friends who are recipients and donors, which are tabulated in Table 4.4, with characteristics of relatives for comparison. The predominance of women is again partly explained by the fact that the majority of households are headed by women: in male-headed households half the recipients and 60 percent of the donors are men. Unsurprisingly, among friends, pensioners and the unemployed are more likely to be

---

6   The dominance of wives' parents over husbands' parents is explained by the fact that the vast majority of household heads were women: in male-headed households the man's parents outweigh those of his wife. The household head was defined as the person primarily responsible for managing the domestic economy. There may be some bias in favour of women since interviewers were asked in the first instance to ask a woman to identify this person.

recipients, and the employed are more likely to be donors, although among relatives it is striking that pensioners are more likely to be donors than recipients. Among friends, the majority of donors and recipients have been friends for more than ten years and normally meet as often as do relatives, at least weekly. About one-third of friends had met through work, one-third as neighbours and only a small minority had met casually. It is clear that the majority of those friends engaged in help relationships are close friends of long standing. We might expect people to be more inclined to give help in the form of a loan to those they know less well, but it is interesting that those friends involved in loan relationships are not significantly different in any respect from those involved in gift relationships.

*Table 4.3    Percentage distribution of help provided by household.*
*(ISITO household survey; 4023 households).*

| Help provided to: | Money | Food | Goods | Loan | All help |
|---|---|---|---|---|---|
| Spouse | 0.5 | 0.4 | 0.4 | 0.2 | 0.3 |
| Parent | 25.8 | 22.1 | 17.5 | 7.9 | 19.9 |
| Of which: | | | | | |
|   Wife's parent | 16.4 | 14.4 | 11.5 | 5.1 | 12.8 |
|   Husband's parent | 9.5 | 7.7 | 6.0 | 2.8 | 7.1 |
| Child | 30.8 | 27.1 | 18.2 | 12.4 | 21.8 |
| Sibling | 10.4 | 12.2 | 11.4 | 14.2 | 11.6 |
| Grandparent | 1.2 | 1.2 | 0.7 | 0.2 | 0.9 |
| Grandchild | 5.5 | 3.4 | 4.5 | 0.3 | 4.0 |
| Other relatives | 12.4 | 13.4 | 15.0 | 12.6 | 14.3 |
| Not relatives | 13.4 | 20.3 | 32.4 | 52.3 | 27.3 |
| Total | 100 | 100 | 100 | 100 | 100 |
| N | 1 425 | 1 718 | 1 069 | 572 | 2 770 |

To analyse the importance of kinship and social networks in determining the opportunities and constraints facing households which need material help we would need information about their social networks beyond those connections already activated. Unfortunately we have very little such information although, as already noted, in the ISITO survey individuals were asked a number of questions about significant others. Table 4.5 shows that almost one in five of these significant others had in fact been tapped for or had been given material help in the course of the previous year.

*Table 4.4:*   *Characteristics of relatives and friends who are recipients and donors of help (ISITO household survey).*

| | Relatives | | | | Friends | | | |
| | Recipients | | Donors | | Recipients | | Donors | |
| | N | Percent | N | Percent | N | Percent | N | Percent |
| Men | 663 | 32.9 | 628 | 31.1 | 188 | 24.9 | 138 | 30.9 |
| Women | 1 352 | 67.1 | 1 390 | 68.9 | 567 | 75.1 | 308 | 69.1 |
| Total | 2 015 | 100 | 2 018 | 100 | 755 | 100 | 446 | 100 |
| **Employment status** | | | | | | | | |
| Working | 945 | 46.9 | 1203 | 59.6 | 437 | 57.9 | 350 | 78.5 |
| Unemployed | 294 | 14.6 | 120 | 5.9 | 126 | 16.7 | 29 | 6.5 |
| Pensioner | 615 | 30.5 | 693 | 34.3 | 149 | 19.7 | 62 | 13.9 |
| Student | 138 | 6.8 | 2 | 0.1 | 38 | 5.0 | 5 | 1.1 |
| Other | 23 | 1.1 | 0 | 0.0 | 5 | 0.7 | 0 | 0.0 |
| Total | 2 015 | 100 | 2 018 | 100 | 755 | 100 | 446 | 100 |
| **Frequency of meeting** | | | | | | | | |
| Daily | 459 | 23.4 | 487 | 24.5 | 256 | 34.3 | 166 | 37.5 |
| Weekly | 731 | 37.3 | 679 | 34.1 | 227 | 30.4 | 134 | 30.2 |
| Monthly | 373 | 19.0 | 411 | 20.7 | 98 | 13.1 | 57 | 12.9 |
| From time to time | 397 | 20.3 | 413 | 20.8 | 165 | 22.1 | 86 | 19.4 |
| Total | 1 960 | 100 | 1 990 | 100 | 746 | 100 | 443 | 100 |
| **Method of acquaintance** | | | | | | | | |
| Education | | | | | 89 | 12.0 | 47 | 10.7 |
| Work | | | | | 215 | 29.0 | 147 | 33.3 |
| Through relatives | | | | | 81 | 10.9 | 43 | 9.8 |
| Through friends | | | | | 61 | 8.2 | 56 | 12.7 |
| A neighbour | | | | | 238 | 32.1 | 118 | 26.8 |
| Casual | | | | | 58 | 7.8 | 30 | 6.8 |
| Total | | | | | 742 | 100 | 441 | 100 |
| **Length of acquaintance** | | | | | | | | |
| Less than five years | | | | | 187 | 24.8 | 83 | 18.7 |
| Five to nine years | | | | | 175 | 23.2 | 109 | 24.5 |
| 10 to nineteen years | | | | | 226 | 30.0 | 132 | 29.7 |
| 20 years or more | | | | | 166 | 22.0 | 121 | 27.2 |
| Total | | | | | 754 | 100 | 445 | 100 |

*Table 4.5:*   *Number of significant others identified by individual household members who were also in help relationships with the household (and total number of significant others identified by members of 1849 households; ISITO household survey).*

|  | Give help to | Get help from | Total number of individuals nominated |
|---|---|---|---|
| Job choice | 17 | 18 | 95 |
| Spend time | 175 | 177 | 1777 |
| Problem at work | 57 | 69 | 863 |
| Get new job | 33 | 56 | 690 |
| N | 282 | 320 | 3 425 |

# ARE GIFT NETWORKS SYMMETRICAL?

The reciprocal exchange of goods and services is a normal feature of any society, embedded in its social norms and cultural traditions and making an important contribution to social cohesion and to the emotional and material support of the members of society. Such exchange is not typically motivated by calculations of rational self-interest but by principles of reciprocity expressed through emotional attachments and normative and cultural commitments. Nevertheless, the persistence of networks of reciprocity, and of the norms and emotions that sustain them, presupposes a degree of symmetry in the exchange relationships.[7]

Calculations of self-interest may begin to intrude if giving help imposes a sustained drain on household resources. Thus, we would expect gift relationships to be more stable and persistent if they were symmetrical: individuals would be more inclined to give to others if they expected that they would eventually be recompensed. Such reciprocity may be immediate, as with an exchange of gifts at New Year, in giving material support to someone who helps in the home, or

[7]   Asymmetrical exchange relationships may be stable if they are an expression of correlatively asymmetrical power relationships, acceptance of an unreciprocated gift signifying the recognition of an unequal power relationship (Blau, 1964; Emerson, 1976). Nevertheless, we would still expect there to be a limit to the extent to which people would incur material hardship in order to sustain such a power relationship.

in giving some agricultural produce to someone who helps work the land. It may be intergenerational, as young people help the older generation in the expectation that they will receive help in return, or as children help their aged parents in the expectation that their children will help them in their turn or, conversely, parents help their children because they were helped by their parents when they were young.[8] It may be probabilistic, as when a friend provides help in the event of sickness or unemployment, in the implicit expectation that the help would be reciprocated if the roles were reversed. Such expectations of reciprocity are not normally embodied in any contractual relationship, or even an informal agreement, but they are embedded in the norms that regulate social interaction and they are supported by the emotional ties that sustain close personal relationships. Such relationships can come under pressure if expectations of reciprocity are not realised, as may be the case if social inequality becomes systematic in a formerly more egalitarian society. We have a limited amount of data that enables us to explore some aspects of the reciprocal character of gift relationships in contemporary Russia.

About one-third of those who gave or received help in the RLMS surveys also received or gave help (Table 4.1), so were involved in reciprocal exchange relations, although obviously not necessarily with the same individuals: exchange typically takes place within open networks of kin and friends rather than in closed dyadic exchanges. Over half of the 1 200 households which responded to the question in all five rounds of RLMS had received help and almost two-thirds had given help in at least one of the five years. Only 15 percent of households had not been involved in private transfers in any of the five years, but only 3 percent of households had been recipients and 2 percent donors in all five years, although the data in each case related only to the month prior to the interview. Two-thirds of those who reported receiving help in at least one round also reported having been donors in at least one of the five surveys, and 58 percent of donors had also reported being recipients on at least one occasion. Thus it would appear that help-giving relationships are episodic and do not tend to involve chronic asymmetries, but nor are they strongly reciprocal: those who had given help in the previous round were no more likely than others to be recipients in the subsequent round, but those who had

8    There may also be an element of power involved in asymmetrical exchange between generations, as parents assert their power over their children, a relationship which is reversed as parents eventually accept their dependence on their children in old age.

received help in the previous round were much more likely also to receive help in the current year. Similarly, those who had given, but not those who had received, help in the previous round were much more likely to have given help in the subsequent round, so there is some tendency for households to divide into sustained donors and sustained recipients, at least in the relatively short term.[9]

The ISITO survey identifies the donors and recipients of help, as well as a number of significant others who interact with household members. In the ISITO survey, 25 percent of households reported giving but not receiving money, food, goods or loans, 20 percent reported receiving but not giving and 22 percent reported that they both gave and received.[10] In over a third of the latter households there was a direct exchange of help, with one of the three people nominated as donors of help also being identified as one of the three people to whom the household had extended help (in a handful of households all three donors and recipients were the same individuals). Thus there appears to be quite a high degree of reciprocity in these relationships.

The ISITO survey also allows us to investigate the extent to which material assistance is given in exchange for help in the home and on the dacha. Of the 84 non-household members identified as looking after children, 20 were given help (three of whom were non-relatives), which might be considered to reciprocate for services rendered, but 26 (23 of whom were a parent or grandparent) gave material help to the household, in addition to helping with childcare. Of the 48 non-household members who helped look after the elderly, 11 (five a son or daughter) received material help but 26 (14 of whom were a son or daughter) gave it. Helping to care for the young or the infirm is, therefore, slightly more often part of a wider package of support for the household than it is a part of an exchange relationship.

---

[9]  Those who had been donors in the previous round were about twice as likely as others to be donors in the current round, those who had been recipients in the previous round were between two and a half and three times as likely to be recipients in the current round. Even those who had given or received help in 1994 were more than 70 percent more likely to have given or received help in 2000. The only significant reciprocal relationship between giving and receiving in successive rounds is between 1995 and 1996, where those who received in 1995 were marginally more likely to give in 1996 (p<.05) and those who gave in 1995 were marginally more likely to receive in 1996 (p<.01), but those who received in 1996 were a little less likely to have given in 2000 (p<.05).

[10]  Directly reciprocal connections were more common in Kemerovo and Syktyvkar (27 percent and 26 percent – 37 percent of all households engaged in private transfers in each case), the cities with much more widespread dacha use and a higher level of demonetisation of the economy, than in Samara and Moscow (19 percent and 15 percent – 30 percent and 25 percent of all households engaged in transfers).

Domestic agriculture does not only involve household members, but is at the centre of a web of reciprocal relationships.[11] However, giving food from the dacha to friends and relatives is not usually considered to be providing material help and tends not to be reported as such. In the ISITO survey, the head of household was asked who was mainly responsible for a number of tasks connected with domestic agriculture (who decides what and how much to produce; who does the most work; who prepares the produce; who sells it). In around 20 percent of households which worked a dacha, non-members of the household played a major role in the dacha and the traditional expectation would be that they would share in the produce. We cannot investigate whether these people were among the reported beneficiaries of help because they were not identified by name, but households in which a non-member played a significant role in exploiting the dacha were not any more likely to report having given food to anybody, supporting the suggestion that this is not considered to be a form of material assistance. This suggestion is also supported by the fact that, apart from a handful of 'don't knows', everybody with a dacha gave away part of their produce to friends or relatives, but when asked about giving help to others, fewer than one-third of them reported having given help in the form of food to others in the past year. Similarly, only two-thirds of those who reported that some of their food consumption was met by gifts from others reported receiving food when asked about help received. In the RLMS data, 27 percent of respondent households in 1998 and 22 percent in 2000 reported having given some of their own produce to friends and relatives, but only 40 percent of these donor households in 1998 and 47 percent in 2000 reported having given any help to anybody in the 30 days prior to the interview.

## HOW MUCH DO HOUSEHOLDS RELY ON THE HELP OF OTHERS?

According to the RLMS data, private transfers in money and in kind made up an average of 8–10 percent of the total money income of all households (including net assistance) in the month prior to the survey

[11] The New Russia Barometer VII, administered by VTsIOM, found that in the spring of 1998 a majority of respondents helped friends and relatives grow food at some time or another, 12 percent doing so often and 19 percent regularly, while 58 percent received food at some time or another from friends and relatives, though only 7 percent were regularly given such food (Rose, 1998).

between 1994 and 2000, with the peak being in 1996, when the non-payment of wages was at its height.[12] Many households were very dependent on such transfers to survive: assistance (including both gifts and loans) as a proportion of the total income of households which were net recipients of such transfers increased from a median of 28 percent in 1994 to 36 percent in 1996, falling back to 22 percent in 2000 as the economic situation improved. In 1996, almost one in ten households reported no income at all the previous month, in money or in kind, and almost three-quarters of these households reported having received gifts or, more often, loans in cash or in kind from others, some receiving enough to raise them into the higher income quintiles. In spring 1998, 4 percent of respondents to the New Russia Barometer VII survey replied that what they got as favours or with the help of friends and relatives was their most important source of income and 14 percent identified these as their second most important income source (Rose, 1998). In general, and not surprisingly, gifts and loans make a much greater relative contribution to the household income of the lowest income groups, but lower income groups are not much more likely than the richest households to be net recipients of assistance, and a substantial proportion of the poorest households are in fact net donors (Table 4.6).

Table 4.6 (which includes loans) and Table 4.7 (which relates to gifts only) do not show any clear pattern of change in the incidence or the relative scale of private transfers over time, although comparison between rounds is difficult because the questions asked in successive rounds were not identical, while interviewing was in different months and there is a high degree of seasonality in giving (peak times being the start of the school year, harvest, New Year, etc.). Bursts of inflation and the irregular payment of wages and benefits have a substantial impact on money incomes, so that the increasing dependence on private transfers is more a result of declining real incomes than of increasing private transfers.

[12] According to the Goskomstat data, private transfers amounted to 4 percent of total money income and about 9 percent of the money income of the lowest decile, those in extreme poverty, in the fourth quarter of 1996 (Ministry of Labour and Social Development and Goskomstat Rossii, 1997). Since 1997 Goskomstat has only reported the value of receipts of foodstuffs from friends and relatives. This amounted to an average of 2.2 percent of consumption spending, and 4.0 percent of that of the lowest expenditure decile, in 1999 (Goskomstat, 2000b). A survey of 1 250 Jewish emigrant families of the mid-1970s found that assistance from relatives had amounted to 1.9 percent of household income and 1.2 percent of household expenditure (Ofer and Vinokur, 1992, pp. 345, 354).

*Table 4.6:*   *Median percentage of household income given and received as gifts and loans by households which are net donors and net recipients by income quintiles.*

|  |  | First | Second | Third | Fourth | Fifth | Total |
|---|---|---|---|---|---|---|---|
|  |  | | | Income quintiles | | | |
| **Net donors** | | | | | | | |
| 1992–94 | % of households | 14 | 19 | 21 | 23 | 27 | 21 |
|  | Median % of income | 26 | 19 | 13 | 10 | 7 | 12 |
| 1994 | % of households | 20 | 24 | 34 | 32 | 38 | 30 |
|  | Median % of income | 35 | 19 | 14 | 10 | 8 | 14 |
| 1995 | % of households | 16 | 19 | 24 | 27 | 32 | 24 |
|  | Median % of income | 40 | 19 | 17 | 12 | 8 | 15 |
| 1996 | % of households | 15 | 17 | 21 | 26 | 35 | 23 |
|  | Median % of income | 70 | 23 | 19 | 13 | 9 | 16 |
| 1998 | % of households | 15 | 16 | 23 | 28 | 31 | 23 |
|  | Median % of income | 40 | 18 | 14 | 11 | 8 | 13 |
| 2000 | % of households | 19 | 24 | 24 | 28 | 33 | 26 |
|  | Median % of income | 28 | 20 | 16 | 10 | 7 | 13 |
| **Net recipients** | | | | | | | |
| 1992–94 | % of households | 13 | 15 | 15 | 18 | 21 | 16 |
|  | Median % of income | 39 | 26 | 21 | 16 | 11 | 19 |
| 1994 | % of households | 28 | 29 | 27 | 32 | 31 | 30 |
|  | Median % of income | 43 | 32 | 25 | 20 | 23 | 28 |
| 1995 | % of households | 28 | 33 | 30 | 27 | 32 | 30 |
|  | Median % of income | 67 | 38 | 33 | 23 | 22 | 33 |
| 1996 | % of households | 32 | 38 | 35 | 32 | 32 | 34 |
|  | Median % of income | 100 | 35 | 28 | 19 | 28 | 35 |
| 1998 | % of households | 35 | 37 | 34 | 31 | 30 | 33 |
|  | Median % of income | 68 | 33 | 26 | 20 | 18 | 28 |
| 2000 | % of households | 30 | 34 | 37 | 33 | 31 | 33 |
|  | Median % of income | 31 | 26 | 21 | 17 | 15 | 22 |

*Source: RLMS data, 1992–2000. Income in phase one (1992–94) is the household money income reported by the head of household. In phase two (1994–2000) it is the total income in money and in kind calculated by RLMS. The two phases are not comparable.*

*Table 4.7:*   *Percentage of households receiving help and net help received by net beneficiaries (as a percentage of last month's household money income; RLMS data).*

| Round | Percentage of households receiving help | Percentage of households giving help | Of which, percentage both giving and receiving help | Percentage of households receiving positive net help | Median net help as percentage of recipient household's money income |
|---|---|---|---|---|---|
| 7–10/92 | 26.0 | 17.0 | 5.5 | 21.8 | 21 |
| 12/92–3/93 | 20.5 | 26.2 | 8.5 | 13.6 | 20 |
| 7/93–9/93 | 22.3 | 25.2 | 7.2 | 15.1 | 15 |
| 10/93–1/94 | 17.6 | 27.2 | 7.7 | 15.3 | 20 |
| 11–12/94 | 23.6 | 31.0 | 8.9 | 18.0 | 28 |
| 10–12/95 | 21.5 | 23.2 | 5.6 | 17.3 | 29 |
| 10–12/96 | 24.9 | 23.8 | 6.8 | 20.8 | 33 |
| 10/98–1/99 | 26.6 | 25.2 | 7.6 | 21.3 | 32 |
| 9–12/2000 | 29.2 | 26.5 | 7.8 | 24.4 | 22 |

*Note: Household money income in the first four rounds (phase one) is the total money income reported by the head of household. In phase two it is the sum of the components of household money income last month reported by the head of household, including net transfers but not including income from the sale of property. Help given and received includes transfers both in money and in kind, except that in phase one donations to others in kind in the previous month were not reported. Help does not include loans given and received. In the first round, a further 13.6 percent of households said that they had given away some agricultural produce in the course of the previous year. The value of transfers in kind is as reported by respondents. In 1992 about two-thirds of transfers were in kind. In the second phase, respondents were not asked to distinguish between transfers in cash and transfers in kind.*

Table 4.1 shows a sharp fall in the real value of the amount given and received after the 1998 crisis, but comparison with Table 4.6 makes it clear that this is a result of the inflationary erosion of income rather than a reduction in the proportion of income given and received.[13] Similarly, the recovery of incomes after the crisis meant that although the real value of help had increased in 2000, it

---

[13]   Note that the estimates of the amount received are substantially greater than the estimates of the amount given, suggesting that donors undervalue and/or recipients overvalue the donations. Exactly the same relationship is found in the ISITO data and in Ofer and Vinokur, 1992.

constituted a substantially lower proportion of the household income of recipients.

Table 4.6 relates only to help given and received in the form of a gift, but many households also receive help in the form of loans. We have seen that friends are much more likely to provide help in the form of a loan than a gift, although the majority of loans are still extended by relatives (see Table 4.2) and many of those who extend loans also provide help in the form of gifts. In the RLMS data, in 1992 a further 6.8 percent, and over 1994–2000 a further 7–10 percent of households had loaned money to others. Receipts of loans were not reported in 1992, but over 1994–2000, 17–21 percent of households reported having received loans, around a third of whom also received help in the form of gifts. The average size of borrowings reported was much larger than the average size of loans (see Table 4.1), which suggests, as in the case of gifts, that recipients overvalue and/or donors undervalue the loans (rather than that those who borrow tend to draw on several sources, since more households reported borrowing than reported lending). The average size of loans received was about twice the average amount of help. For those who received both gifts and a loan, the loan accounted for a little over half the total assistance received.

It appears from the data in Table 4.1 that there has been a slight tendency for both the scale and the extent of lending to have declined fairly steadily through the second half of the 1990s, but no such trend is evident when we look at the net amounts given and received by households in the form of both gifts and loans (Table 4.7).

In an analysis of the first phase RLMS data (Rounds One and Three), covering the period 1992–94, Cox et al., 1997 found that, in Round One, gross transfer receipts made up 6.9 percent of total household income, but had only a small impact on the poverty headcount, reducing it from 38.2 percent to 36.6 percent of households (public transfers had a much bigger impact on poverty, the incidence of which without any transfers would have been 58.7 percent). However, the impact on net recipients was much more substantial, private transfers comprising on average 30.7 percent of the household income of net recipients, reducing the incidence of poverty among the latter from 44.9 percent to 29.1 percent.

Private transfers in the second phase of RLMS had a similarly modest impact on the poverty headcount, only 3–4 percent of households being lifted out of poverty (based on the reported total income of the household, including income in kind), with 1–2 percent of households being thrust into poverty as a result of their donations to others (Table 4.8).

*Table 4.8:    Impact of private transfers on the incidence of poverty.*

| Percentage of households | 1994 | 1995 | 1996 | 1998 | 2000 |
|---|---|---|---|---|---|
| Not in poverty | 83 | 69 | 63 | 58 | 68 |
| Thrust into poverty by giving | 1 | 2 | 2 | 2 | 2 |
| Lifted out of poverty by help | 3 | 3 | 4 | 3 | 4 |
| In poverty regardless of help | 13 | 26 | 31 | 37 | 26 |
| N | 3 973 | 3 781 | 3 750 | 3 622 | 3 777 |

*Source: RLMS data, 1994–2000*

Private transfers have relatively little impact on poverty because they have little impact on the overall distribution of income. This is partly because the majority of households are not recipients of help, but it is also because private transfers are not so much a form of charitable donation as a part of the normal reciprocal relationships among friends and, above all, close relatives at all income levels. Thus, those households with the highest incomes tend to give the most, but they also tend to receive the most, although donations are pretty evenly distributed across the income range. Those households fortunate enough to have more wealthy (or generous) connections move up the income scale as a result of the help received, so that more than half the total help given to all households ends up in the hands of the richest 20 percent of households (Table 4.9).

Many donor households are themselves on or below the poverty line, 9 percent of net donors being thrust in to poverty as a result of their generosity in 1992 and 5 to 6 percent between 1994 and 2000. On the other hand, net donors do tend to have significantly higher money incomes (before private transfers) than do net recipients, so there is some tendency for private transfers to flow from relatively better-off to relatively worse-off households and so to reduce inequality between them: the household money income of recipient households between 1994 and 2000 was not significantly lower than that of donor households after transfers, while both donors and recipients on average had significantly higher incomes than those not engaged in private transfers at all.

Age and kinship differentiated donors from recipients much more sharply than did income in the 1992 and 1993 data. Households headed by older people were more likely to be donors, although the amount given declined with age. Households headed by younger people were much more likely to be recipients, the amount received again declining with age. Parents were much more likely to be donors and children recipients. To examine these questions further, and to compare the subsequent data with the analysis of the 1992 data by Cox and his colleagues, we need to turn to the multivariate analysis of the more recent RLMS data, which can be supplemented with analysis of the ISITO survey data.

*Table 4.9:*   *Percentage of total transfers given and received by household income quintiles, 1992–2000.*

| | 1992–94 | | 1994–2000 | | 1994–2000 | |
|---|---|---|---|---|---|---|
| | Money income reported by household head | | Total income quintiles, before private transfers | | Total income quintiles, after private transfers | |
| Income quintiles | Percentage of | | Percentage of | | Percentage of | |
| | transfers given | transfers received | transfers given | transfers received | transfers given | transfers received |
| Lowest | 10 | 7 | 2 | 20 | 8 | 4 |
| Second | 12 | 9 | 6 | 19 | 13 | 9 |
| Third | 15 | 13 | 11 | 18 | 16 | 14 |
| Fourth | 21 | 20 | 19 | 20 | 22 | 19 |
| Fifth | 42 | 51 | 62 | 24 | 41 | 55 |
| Total | 100 | 100 | 100 | 100 | 100 | 100 |

*Sources: author's calculations from RLMS data.*
*Note: In 1992 respondents were asked what help they received in money and in kind (two-thirds of help was in kind), but only about monetary donations in the last month. Subsequently respondents have been asked the total value of all help given and received in money or in kind. Cox et al., 1997, p. 222 gives a rather different distribution for 1992, based on netting all public and private transfers out of income, which increases the share of the bottom quintile and reduces the share of the top quintile. Total income since 1994 includes the net value of domestic agricultural production imputed by RLMS (because help also includes help in kind). The value of non-cash income from home production and the informal sector amounted to 8 percent of total household income (in money and in kind) across all households in 1992, 11 percent in 1994, 8 percent in 1995, 16 percent in 1996, 18 percent in 1996, falling back to 12 percent in 2000 (Mroz et al., 2001, Table 2), but only about half of all households have such income.*

# PRIVATE TRANSFERS: CHARITY OR RECIPROCITY?

We have noted that private transfers tend to be embedded in networks of reciprocity between friends and relatives, whatever their income level. At the same time, the receipt of gifts and loans from others is an important resource for those households on the margins of subsistence. If we want to understand the role of private transfers in households' survival strategies we have to ask to what extent these networks can be tapped for assistance in times of particular hardship. To what extent have networks of reciprocity been transformed into asymmetrical relationships of provision of assistance from the more to the less prosperous households and to what extent can households rely on such networks for support in times of hardship? To address this question we need to undertake a multivariate analysis of the data at our disposal in order to discover the relative strength of economic and social factors in determining private transfers. The RLMS data allows us to generalise to the Russian population as a whole and to look at the impact of changes in household circumstances on reciprocity. The ISITO data has the advantage of providing information about a more homogeneous population, that of four large cities, and covering transfers over the previous year, rather than just over the previous month.[14] The ISITO data also has the advantage of distinguishing between different types of transfer (money, food, goods and loans) and containing some information on the source and destination of transfers as well as other relationships with non-members of the household.[15]

Unfortunately we have only very limited data regarding the social framework within which households subsist, but we can explore the impact of a variety of socio-demographic factors which we might expect would affect the probability of households engaging in symmetrical or asymmetrical exchange relations. For this purpose we distinguish between donor households, recipient households and those households that both give and receive help.[16] The regression results are shown in Tables 4.10 to 4.18 at the end of this chapter.

---

[14] None of the coefficients in the regressions run separately for each city are significantly different from those in the regression for all cities together.

[15] In both surveys the relevant questions related specifically to the provision of help, rather than to transfers in general.

[16] The distinctiveness of the latter is confirmed by the marked increase in explanatory power of the models which is achieved by differentiating them from pure donor and recipient households.

If private transfers are primarily a form of assistance to those households most in need, we would expect that the incidence and scale of such transfers would be strongly related to the level of the household income per head, with the rich more likely to give, and giving more, and the poor more likely to receive, and receiving more. If private transfers are primarily an element of the reciprocal relations between friends and relatives, we would not expect the probability of transfers to be so much affected by income, although it is necessary to have a minimum of resources to be able to give or to engage in reciprocal exchange, and, to the extent that members of social networks tend to have similar levels of income, we would expect the size of both gifts and receipts to be positively related to income.[17]

In both data sets we find that it is indeed the case that lower income households tend to be recipients of both gifts and loans while those with a higher income per head are much more likely to be donors, but the relationship to income is not very strong and there is not much variation, except at the top and bottom of the income scale.[18] Those in the RLMS data set who had reported no money income in the previous month were not significantly more likely than all but the richest households to have received help from others, although they did receive significantly more than did middle income households. They, like other low-income households, were substantially more likely to have borrowed money to get them through difficult times, suggesting that borrowing is more significant than the receipt of gifts for those in difficulties.

When we turn to the amount given and received, in both data sets the amount given and, to a lesser extent, the amount received as gifts and loans is an increasing function of income, though the relationship is not very strong and the top income decile both gives *and receives* substantially more than all others. This is contrary to what an altruistic interpretation of help would expect, but is not unexpected if giving help is an aspect of reciprocity within social networks.

---

17  Note that this assumption is unlikely to hold, particularly in the relation between parents and children. Nevertheless, the important consideration in the latter case is whether the transfers are motivated primarily by the kinship relation or primarily by differences in economic circumstances.

18  We use total money income per head (without including help given and received) as the independent variable in the regressions. Because there is no significant functional relationship to income in the RLMS data, and some households have zero income, we use dummy variables for income deciles relative to the region and round in the regressions. Coefficients for the log of household income per head from a separate regression, which of course excludes those with no income, are also cited.

The level of current reported household income may not be a very good indicator of the perceived level of need of the household. On the one hand, we can use subjective indicators of the level of perceived need of the household. On the other hand, we can use indicators of changes in the household's circumstances. In the ISITO survey the head of household was asked whether the household income was sufficient to cover the purchase of food, whether they had enough for food but not for clothing, whether they could just afford food and clothing, whether they could afford to buy durables or whether they wanted for nothing. In the RLMS survey individual respondents were asked to rank themselves as poor or rich on a scale of 1 to 9, the household indicator used here being the mean of the individual scores.[19] In the RLMS survey this subjective indicator adds nothing to the explanatory power of the objective income measure in determining the probability of receiving help or engaging in reciprocal exchange, but those who felt themselves richer were more likely to be donors and there is a significant positive relationship with the amount given. In the ISITO data those who considered themselves relatively more in need were more likely to receive help and were also more likely to be involved in reciprocal exchange, which weakens the positive relationship with the objective income measure, while the subjective indicator reinforces the objective measure in relation to the probability of being a donor. The subjective indicator also reinforces the objective measure in relation to the amount given and received. Overall, it seems that subjective indicators of need are even weaker determinants of the probability of receiving help than are objective indicators of income.

If we turn to the various changes in household circumstances which might be expected to increase the need for help, we find that in the RLMS data those households whose income relative to others had fallen since 1996 (indicated by the difference in income decile rank between surveys) were no more likely to be recipients, while those whose income had increased were *less* likely to be donors in 1998, and relative income change had no significant effect on the amount given and received. RLMS asked respondents whether their situation had got worse in the past five years and whether they expected the situation to

---

[19] There is a strong correlation between subjective indicators and reported household income per head. In the ISITO data, 96 percent of the bottom income quintile, against 40 percent of the top quintile, said that they could at best meet their basic subsistence needs, but had difficulty in affording clothing. For this reason, the subjective indicators are not included in the regressions reproduced here.

improve in the next year (not included in the regression results reported here). We would expect the former to have a greater need of help, while the latter might be more willing to solicit help since they would have more expectation of being able to reciprocate. Those who thought that they lived worse than they did five years ago were indeed a little more likely to be recipients of help, but people's expectations of the future had no significant impact on the likelihood of engaging in help relations.

Those households which had sold household property in the last year were no more likely to be donors or recipients in the RLMS data, but were significantly more likely to have been involved in reciprocal exchange, perhaps because those more involved in networks of reciprocal exchange are best placed to find a buyer for their property (these households also received a little less help than others). In the ISITO data too, those who had sold property were more likely to have been involved in mutual exchange, but they were also more likely to have been donors and less likely to have been recipients of help. The data suggests that the sale of property is a normal feature of everyday life and only exceptionally is the last recourse of those who are not able to obtain help.

To what extent do gifts and loans enable households to overcome temporary hardships? We have seen that those with the lowest incomes are more likely than the average household to receive all forms of help. However, misfortunes such as the non-payment of wages, being sent on unpaid leave, being paid in kind or suffering a lay-off and unemployment have only a very small impact on the likelihood of receiving help or on the scale of help received. In the ISITO data, administrative leave, unemployment, the non-payment of wages and payment in kind had no significant impact on the likelihood of the household receiving any kind of gifts or loans or on the scale of help received, except that households whose members had been sent on administrative leave were more likely to have been recipients of help. In the RLMS data, none of these variables (either of the existence or of the scale of such phenomena in the household) increased the likelihood of receiving help to a statistically significant degree in any of the regressions, although if we omit the income variables, those households which had suffered from unpaid wages or the payment of wages in kind and those with a larger number of unemployed were significantly more likely to have received help. This would suggest that it is primarily the loss of income, rather than the particular circumstance, that explains the increased likelihood of receiving help, but it also suggests that exchange relations between households are reasonably stable and do not respond rapidly to temporary misfortune. Paradoxically, those households whose members had experienced a spell of administrative leave in the RLMS data were more likely to have *given* help in the previous month and those who gave help gave more the more household members were unemployed.

We have already noted that in the RLMS data, those without income were more likely to borrow than to receive gifts to tide them over. We find here again, in the RLMS data, that those households that had suffered from unpaid wages or from administrative leave were more likely to have been borrowers, although those who had been paid in kind were less likely to have borrowed and, if they did, had borrowed less. When (and only when) we control for income, those households suffering from unpaid wages were also more likely to have been lenders. This endorses the suggestion that the mutual support of households is reciprocal, since the non-payment of wages is highly clustered (Earle and Sabirianova, 1999), so those who have suffered from unpaid wages are very likely to have friends and relatives in the same situation, lending to one another to the extent that they are able and repaying loans when they receive their wages.

Household resources would be expected to play a significant role in involvement in exchange relations. Having a car or a dacha are indicators of the resources at the disposal of the household, but are also important foci of reciprocal relationships, as we have already noted in relation to the dacha. A car can equally be an important resource in the exchange network, for example in transporting friends and their produce to and from their dachas. In fact, ownership of a car does not have much impact on the probability or scale of transfers, except that, even controlling for income, car owners were more likely to give help, particularly in the form of money and food, and, in the RLMS data, those who gave help gave significantly more than non-owners and, in the ISITO data, those who received, received more, while in RLMS car-owners also both lent and borrowed more than non-owners. This suggests that car ownership serves to widen the web of reciprocity, in addition to any impact it may have through its contribution to the household's prosperity.

Because of the important role of gifts of food in private transfers, we would expect those with a dacha to be less likely to receive help and more likely to give help or engage in reciprocal exchange although, as noted above, gifts of food are often not considered to be a form of help. These expectations are supported by the data. In both data sets, dacha owners, particularly in the countryside,[20] were less likely to be recipients of help and urban dacha owners were more likely to be donors, particularly of food, but dacha ownership had no impact on the scale of giving or receiving help. Those households in the ISITO data in which a non-household member played a significant role in exploiting their dacha were substantially more likely to be recipients of food and money and to engage in reciprocal exchange, probably because, as we saw above, help with the dacha is sometimes reciprocated, but it is often part of a wider package of help for the household. Even though it is usual to share the produce of the dacha with those who help to exploit it, these households were not significantly more likely to be donors, confirming the supposition above that such transfers are not usually considered as help.[21]

The socio-demographic composition of the household affects both the need for help and the possibility of engaging in exchange networks. We allow for the impact of the size of the household on the need for income by using the household income per head as our income indicator. A household with more adult members might be expected to have a more extensive social network, but in both data sets, larger households are actually significantly *less* likely to be recipients of any kind of gifts, and, in the RLMS data, are also less

---

[20] We might expect the scope for giving food to be reduced in rural districts, where agricultural production is more diversified and most households are largely self-sufficient. In the 1992 RLMS data, urban households were much more likely to be recipients, and a bit more likely to be donors, than were rural households (Cox et al., 1997, pp. 223–5), but in the second phase data there is no significant difference between urban and rural household in any respect. There were very substantial regional variations in the 1992 data, which were much less significant in the subsequent data. It is likely that the earlier variation was primarily due to marked regional variations in the rate of inflation following price liberalisation and to unevenness in the quality of the data in the first phase of RLMS. Apart from this, the patterns identified in the 1994–2000 data are similar to those identified by Cox et al., 1997 for 1992 and 1993.

[21] In the ISITO data there is a very marked difference in behaviour between those who sell some of the produce of the dacha and those who do not. Those who sold some of the produce of their dacha were substantially more likely and those who did not sell any produce were less likely than non-dacha owners to be donors or involved in reciprocal exchange. In the RLMS data there is a similar, though less substantial, difference, particularly in relation to urban households.

Only a handful of households regard their dacha as a source of income. The difference between those who do and those who do not sell their product may be related to the scale of their dacha activity. Certainly, those who sold some of the produce also reported that they met more of their own needs from their dacha. In the RLMS data, those urban dacha owners who sold some of their produce grew significantly, and often substantially, more than those who did not.

likely to give and to lend to others, although when they do give to others, larger households tend to give more in both data sets. This is probably a result of the household composition, larger households being likely to be multi-generational: since a substantial proportion of transfers are between close relatives, these transfers will not be recorded in an extended household because they will be internal to the household, while the larger household will be better able to spare more resources to give to others. In the ISITO data, those households which included parents of the head of household were markedly less likely to receive help from others and those with co-resident adult children were less likely to give help and gave significantly less.

The common supposition that women play a predominant role in mediating exchange relations between households is supported by the fact that male-headed households were much less likely both to give and receive help and, in the RLMS data, to lend (but not to borrow) than were female-headed households. The supposition is also supported by the fact that, in the ISITO data, more than two-thirds of the exchange partners were women (71 percent when the household was headed by a woman and 63 percent when it was headed by a man). The most likely explanation for this is that it is women who are predominantly responsible for the management of the household budget (Clarke, 2002) and so for managing exchanges between households.

We would expect a household with relatively more wage-earners to be better placed to give to others and to have less need of help. Controlling for household size, the more adults are working in the household, the less likely is the household to receive help and, in the RLMS data, the more likely it is to give help and the more it gives. The fact that transfers tend to be from parents to children means that the presence of pensioners in the household has as large an impact as the presence of workers. In the RLMS data, the more pensioners there are in the household the more likely is the household to give and the less likely it is to receive help, while the household gives more and receives less. The household with more pensioners is less likely to borrow and, especially, to lend. In the ISITO data too, households in which there are more pensioners are more likely to be donors of help, unless the pensioners have stopped work, in which case they are much more likely to be recipients.

A single parent is likely to be in particular need because of the limited opportunities for earning income, but is likely to have a narrower network of kin and friends. In both data sets, single parents are not significantly more likely to receive help, although in the RLMS data a single parent is marginally less likely to give help and receives a little more than average. There is no significant difference between male and female single parents in this respect.

We have already seen that transfers are predominantly between parents and children. Young adult children receive help from their parents, partly as an expression of the power relation between the generations but also in the expectation that the children will help their parents when the latter are elderly. As the proportion of older people in the household increases, the probability of giving help increases, the probability of receiving help declines, the amount given increases and the amount received falls. Similarly, as the age of the household head increases, the household becomes progressively less likely to be a recipient, slightly less likely to be involved in reciprocal exchange and more likely to be a donor (and to give a bit more and to receive a bit less), although in each case at a diminishing rate. In the ISITO data, without controlling for other variables, the highest probability of being a donor is when the household head is aged 47, and the lowest probability of being a recipient is reached at age 62, with the probability of being involved in reciprocal exchange falling continuously, but at a decreasing rate. In the RLMS data the maxima and minima for donors and recipients of help are reached at age 55 and 61 respectively. In the ISITO data, giving and receiving loans does not vary significantly with age, but in the RLMS data the probability of borrowing reaches a maximum at 34, while the probability of being a lender falls continuously. There is no significant difference between male and female-headed households in either data set. In the RLMS, 58 percent of the young households (average age of all adult members under 25), but only 13 percent of those aged over 60, received help (including reciprocal exchange). In the ISITO data three-quarters of young households received help against fewer than a third of the over-60s. This data suggests that the flow of help between parents and children does not reverse its direction until the parents are over, or even considerably over, the pension age.

Children impose heavy demands on the family, especially at New Year and the start of the school year, while we would expect the presence of children, and particularly young children, in the household to increase the probability of receiving support from relatives. In the RLMS data, households with more young children were more likely to receive help, while those with more older children were less likely to give help. However, in the ISITO data, households with more young children were significantly less likely to be recipients of help, otherwise the number of children does not influence the probability or the scale of giving or receiving help. This may be because many Russians starting a family, particularly in the large cities covered by the ISITO survey, continue to live with their parents, so that transfers are within the household. In the ISITO sample, a third of the children under seven and just over a fifth of those aged between seven and 16 lived in a household which included one or more of their grandparents and/or great-grandparents.

If social networks and social norms play an important role in determining private transfers, then we might expect such networks and norms to be different in different social strata. In fact we find that there are very few significant differences according to such factors as the education and employment status of household members. The mean level of education of household members does not affect the probability of giving or receiving help, although in the RLMS data the amount received in help increases with the average educational level of the household. In both data sets, those with higher education are more likely to be involved in all forms of help relationship. This may be because many significant friendships are formed as students, so that those with higher education are likely to have a wider range of social contacts and, in particular, those in need are more likely to have more successful friends willing and able to help, and vice versa.[22]

Although we might expect different occupational groups to be marked by relatively more or less solidary social relations, and we know that professional advance depends on having appropriate connections, the socio-economic status of household members (as managerial/professional, clerical and skilled and unskilled manual workers) is not significant in any of the regressions. Those with stable employment might be expected to have more developed work-based friendships but in fact (as indicated by the average tenure of household members in the current job or the tenure of the head of household), they are neither more nor less likely to engage in private transfers. As we have seen, access to secondary employment depends heavily on

[22] Cox et al., 1997 provide a more narrowly economic explanation, suggesting that those with a higher level of education may have better future earning possibilities and greater aspirations for expenditure, so that donors will have more expectation of favours being returned in the future.

integration into social networks and we do find that the more household members have second jobs, the more likely is the household to engage in private transfers, although only to a statistically significant extent in reciprocal exchange and, in the RLMS data, in giving.

Those born elsewhere might be expected to have a less extensive local social network, although they may have retained connections with their district of birth that provide opportunities for complementary exchange (for example of products not readily available locally). In the RLMS data, those who are in-migrants to the region are no less likely to engage in private transfers than those still living in their place of birth (although many of the former will have moved as children, so will have had plenty of time to build their local social networks). Charity is often associated with religious commitment. RLMS asks respondents about the depth of their religious belief, but religious affiliation does not appear to impinge on the extent or the scale of private transfers.

We have already seen that many of the differences in the behaviour and experience of households are consistent with the supposition that the character and extent of a household's social network is an important factor in facilitating or inhibiting the provision of help from the more to the less fortunate households. In the ISITO survey, as noted above (page 181), individual household members and the household head were asked about a number of connections with non-members of the household. From the regression results it can be seen that the number of contacts identified is a strong predictor of the likelihood of being engaged in all forms of private transfer.[23] Contact with relatives has more weight than contact with friends, unsurprisingly since the majority of private transfers are between relatives, except in the case of giving and receiving loans.[24]

In addition to asking household heads about help with the dacha, heads of those households with young children or elderly or infirm adults in need of care were asked in the ISITO survey who provided this care, and on occasion this was someone who was not a member of

---

[23]   The extent of the network is indicated by the number of links per respondent. Non-respondents were absentees and refusals and pensioners who had not worked in the last three years.

[24]   Those whose contacts included relatively more pensioners were more likely to give and to receive help. Those with more contacts working in the new private sector, which tends to pay higher wages and more often to pay on time, were not significantly different from others.

the household. We have already noted that those households in which outsiders participated in exploiting the dacha were significantly more likely to have received help or been engaged in reciprocal exchange. Those households which called on an outsider to help with care of children or the elderly were more likely to be engaged in all forms of transfer, but the difference is not statistically significant, except in Samara, where such households were more likely to give help.

Cox et al., 1997, working under the aegis of the World Bank, were primarily concerned to investigate whether private and public transfers were complementary or competitive, and found that those receiving pensions were less likely to receive private help, while receiving other public transfers increased the likelihood of receiving help, but the coefficient of determination was quite small so there was no evidence that private transfers could play a significant role in relieving poverty if public transfers were reduced, or that increasing public transfers would 'crowd out' private transfers.

In the RLMS data there is a weak inverse relationship between the amount received by the household as pension income and the probability of receiving help and loans and a weak positive relationship with the likelihood of giving loans. There is no significant relationship between other benefit income (unemployment benefit, child benefit, stipends and apartment and fuel benefits) and the likelihood of giving or receiving help. In the ISITO data there is a positive relationship between the amount of the household's non-pension benefit income and the probability of receiving help, primarily in the form of food, and between the size of pension income and the probability of giving all forms of help. This is consistent with the idea that pensions (and to a lesser extent other social benefits) are an important source of money income in a demonetised economy and that pensioners tend to redistribute some of their income to others (c.f. Burawoy et al., 2000, n.9, pp. 62–3). Neither pension income nor other benefits have any significant impact on the amount given or received by the household. These findings reinforce Cox's conclusion that there is little relationship between private and public transfers, so that there is no evidence that the former can substitute for the latter and give force to Burawoy's suggestion that 'if the state wanted to distribute income to the needy, perhaps one of the rational ways of doing this is indeed to use pensioners as their agents' (ibid., p. 62).

## CONCLUSION

The evidence reviewed in this chapter points to the conclusion that giving and receiving help is embedded in the normative structure of reciprocal relations of kinship and friendship, and perhaps inter-generational relations of subordination and dependence, with resources flowing particularly from parents to children until parents are well past pension age. Within this structure there is only a small tendency for resources to flow from richer to poorer households, which is probably largely a reflection of intra-family inter-generational inequality, and the richest households both give and receive the most. Giving and receiving help is heavily concentrated in relations between close kin, suggesting that reciprocity is not the legacy of some specifically Russian traditions of communality but is rather an expression of the narrowing of social support to close family connections characteristic of the Soviet period.

The fact that private transfers are deeply embedded in social relations of close friendship and, particularly, kinship means that they are not particularly sensitive to the specific circumstances of the parties to the relationship. Thus, the poorest households are not much less likely to give money and goods to others than are the richest households, even if their generosity imposes hardship on them, and there is virtually no evidence that private transfers respond to temporary difficulties or income shortfalls. Almost as many households are thrust into poverty by giving as are lifted out of poverty by the help they receive. More generally, various indicators of need and opportunity for households to receive and provide help generally prove to be insignificant determinants of the probability or scale of private transfers, reinforcing the conclusion that such transfers are predominantly not situational.

While the receipt of private transfers for those fortunate enough to receive them can make an important contribution to the well-being of the household, there is no evidence that private transfers constitute a significant component of a household survival strategy, in the sense that households in difficulty are able to mobilise their kin and social connections to supplement the household income. Ethnographic evidence also suggests that private transfers are generally unsolicited and people are very reluctant to ask even their close kin for help. Those households for whom the help of others is a critical factor in their survival get such help not so much because of their hardship as because they are inserted in appropriate social networks. Those in hardship who do not have the appropriate social connections do not receive help.

The partial exception to this conclusion relates to loans. While it is always difficult to solicit support in the form of a gift, even from close kin, it is somewhat easier to solicit such support with a promise to repay, and the data suggests that it is possible to tap a wider network of support in search of a loan, with friends playing a more significant role than in the case of gifts. The RLMS data, at least, suggests that those in temporary difficulty as a result of a loss of income, particularly as a result of being sent on unpaid administrative leave or not receiving wages due, are more able than others to get support from friends and relatives in the form of a loan. However, the determinants of lending suggested by the regression results are not very different from those of giving, suggesting that loans and gifts do not pass through very different channels, both being dominated by transfers between close kin, and are not sharply distinguished from one another by their executors. On the one hand, both a gift and a loan impose a drain on the resources of the giver. On the other hand, the virtual absence of inflation in the Soviet Union means that Russia has not yet established a tradition of repaying loans with interest. In the highly inflationary conditions of the transition economy this means that anything other than a short-term loan is indeed little different from a gift if repayment is to be expected, if at all, in a sharply devalued currency.

The norms which govern the relations between friends and kin are likely to be reasonably stable so long as the expectations of reciprocity in which they are embedded continue to correspond to the obligations which they entail. For example, if personal misfortune is a random and relatively rare event the obligations between friends will be mutual and not especially burdensome, but if misfortune becomes chronic, systematic and persistent the obligations are likely to become heavy and the expectations of reciprocity to be diminished, putting relations of friendship under heavy pressure. Friendship may be strengthened by regular reciprocal transfers between friends whose wages or pensions are paid irregularly, but it may be severely strained where the non-payment of wages, low pay or unemployment is chronic and persistent. A decline in the level of pensions, a sharp increase in the cost of medical care or education or a decline in the incomes of a significant portion of the population of working-age is similarly likely to put inter-generational relationships under severe pressure. Once some people start to abrogate their social obligations to friends and kin, expectations begin to change and apparently deeply rooted traditions of mutual assistance can turn out to be very vulnerable.

The conditions of stability and relative equality which have sustained the traditional networks of support have been eroded with the collapse of the Soviet system and the transition to a market economy, so we would anticipate that the expectations of reciprocity which underpin the safety net of private transfers will be eroded over time, so that Russia will become more like other developed capitalist economies in the limited role of private assistance in the provision of social support. This is not an expectation that we can investigate empirically because we do not have data covering a sufficiently long time span, but there is certainly no evidence of any increase in mutual support to limit the impact of the deepening crisis. The RLMS data suggests that there may have been a decline in the real value of the amount given and received by households since 1994 and, in particular, in the wake of the August 1998 crisis, when the real value of private transfers fell even more sharply than did real incomes.

Table 4.10: *Logistic regression – probabilities of being a recipient, both recipient and donor and being a donor of all forms of help (ISITO household survey data).*

| | Recipient | | | Recipient and Donor | | | Donor | | |
|---|---|---|---|---|---|---|---|---|---|
| | Coefficient | RRR | P>z | Coefficient | RRR | P>z | Coefficient | RRR | P>z |
| Log of household income per head | −0.53 | 0.59 | .000 | 0.18 | 1.20 | .098 | 1.00 | 2.73 | .000 |
| Income deciles (reference is decile 5) | | | | | | | | | |
| Decile 1 | 0.58 | 1.78 | .034 | 0.16 | 1.18 | .548 | −0.54 | 0.58 | .093 |
| Decile 2 | 0.50 | 1.65 | .064 | −0.14 | 0.87 | .620 | −0.33 | 0.72 | .266 |
| Decile 3 | 0.32 | 1.37 | .264 | 0.22 | 1.24 | .413 | −0.03 | 0.97 | .919 |
| Decile 4 | −0.23 | 0.80 | .465 | −0.04 | 0.96 | .892 | 0.13 | 1.14 | .639 |
| Decile 6 | −0.12 | 0.89 | .678 | −0.01 | 0.99 | .979 | −0.13 | 0.88 | .639 |
| Decile 7 | −0.02 | 0.98 | .938 | 0.51 | 1.66 | .056 | 0.62 | 1.86 | .020 |
| Decile 8 | −0.04 | 0.97 | .906 | 0.50 | 1.64 | .063 | 0.79 | 2.19 | .003 |
| Decile 9 | −0.45 | 0.64 | .139 | 0.34 | 1.41 | .200 | 1.10 | 3.02 | .000 |
| Decile 10 | −0.74 | 0.48 | .021 | 0.30 | 1.35 | .280 | 1.30 | 3.67 | .000 |
| Household pension income | −0.12 | 0.89 | .763 | 0.57 | 1.76 | .072 | 1.35 | 3.85 | .000 |
| Household benefit income | 1.21 | 3.37 | .037 | 0.65 | 1.92 | .271 | 0.50 | 1.64 | .427 |
| Others help on dacha | 0.86 | 2.36 | .000 | 0.60 | 1.83 | .004 | −0.11 | 0.89 | .632 |
| Network contacts per head | 0.16 | 1.17 | .098 | 0.14 | 1.15 | .103 | 0.03 | 1.03 | .741 |
| Proportion of friends in network | 0.34 | 1.41 | .057 | 0.88 | 2.41 | .000 | 0.58 | 1.79 | .000 |

# Table 4.10 (continued)

| | | | | | | | | | |
|---|---|---|---|---|---|---|---|---|---|
| Proportion of relatives in network | 0.88 | 2.42 | .000 | 1.18 | 3.24 | .000 | 0.84 | 2.31 | .000 |
| Household head | | | | | | | | | |
| Male | −0.29 | 0.75 | .069 | −0.20 | 0.82 | .163 | −0.29 | 0.74 | .038 |
| Age | −0.04 | 0.96 | .238 | −0.01 | 0.99 | .648 | 0.07 | 1.07 | .034 |
| Age squared/100 | −0.03 | 0.97 | .522 | −0.04 | 0.96 | .298 | −0.08 | 0.93 | .039 |
| Has higher education | 0.44 | 1.55 | .010 | 0.62 | 1.86 | .000 | 0.53 | 1.69 | .001 |
| Has technical education | 0.06 | 1.06 | .681 | 0.36 | 1.43 | .010 | 0.39 | 1.48 | .006 |
| Proportion of household members: | | | | | | | | | |
| Working | −0.37 | 0.69 | .063 | −0.18 | 0.83 | .335 | 0.10 | 1.11 | .567 |
| With secondary employment | 0.28 | 1.32 | .130 | 0.59 | 1.80 | .001 | 0.30 | 1.35 | .083 |
| Non-working pensioners | 0.15 | 1.17 | .573 | 0.37 | 1.44 | .137 | −0.22 | 0.80 | .338 |
| Owed wages | −0.08 | 0.92 | .712 | −0.12 | 0.89 | .550 | −0.35 | 0.70 | .070 |
| On administrative leave | 0.64 | 1.90 | .040 | 0.53 | 1.69 | .081 | 0.35 | 1.42 | .238 |
| Paid in kind | −0.04 | 0.96 | .881 | −0.10 | 0.90 | .698 | 0.34 | 1.40 | .197 |
| Number of adults in household | −0.31 | 0.73 | .002 | −0.07 | 0.93 | .432 | −0.03 | 0.97 | .716 |
| Number of children under 7 | −0.34 | 0.71 | .026 | 0.10 | 1.11 | .463 | −0.03 | 0.97 | .844 |
| Number of children 7–16 | −0.18 | 0.84 | .078 | 0.02 | 1.02 | .828 | 0.02 | 1.02 | .829 |
| Household: | | | | | | | | | |
| Includes adult children | −0.19 | 0.83 | .317 | −0.35 | 0.70 | .044 | −0.35 | 0.70 | .032 |
| Has sold property | 0.01 | 1.01 | .952 | 0.71 | 2.04 | .000 | 0.20 | 1.22 | .275 |

Table 4.10 (continued)

| | | | | | | | | | |
|---|---|---|---|---|---|---|---|---|---|
| Has a dacha | -0.24 | 0.78 | .097 | 0.43 | 1.53 | .002 | 0.50 | 1.65 | .000 |
| Has a car | 0.03 | 1.03 | .847 | 0.10 | 1.10 | .485 | 0.33 | 1.38 | .016 |
| Includes infirm member(s) | 0.65 | 1.92 | .018 | 0.58 | 1.78 | .021 | 0.05 | 1.05 | .844 |
| Has a non-household carer | 0.23 | 1.26 | .491 | 0.01 | 1.01 | .986 | 0.20 | 1.23 | .591 |
| Includes parent(s) of head | -1.28 | 0.28 | .000 | -1.29 | 0.27 | .000 | -0.49 | 0.61 | .030 |
| Single-parent household | -0.01 | 0.99 | .979 | 0.06 | 1.06 | .767 | -0.09 | 0.92 | .705 |
| Samara | -0.03 | 0.97 | .858 | 0.18 | 1.20 | .312 | -0.01 | 0.99 | .928 |
| Kemerovo | 0.38 | 1.47 | .066 | 0.76 | 2.15 | .000 | 0.13 | 1.14 | .504 |
| Syktyvkar | -0.35 | 0.71 | .100 | 0.37 | 1.45 | .062 | 0.11 | 1.11 | .572 |
| Constant | 2.14 | | .006 | -0.75 | | .315 | -3.44 | | .000 |

Notes: 20 percent of households were recipients, 22 percent of households were both donors and recipients and 25 percent of households were donors of some kind of help (money, food, goods, loans). The coefficient for the log of household income per head is from a separate regression. Household pension and benefit incomes are in thousands of roubles. RRR is the Relative Risk Ratio. All variables are dummies unless otherwise indicated.

Number of observations = 2 639. Model Chi Squared = 989.54. Prob > chi2 = .0000. Log likelihood = –3 129.78. Pseudo R2 = 0.1365

For variable means see Table 4.18

211

*Table 4.11: Logistic regression – probabilities of being a recipient, both recipient and donor and being a donor of money (ISITO household survey data).*

| | Recipient | | | Recipient and Donor | | | Donor | | |
|---|---|---|---|---|---|---|---|---|---|
| | Coefficient | RRR | P>z | Coefficient | RRR | P>z | Coefficient | RRR | P>z |
| Log of household income per head | -0.22 | 0.80 | .018 | 0.37 | 1.45 | .018 | 1.09 | 2.96 | .000 |
| Income deciles (reference is decile 5) | | | | | | | | | |
| Decile 1 | 0.29 | 1.34 | .269 | -0.47 | 0.62 | .248 | -0.41 | 0.67 | .211 |
| Decile 2 | 0.58 | 1.78 | .026 | -0.58 | 0.56 | .178 | -0.36 | 0.70 | .269 |
| Decile 3 | 0.36 | 1.43 | .178 | -0.18 | 0.83 | .633 | -0.07 | 0.93 | .807 |
| Decile 4 | 0.03 | 1.03 | .914 | -0.78 | 0.46 | .095 | 0.11 | 1.12 | .701 |
| Decile 6 | 0.01 | 1.01 | .976 | -0.44 | 0.64 | .263 | 0.17 | 1.19 | .539 |
| Decile 7 | 0.18 | 1.20 | .501 | -0.11 | 0.89 | .769 | 0.68 | 1.98 | .011 |
| Decile 8 | 0.00 | 1.00 | .997 | 0.05 | 1.06 | .881 | 0.87 | 2.39 | .001 |
| Decile 9 | -0.12 | 0.89 | .679 | 0.15 | 1.16 | .691 | 1.35 | 3.86 | .000 |
| Decile 10 | -0.29 | 0.75 | .324 | -0.04 | 0.96 | .909 | 1.39 | 4.02 | .000 |
| Household pension income | 0.30 | 1.35 | .377 | -0.94 | 0.39 | .124 | 0.90 | 2.45 | .000 |
| Household benefit income | 0.16 | 1.18 | .752 | 0.77 | 2.16 | .263 | -0.48 | 0.62 | .434 |
| Others help on dacha | 0.57 | 1.77 | .002 | 0.59 | 1.81 | .018 | 0.12 | 1.13 | .563 |
| Network contacts per head | 0.10 | 1.10 | .251 | 0.10 | 1.11 | .388 | 0.04 | 1.04 | .591 |
| Proportion of friends in network | 0.35 | 1.42 | .039 | 0.85 | 2.34 | .002 | 0.43 | 1.54 | .007 |

*Table 4.11 (continued)*

| | | | | | | | | | |
|---|---|---|---|---|---|---|---|---|---|
| Proportion of relatives in network | 0.99 | 2.68 | .000 | 1.17 | 3.22 | .000 | 0.70 | 2.02 | .000 |
| Household head | | | | | | | | | |
| Male | -0.29 | 0.75 | .054 | -0.12 | 0.89 | .570 | -0.27 | 0.76 | .041 |
| Age | -0.05 | 0.95 | .085 | -0.11 | 0.89 | .006 | 0.11 | 1.12 | .001 |
| Age squared/100 | -0.01 | 0.99 | .869 | 0.09 | 1.10 | .076 | -0.11 | 0.89 | .006 |
| Has higher education | 0.54 | 1.72 | .001 | 0.59 | 1.80 | .016 | 0.33 | 1.39 | .033 |
| Has technical education | 0.08 | 1.08 | .563 | 0.32 | 1.37 | .154 | 0.24 | 1.27 | .086 |
| Proportion of household members: | | | | | | | | | |
| Working | -0.45 | 0.64 | .017 | -0.08 | 0.93 | .782 | 0.16 | 1.17 | .371 |
| With secondary employment | 0.12 | 1.13 | .465 | 0.73 | 2.07 | .003 | 0.22 | 1.25 | .170 |
| Non-working pensioners | 0.08 | 1.08 | .774 | 0.54 | 1.72 | .213 | -0.14 | 0.87 | .554 |
| Owed wages | 0.12 | 1.13 | .539 | -0.44 | 0.64 | .146 | -0.33 | 0.72 | .067 |
| On administrative leave | 0.15 | 1.17 | .600 | 1.12 | 3.07 | .005 | 0.19 | 1.20 | .500 |
| Paid in kind | -0.39 | 0.67 | .134 | -0.72 | 0.49 | .073 | -0.01 | 0.99 | .955 |
| Number of adults in household | -0.34 | 0.71 | .000 | -0.02 | 0.98 | .899 | -0.09 | 0.91 | .313 |
| Number of children under 7 | 0.11 | 1.12 | .385 | 0.06 | 1.06 | .753 | 0.30 | 1.35 | .040 |
| Number of children 7–16 | -0.05 | 0.95 | .575 | -0.45 | 0.64 | .004 | 0.03 | 1.03 | .774 |
| Household: | | | | | | | | | |
| Includes adult children | -0.01 | 0.99 | .951 | -0.79 | 0.45 | .010 | -0.67 | 0.51 | .000 |
| Has sold property | -0.09 | 0.92 | .599 | 0.69 | 1.99 | .001 | -0.06 | 0.94 | .699 |

Table 4.11 (continued)

| | | | | | | | | | |
|---|---|---|---|---|---|---|---|---|---|
| Has a dacha | -0.03 | 0.97 | .839 | 0.28 | 1.32 | .187 | -0.15 | 0.86 | .269 |
| Has a car | 0.09 | 1.09 | .532 | -0.08 | 0.92 | .694 | 0.25 | 1.29 | .047 |
| Includes infirm member(s) | 0.13 | 1.14 | .620 | 0.43 | 1.53 | .278 | -0.23 | 0.80 | .355 |
| Has a non-household carer | -0.20 | 0.82 | .508 | 0.32 | 1.38 | .447 | 0.12 | 1.12 | .734 |
| Includes parent(s) of head | -0.95 | 0.38 | .000 | -0.72 | 0.49 | .079 | 0.07 | 1.08 | .739 |
| Single-parent household | 0.09 | 1.09 | .632 | -0.06 | 0.94 | .840 | -0.38 | 0.68 | .090 |
| Samara | 0.10 | 1.10 | .579 | -0.28 | 0.76 | .310 | -0.06 | 0.94 | .729 |
| Kemerovo | 0.35 | 1.42 | .073 | 0.51 | 1.67 | .077 | 0.40 | 1.49 | .033 |
| Syktyvkar | -0.04 | 0.96 | .843 | 0.35 | 1.42 | .225 | 0.40 | 1.50 | .027 |
| Constant | 1.38 | | .053 | -0.25 | | .797 | -4.82 | | .000 |

Notes: 18 percent of households were recipients, 6 percent of households were both donors and recipients and 20 percent of households were donors of money. The coefficient for the log of household income per head is from a separate regression. Household pension and benefit incomes are in thousands of roubles. RRR is the Relative Risk Ratio. All variables are dummies unless otherwise indicated.

Number of observations = 2639. Model Chi Squared = 794.39. Prob > chi2 = .0000. Log likelihood = –2 633.08. Pseudo R2 = 0.1311

For variable means see Table 4.18

*Table 4.12: Logistic regression – probabilities of being a recipient, both recipient and donor and being a donor of food (ISITO household survey data).*

| | Recipient | | | Recipient and Donor | | | Donor | | |
|---|---|---|---|---|---|---|---|---|---|
| | Coefficient | RRR | P>z | Coefficient | RRR | P>z | Coefficient | RRR | P>z |
| Log of household income per head | -0.39 | 0.67 | .000 | 0.00 | 1.00 | .994 | 0.61 | 1.85 | .000 |
| Income deciles (reference is decile 5) | | | | | | | | | |
| Decile 1 | 0.45 | 1.57 | .085 | 0.01 | 1.01 | .980 | -0.44 | 0.65 | .144 |
| Decile 2 | 0.38 | 1.46 | .153 | -0.05 | 0.95 | .876 | -0.37 | 0.69 | .196 |
| Decile 3 | 0.19 | 1.21 | .493 | 0.22 | 1.24 | .509 | 0.15 | 1.16 | .575 |
| Decile 4 | -0.13 | 0.88 | .665 | -0.06 | 0.94 | .865 | 0.21 | 1.23 | .453 |
| Decile 6 | -0.39 | 0.68 | .170 | -0.12 | 0.88 | .713 | -0.19 | 0.83 | .470 |
| Decile 7 | 0.24 | 1.27 | .375 | 0.12 | 1.13 | .716 | 0.36 | 1.43 | .165 |
| Decile 8 | -0.04 | 0.96 | .871 | 0.16 | 1.17 | .628 | 0.50 | 1.64 | .048 |
| Decile 9 | -0.16 | 0.85 | .563 | -0.20 | 0.82 | .571 | 0.75 | 2.11 | .002 |
| Decile 10 | -0.81 | 0.45 | .006 | 0.13 | 1.14 | .706 | 0.72 | 2.06 | .004 |
| Household pension income | -0.23 | 0.79 | .546 | 0.75 | 2.11 | .047 | 0.90 | 2.47 | .000 |
| Household benefit income | 1.08 | 2.95 | .039 | 0.35 | 1.41 | .608 | 0.52 | 1.69 | .336 |
| Others help on dacha | 1.00 | 2.72 | .000 | 0.61 | 1.83 | .006 | -0.11 | 0.89 | .573 |
| Network contacts per head | 0.00 | 1.00 | .970 | 0.18 | 1.19 | .088 | -0.04 | 0.96 | .568 |
| Proportion of friends in network | 0.36 | 1.44 | .033 | 0.40 | 1.49 | .073 | 0.46 | 1.58 | .003 |

Table 4.12 (continued)

| | 0.83 | 2.30 | .000 | 0.71 | 2.04 | .004 | 0.58 | 1.79 | .002 |
|---|---|---|---|---|---|---|---|---|---|
| Proportion of relatives in network | 0.83 | 2.30 | .000 | 0.71 | 2.04 | .004 | 0.58 | 1.79 | .002 |
| Household head: | | | | | | | | | |
| Male | -0.26 | 0.77 | .083 | -0.35 | 0.70 | .057 | -0.22 | 0.81 | .113 |
| Age | -0.08 | 0.92 | .010 | -0.02 | 0.98 | .566 | 0.08 | 1.08 | .015 |
| Age squared/100 | 0.02 | 1.02 | .593 | -0.03 | 0.97 | .562 | -0.08 | 0.92 | .033 |
| Has higher education | 0.39 | 1.47 | .015 | 0.18 | 1.20 | .390 | 0.30 | 1.34 | .051 |
| Has technical education | 0.07 | 1.07 | .640 | 0.34 | 1.40 | .055 | 0.22 | 1.25 | .109 |
| Proportion of household members: | | | | | | | | | |
| Working | -0.39 | 0.67 | .034 | -0.61 | 0.54 | .013 | -0.25 | 0.78 | .147 |
| With secondary employment | 0.41 | 1.51 | .012 | 0.25 | 1.28 | .262 | 0.41 | 1.51 | .011 |
| Non-working pensioners | 0.38 | 1.46 | .147 | 0.11 | 1.11 | .753 | -0.19 | 0.82 | .382 |
| Owed wages | -0.08 | 0.92 | .671 | 0.05 | 1.05 | .850 | -0.05 | 0.95 | .770 |
| On administrative leave | 0.40 | 1.49 | .166 | 0.43 | 1.53 | .249 | 0.32 | 1.37 | .243 |
| Paid in kind | -0.12 | 0.89 | .650 | -0.11 | 0.90 | .738 | 0.28 | 1.32 | .244 |
| Number of adults in household | -0.32 | 0.72 | .001 | -0.02 | 0.98 | .842 | -0.05 | 0.95 | .578 |
| Number of children under 7 | -0.27 | 0.76 | .045 | 0.00 | 1.00 | .993 | -0.17 | 0.85 | .272 |
| Number of children 7–16 | -0.14 | 0.87 | .129 | -0.10 | 0.91 | .407 | -0.16 | 0.85 | .079 |
| Household: | | | | | | | | | |
| Includes adult children | -0.10 | 0.90 | .596 | -0.25 | 0.78 | .280 | -0.30 | 0.74 | .058 |
| Has sold property | 0.06 | 1.06 | .719 | 0.82 | 2.27 | .000 | 0.34 | 1.40 | .036 |

Table 4.12 (continued)

| | | | | | | | | | |
|---|---|---|---|---|---|---|---|---|---|
| Has a dacha | -0.28 | 0.75 | .046 | 0.61 | 1.84 | .001 | 1.17 | 3.22 | .000 |
| Has a car | 0.08 | 1.08 | .584 | 0.18 | 1.20 | .277 | 0.48 | 1.61 | .000 |
| Includes infirm member(s) | 0.66 | 1.94 | .013 | 0.23 | 1.25 | .495 | 0.00 | 1.00 | .987 |
| Has a non-household carer | -0.17 | 0.84 | .563 | 0.02 | 1.02 | .961 | -0.10 | 0.91 | .791 |
| Includes parent(s) of head | -1.84 | 0.16 | .000 | -1.00 | 0.37 | .001 | -0.55 | 0.57 | .015 |
| Single-parent household | 0.07 | 1.08 | .693 | -0.38 | 0.68 | .162 | 0.07 | 1.07 | .750 |
| Samara | -0.07 | 0.93 | .692 | 0.25 | 1.28 | .345 | -0.24 | 0.79 | .152 |
| Kemerovo | 0.14 | 1.15 | .478 | 0.81 | 2.24 | .003 | -0.13 | 0.88 | .489 |
| Syktyvkar | -0.20 | 0.82 | .294 | 0.49 | 1.63 | .075 | -0.14 | 0.87 | .437 |
| Constant | 2.44 | | .001 | -1.35 | | .138 | -3.97 | | .000 |

Notes: 20 percent of households were recipients, 8 percent of households were both donors and recipients and 21 percent of households were donors of some kind of help (money, food, goods, loans). The coefficient for the log of household income per head is from a separate regression. Household pension and benefit incomes are in thousands of roubles. RRR is the Relative Risk Ratio. All variables are dummies unless otherwise indicated.

Number of observations = 2 639. Model Chi Squared = 881.66. Prob > chi2 = .0000. Log likelihood = –2 799.19. Pseudo R2 = 0.1361

For variable means see Table 4.18

Table 4.13: Logistic regression – probabilities of being a recipient, both recipient and donor and being a donor of goods (ISITO household survey data).

| | Recipient | | | Recipient and Donor | | | Donor | | |
|---|---|---|---|---|---|---|---|---|---|
| | Coefficient | RRR | P>z | Coefficient | RRR | P>z | Coefficient | RRR | P>z |
| Log of household income per head | -0.46 | 0.63 | .000 | 0.30 | 1.35 | .117 | 0.69 | 1.99 | .000 |
| Income deciles (reference is decile 5) | | | | | | | | | |
| Decile 1 | 0.16 | 1.17 | .568 | 0.33 | 1.38 | .532 | -0.43 | 0.65 | .150 |
| Decile 2 | 0.14 | 1.14 | .631 | 0.04 | 1.04 | .947 | -0.43 | 0.65 | .142 |
| Decile 3 | -0.05 | 0.95 | .850 | 0.38 | 1.46 | .456 | -0.17 | 0.84 | .540 |
| Decile 4 | -1.02 | 0.36 | .006 | 0.28 | 1.32 | .607 | 0.03 | 1.03 | .906 |
| Decile 6 | -0.14 | 0.87 | .637 | 0.49 | 1.63 | .358 | -0.08 | 0.93 | .776 |
| Decile 7 | -0.11 | 0.89 | .705 | 1.03 | 2.80 | .036 | 0.43 | 1.54 | .092 |
| Decile 8 | -0.63 | 0.53 | .044 | 0.98 | 2.67 | .045 | 0.49 | 1.63 | .054 |
| Decile 9 | -0.98 | 0.38 | .003 | 0.20 | 1.22 | .719 | 0.64 | 1.89 | .010 |
| Decile 10 | -1.05 | 0.35 | .001 | 0.71 | 2.03 | .185 | 0.93 | 2.54 | .000 |
| Household pension income | 0.04 | 1.04 | .919 | 0.24 | 1.28 | .657 | 0.50 | 1.66 | .040 |
| Household benefit income | 0.53 | 1.69 | .369 | 0.80 | 2.23 | .288 | 0.17 | 1.18 | .749 |
| Others help on dacha | 0.20 | 1.22 | .343 | 0.50 | 1.65 | .092 | -0.17 | 0.84 | .397 |
| Network contacts per head | 0.16 | 1.17 | .106 | 0.29 | 1.33 | .028 | 0.10 | 1.10 | .200 |
| Proportion of friends in network | 0.23 | 1.25 | .260 | 0.33 | 1.39 | .299 | 0.54 | 1.71 | .001 |

*Table 4.13 (continued)*

| | | | | | | | | | |
|---|---|---|---|---|---|---|---|---|---|
| Proportion of relatives in network | 0.63 | 1.89 | .003 | 0.69 | 2.00 | .042 | 0.54 | 1.72 | .005 |
| Household head | | | | | | | | | |
| Male | -0.34 | 0.71 | .052 | -0.36 | 0.70 | .167 | -0.44 | 0.64 | .002 |
| Age | -0.06 | 0.94 | .061 | -0.05 | 0.95 | .250 | 0.08 | 1.09 | .012 |
| Age squared/100 | 0.02 | 1.02 | .563 | 0.05 | 1.05 | .382 | -0.08 | 0.92 | .038 |
| Has higher education | 0.55 | 1.73 | .003 | 0.59 | 1.80 | .049 | 0.66 | 1.94 | .000 |
| Has technical education | 0.15 | 1.16 | .361 | 0.42 | 1.53 | .113 | 0.32 | 1.38 | .025 |
| Proportion of household members: | | | | | | | | | |
| Working | -0.37 | 0.69 | .072 | -0.30 | 0.74 | .371 | -0.33 | 0.72 | .062 |
| With secondary employment | 0.48 | 1.62 | .007 | -0.02 | 0.98 | .951 | 0.38 | 1.47 | .019 |
| Non-working pensioners | 0.09 | 1.09 | .774 | 0.70 | 2.02 | .094 | -0.18 | 0.84 | .475 |
| Owed wages | -0.08 | 0.92 | .711 | -0.56 | 0.57 | .115 | -0.12 | 0.88 | .513 |
| On administrative leave | 0.02 | 1.03 | .940 | 0.35 | 1.41 | .505 | 0.31 | 1.36 | .259 |
| Paid in kind | 0.18 | 1.19 | .538 | 0.04 | 1.04 | .935 | 0.23 | 1.25 | .339 |
| Number of adults in household | -0.47 | 0.63 | .000 | 0.00 | 1.00 | .989 | 0.08 | 1.09 | .320 |
| Number of children under 7 | 0.16 | 1.18 | .263 | 0.28 | 1.33 | .215 | 0.13 | 1.14 | .364 |
| Number of children 7–16 | -0.06 | 0.94 | .594 | 0.23 | 1.26 | .131 | 0.04 | 1.04 | .685 |
| Household: | | | | | | | | | |
| Includes adult children | -0.39 | 0.68 | .097 | -1.04 | 0.35 | .007 | -0.10 | 0.91 | .535 |
| Has sold property | 0.16 | 1.17 | .397 | 0.86 | 2.36 | .001 | 0.69 | 2.00 | .000 |

219

*Table 4.13 (continued)*

| | | | | | | | | | |
|---|---|---|---|---|---|---|---|---|---|
| Has a dacha | 0.10 | 1.10 | .541 | 0.23 | 1.26 | .360 | 0.14 | 1.15 | .286 |
| Has a car | 0.03 | 1.03 | .877 | 0.03 | 1.03 | .903 | 0.14 | 1.15 | .265 |
| Includes infirm member(s) | 0.18 | 1.20 | .566 | 0.14 | 1.16 | .747 | 0.08 | 1.08 | .742 |
| Has a non-household carer | 0.18 | 1.20 | .565 | 0.14 | 1.15 | .776 | -0.10 | 0.91 | .793 |
| Includes parent(s) of head | -0.78 | 0.46 | .013 | -0.47 | 0.63 | .300 | -0.05 | 0.95 | .824 |
| Single-parent household | 0.16 | 1.18 | .446 | 0.51 | 1.67 | .109 | -0.04 | 0.96 | .849 |
| Samara | -0.46 | 0.63 | .023 | 0.20 | 1.23 | .631 | -0.31 | 0.73 | .057 |
| Kemerovo | 0.00 | 1.00 | 1.000 | 1.21 | 3.34 | .005 | 0.10 | 1.10 | .602 |
| Syktyvkar | -0.32 | 0.73 | .151 | 1.19 | 3.27 | .005 | 0.14 | 1.15 | .442 |
| Constant | 1.31 | | .080 | -3.76 | | .002 | -4.56 | | .000 |

*Notes: 12 percent of households were recipients, 4 percent of households were both donors and recipients and 16 percent of households were donors of goods. The coefficient for the log of household income per head is from a separate regression. Household pension and benefit incomes are in thousands of roubles. RRR is the Relative Risk Ratio. All variables are dummies unless otherwise indicated.*

*Number of observations = 2 639. Model Chi Squared = 582.93. Prob. > chi2 = .0000. Log likelihood = –2 291.03. Pseudo R2 = 0.1129.*

*For variable means see Table 4.18*

Table 4.14: Logistic regression – probabilities of being a recipient, both recipient and donor and being a donor of loans (ISITO household survey data).

| | Recipient | | | Recipient and Donor | | | Donor | | |
|---|---|---|---|---|---|---|---|---|---|
| | Coefficient | RRR | P>z | Coefficient | RRR | P>z | Coefficient | RRR | P>z |
| Log of household income per head | -0.39 | 0.68 | .000 | 0.44 | 1.55 | .012 | 0.55 | 1.73 | .000 |
| Income deciles (reference is decile 5) | | | | | | | | | |
| Decile 1 | 0.59 | 1.80 | .056 | -0.25 | 0.78 | .609 | -0.91 | 0.40 | .024 |
| Decile 2 | 0.36 | 1.43 | .257 | -0.06 | 0.95 | .907 | -1.15 | 0.32 | .006 |
| Decile 3 | 0.52 | 1.68 | .094 | -0.27 | 0.76 | .591 | -0.59 | 0.55 | .101 |
| Decile 4 | 0.02 | 1.02 | .959 | -0.10 | 0.90 | .837 | -0.58 | 0.56 | .123 |
| Decile 6 | 0.00 | 1.00 | .991 | 0.22 | 1.25 | .631 | -0.29 | 0.75 | .392 |
| Decile 7 | 0.18 | 1.20 | .575 | 0.29 | 1.34 | .515 | 0.04 | 1.04 | .905 |
| Decile 8 | 0.08 | 1.08 | .815 | 0.80 | 2.23 | .056 | -0.20 | 0.82 | .542 |
| Decile 9 | -0.49 | 0.61 | .154 | 0.04 | 1.05 | .924 | 0.00 | 1.00 | .999 |
| Decile 10 | -0.21 | 0.81 | .543 | 0.51 | 1.66 | .257 | 0.33 | 1.39 | .294 |
| Household pension income | -0.61 | 0.54 | .147 | -0.51 | 0.60 | .417 | 1.20 | 3.32 | .000 |
| Household benefit income | 0.37 | 1.45 | .525 | 0.11 | 1.11 | .915 | 0.95 | 2.58 | .083 |
| Others help on dacha | 0.16 | 1.17 | .446 | -0.20 | 0.82 | .529 | 0.06 | 1.06 | .809 |
| Network contacts per head | 0.11 | 1.12 | .279 | 0.53 | 1.69 | .000 | 0.10 | 1.11 | .351 |
| Proportion of friends in network | 0.57 | 1.78 | .006 | 0.30 | 1.34 | .339 | 0.42 | 1.53 | .063 |

Table 4.14 (continued)

| | | | | | | | | | |
|---|---|---|---|---|---|---|---|---|---|
| Proportion of relatives in network | 0.55 | 1.73 | .018 | 0.15 | 1.16 | .667 | 0.22 | 1.24 | .417 |
| Household head | | | | | | | | | |
| Male | -0.09 | 0.91 | .584 | -0.14 | 0.87 | .570 | 0.12 | 1.13 | .502 |
| Age | 0.05 | 1.05 | .254 | 0.06 | 1.06 | .307 | 0.07 | 1.07 | .142 |
| Age squared/100 | -0.10 | 0.90 | .066 | -0.14 | 0.87 | .076 | -0.09 | 0.92 | .113 |
| Has higher education | 0.10 | 1.11 | .572 | -0.22 | 0.80 | .407 | 0.32 | 1.38 | .137 |
| Has technical education | -0.26 | 0.77 | .098 | -0.04 | 0.97 | .878 | 0.36 | 1.43 | .068 |
| Proportion of household members: | | | | | | | | | |
| Working | -0.07 | 0.93 | .761 | -0.02 | 0.98 | .963 | -0.14 | 0.87 | .548 |
| With secondary employment | 0.68 | 1.97 | .000 | 0.20 | 1.23 | .459 | 0.49 | 1.64 | .023 |
| Non-working pensioners | 0.09 | 1.09 | .822 | 1.48 | 4.39 | .001 | -0.60 | 0.55 | .107 |
| Owed wages | 0.21 | 1.24 | .339 | 0.37 | 1.45 | .220 | -0.48 | 0.62 | .070 |
| On administrative leave | 0.37 | 1.45 | .238 | 0.68 | 1.97 | .110 | 0.20 | 1.23 | .595 |
| Paid in kind | -0.39 | 0.68 | .180 | -0.43 | 0.65 | .270 | -0.33 | 0.72 | .356 |
| Number of adults in household | 0.03 | 1.03 | .756 | 0.14 | 1.15 | .424 | 0.01 | 1.01 | .961 |
| Number of children under 7 | -0.13 | 0.88 | .402 | 0.14 | 1.15 | .521 | 0.22 | 1.24 | .226 |
| Number of children 7–16 | -0.02 | 0.98 | .850 | 0.04 | 1.04 | .823 | 0.11 | 1.12 | .361 |
| Household: | | | | | | | | | |
| Includes adult children | 0.07 | 1.08 | .714 | -0.55 | 0.58 | .127 | -0.11 | 0.89 | .621 |
| Has sold property | 0.28 | 1.32 | .111 | 0.65 | 1.92 | .006 | 0.00 | 1.00 | .996 |

222

*Table 4.14 (continued)*

| | | | | | | | | | |
|---|---|---|---|---|---|---|---|---|---|
| Has a dacha | 0.22 | 1.24 | .175 | 0.23 | 1.26 | .305 | 0.41 | 1.51 | .022 |
| Has a car | -0.14 | 0.87 | .396 | 0.04 | 1.04 | .844 | -0.11 | 0.90 | .533 |
| Includes infirm member(s) | 0.06 | 1.06 | .869 | 0.56 | 1.75 | .194 | 0.10 | 1.10 | .768 |
| Has a non-household carer | -0.11 | 0.89 | .761 | -0.01 | 0.99 | .987 | -0.48 | 0.62 | .375 |
| Includes parent(s) of head | -0.51 | 0.60 | .097 | -1.43 | 0.24 | .003 | -0.50 | 0.60 | .125 |
| Single-parent household | -0.01 | 0.99 | .977 | 0.37 | 1.45 | .257 | -0.03 | 0.98 | .929 |
| Samara | -0.13 | 0.87 | .527 | 0.40 | 1.49 | .254 | 0.63 | 1.88 | .015 |
| Kemerovo | 0.60 | 1.83 | .007 | 0.71 | 2.04 | .055 | 0.72 | 2.05 | .012 |
| Syktyvkar | -0.10 | 0.90 | .659 | 0.66 | 1.93 | .071 | 1.00 | 2.73 | .000 |
| Constant | -3.09 | | .001 | -4.71 | | .000 | -4.72 | | .000 |

*Notes: 9 percent of households were recipients, 4 percent of households were both donors and recipients and 7 percent of households were donors of loans. The coefficient for the log of household income per head is from a separate regression. Household pension and benefit incomes are in thousands of roubles. RRR is the Relative Risk Ratio. All variables are dummies unless otherwise indicated.*

*Number of observations = 2 639. Model Chi Squared = 384.39. Prob. > chi2 = .0000. Log likelihood = -1 959.17. Pseudo R2 = 0.0893.*

*For variable means see Table 4.18*

Table 4.15: Logistic regression – probabilities of being a recipient, both recipient and donor and being a donor of help (RLMS data, 1994–2000).

| | Recipient | | | Recipient and Donor | | | Donor | | |
|---|---|---|---|---|---|---|---|---|---|
| | Coefficient | RRR | P>z | Coefficient | RRR | P>z | Coefficient | RRR | P>z |
| Number of adults | -0.48 | 0.62 | .000 | -0.50 | 0.61 | .000 | -0.09 | 0.92 | .010 |
| Number of children under 7 | 0.24 | 1.27 | .000 | 0.10 | 1.10 | .257 | -0.09 | 0.92 | .181 |
| Number of children 7–17 | -0.05 | 0.96 | .242 | -0.10 | 0.91 | .081 | -0.16 | 0.85 | .000 |
| Male-headed household | -0.16 | 0.85 | .017 | -0.52 | 0.59 | .000 | -0.25 | 0.78 | .000 |
| Single-parent household | 0.07 | 1.07 | .550 | -0.22 | 0.80 | .179 | -0.32 | 0.73 | .020 |
| Urban household | -0.18 | 0.83 | .163 | -0.21 | 0.81 | .265 | -0.08 | 0.92 | .627 |
| Proportion of adults: | | | | | | | | | |
| Under 25 | -0.08 | 0.92 | .773 | -0.50 | 0.60 | .192 | -0.38 | 0.69 | .273 |
| 25–39 | -1.10 | 0.33 | .000 | -1.24 | 0.29 | .001 | 0.03 | 1.03 | .936 |
| 40 – pension age | -1.94 | 0.14 | .000 | -1.68 | 0.19 | .000 | 0.81 | 2.24 | .015 |
| Of pension age | -2.28 | 0.10 | .000 | -2.18 | 0.11 | .000 | 0.79 | 2.19 | .021 |
| With higher education | 0.44 | 1.55 | .000 | 0.72 | 2.06 | .000 | 0.27 | 1.31 | .001 |
| Born in the countryside | 0.03 | 1.03 | .716 | 0.32 | 1.37 | .003 | 0.05 | 1.05 | .476 |
| Who are disabled | -0.09 | 0.92 | .695 | 0.12 | 1.13 | .740 | -0.04 | 0.96 | .871 |
| On paid leave | 0.00 | 1.00 | .994 | 0.57 | 1.76 | .219 | 0.47 | 1.59 | .226 |
| On leave without pay | -0.63 | 0.53 | .165 | -0.50 | 0.61 | .391 | 0.10 | 1.10 | .838 |

*Table 4.15 (continued)*

| | | | | | | | | | |
|---|---|---|---|---|---|---|---|---|---|
| On maternity leave or housewife | −0.06 | 0.95 | .733 | 0.35 | 1.42 | .192 | 0.54 | 1.72 | .007 |
| Currently working | −0.41 | 0.66 | .000 | −0.03 | 0.97 | .835 | 0.51 | 1.66 | .000 |
| With second jobs | 0.28 | 1.32 | .144 | 0.61 | 1.83 | .005 | 0.36 | 1.43 | .047 |
| With IEA | 0.21 | 1.24 | .063 | 0.93 | 2.53 | .000 | 0.48 | 1.62 | .000 |
| In self-employment | −0.59 | 0.55 | .002 | −0.35 | 0.70 | .204 | −0.25 | 0.78 | .186 |
| Owed unpaid wages | 0.11 | 1.11 | .091 | 0.05 | 1.06 | .562 | 0.04 | 1.04 | .527 |
| Paid in kind | 0.20 | 1.22 | .144 | 0.11 | 1.11 | .579 | 0.24 | 1.27 | .061 |
| Sent on administrative leave | 0.14 | 1.15 | .249 | 0.65 | 1.91 | .000 | 0.27 | 1.30 | .024 |
| Urban household has a dacha | −0.73 | 0.48 | .000 | −0.39 | 0.68 | .038 | 0.24 | 1.27 | .146 |
| Rural household has a dacha | −0.19 | 0.83 | .003 | 0.09 | 1.10 | .304 | 0.29 | 1.33 | .000 |
| Household owns a car | −0.10 | 0.90 | .131 | 0.05 | 1.05 | .588 | 0.29 | 1.33 | .000 |
| No money income last month | 0.10 | 1.11 | .320 | −0.60 | 0.55 | .001 | −0.18 | 0.83 | .120 |
| Income deciles (reference is decile 5) | | | | | | | | | |
| Decile 1 | 0.18 | 1.20 | .125 | −0.35 | 0.70 | .063 | −0.27 | 0.76 | .066 |
| Decile 2 | 0.22 | 1.24 | .027 | −0.29 | 0.75 | .057 | −0.33 | 0.72 | .003 |
| Decile 3 | 0.02 | 1.03 | .798 | −0.06 | 0.94 | .659 | −0.07 | 0.93 | .487 |
| Decile 4 | 0.11 | 1.12 | .229 | −0.25 | 0.78 | .084 | −0.03 | 0.97 | .759 |
| Decile 6 | −0.01 | 0.99 | .913 | −0.09 | 0.91 | .514 | 0.26 | 1.29 | .004 |
| Decile 7 | −0.16 | 0.85 | .101 | 0.10 | 1.11 | .479 | 0.33 | 1.40 | .000 |
| Decile 8 | −0.30 | 0.74 | .006 | −0.08 | 0.92 | .579 | 0.41 | 1.51 | .000 |

Table 4.15 (continued)

| | | | | | | | | | |
|---|---|---|---|---|---|---|---|---|---|
| Decile 9 | -0.37 | 0.69 | .001 | 0.18 | 1.20 | .190 | 0.60 | 1.82 | .000 |
| Decile 10 | -0.57 | 0.56 | .000 | 0.25 | 1.28 | .085 | 0.89 | 2.44 | .000 |
| Log of household money income per head | -0.18 | 0.83 | .000 | 0.16 | 1.17 | .001 | 0.40 | 1.50 | .000 |
| Household non-pension income benefit | 0.08 | 1.08 | .072 | 0.11 | 1.12 | .041 | -0.01 | 0.99 | .858 |
| Household pension income | -0.10 | 0.91 | .007 | -0.06 | 0.94 | .202 | 0.02 | 1.02 | .337 |
| Round (reference is Round 5 1994) | | | | | | | | | |
| 1995 | 0.04 | 1.04 | .535 | -0.51 | 0.60 | .000 | -0.36 | 0.70 | .000 |
| 1996 | 0.23 | 1.26 | .001 | -0.24 | 0.79 | .012 | -0.38 | 0.69 | .000 |
| 1998 | 0.28 | 1.32 | .000 | -0.11 | 0.90 | .258 | -0.27 | 0.77 | .000 |
| 2000 | 0.52 | 1.69 | .000 | 0.07 | 1.07 | .459 | -0.12 | 0.89 | .067 |
| Constant | 1.61 | | | 0.87 | | | -1.84 | | |

Notes: 16 percent of households were recipients, 6 percent of households were both donors and recipients and 19 percent of households were donors of help. The coefficient for the log of household income per head is from a separate regression. Household pension and benefit incomes are in thousands of roubles. RRR is the Relative Risk Ratio. All variables are dummies unless otherwise indicated. Standard errors are corrected for panels. The regression also included seven regional dummies.

Number of observations =18 170. Model Chi Squared = 2 548.9. Prob. > chi2 = .0000. Log likelihood = −18 208.5. Pseudo R2 = 0.0888.

For variable means see Table 4.17.

*Table 4.16: Logistic Regression. Probabilities of household being a lender, lender and borrower or borrower. RLMS data, 1994–2000*

| | Lend | | | Lend and borrow | | | Borrow | | |
|---|---|---|---|---|---|---|---|---|---|
| | Coefficient | RRR | P>z | Coefficient | RRR | P>z | Coefficient | RRR | P>z |
| Number of adults | -0.14 | 0.87 | .000 | -0.15 | 0.86 | .069 | 0.03 | 1.03 | .366 |
| Number of children under 7 | 0.14 | 1.14 | .027 | 0.39 | 1.48 | .000 | 0.15 | 1.17 | .002 |
| Number of children 7–17 | 0.03 | 1.03 | .422 | 0.17 | 1.19 | .028 | 0.14 | 1.15 | .000 |
| Male-headed household | 0.03 | 1.03 | .640 | 0.13 | 1.14 | .371 | -0.24 | 0.79 | .000 |
| Single-parent household | 0.24 | 1.27 | .060 | -0.01 | 0.99 | .957 | 0.14 | 1.15 | .194 |
| Urban household | 0.29 | 1.33 | .068 | 0.35 | 1.42 | .246 | -0.01 | 0.99 | .910 |
| Proportion of adults: | | | | | | | | | |
| Under 25 | -0.33 | 0.72 | .313 | -1.25 | 0.29 | .010 | -0.20 | 0.82 | .467 |
| 25–39 | -0.63 | 0.53 | .052 | -1.83 | 0.16 | .000 | -0.16 | 0.85 | .540 |
| 40 – pension age | -1.07 | 0.34 | .001 | -2.42 | 0.09 | .000 | -0.13 | 0.88 | .641 |
| Of pension age | -1.11 | 0.33 | .001 | -3.19 | 0.04 | .000 | -0.62 | 0.54 | .027 |
| With higher education | 0.01 | 1.01 | .879 | -0.35 | 0.71 | .066 | -0.11 | 0.89 | .213 |
| Born in the countryside | 0.05 | 1.05 | .557 | 0.01 | 1.01 | .933 | 0.07 | 1.07 | .296 |
| Who are disabled | 0.06 | 1.06 | .842 | 1.21 | 3.37 | .012 | 0.82 | 2.28 | .000 |

*Table 4.16 (continued)*

|  | | | | | | | | | |
|---|---|---|---|---|---|---|---|---|---|
| On paid leave | 0.78 | 2.18 | .035 | 1.79 | 5.98 | .004 | 0.11 | 1.11 | .765 |
| On leave without pay | −0.42 | 0.65 | .420 | −0.66 | 0.52 | .591 | −0.18 | 0.83 | .667 |
| On maternity leave or housewife | 0.14 | 1.15 | .472 | −1.05 | 0.35 | .014 | −0.62 | 0.54 | .001 |
| Currently working | 0.24 | 1.27 | .022 | 0.26 | 1.29 | .263 | 0.02 | 1.02 | .842 |
| With second jobs | 0.80 | 2.22 | .000 | 0.90 | 2.46 | .003 | 0.76 | 2.14 | .000 |
| With IEA | 0.36 | 1.44 | .004 | 1.08 | 2.95 | .000 | 0.61 | 1.83 | .000 |
| In self-employment | 0.00 | 1.00 | .986 | 0.74 | 2.10 | .034 | 0.00 | 1.00 | .986 |
| Owed unpaid wages | 0.19 | 1.21 | .007 | 0.34 | 1.41 | .017 | 0.28 | 1.33 | .000 |
| Paid in kind | 0.18 | 1.20 | .228 | 0.19 | 1.21 | .470 | −0.32 | 0.72 | .012 |
| Sent on administrative leave | 0.02 | 1.02 | .876 | 0.56 | 1.75 | .029 | 0.34 | 1.40 | .001 |
| Urban household has a dacha | 0.23 | 1.26 | .146 | 0.16 | 1.17 | .621 | −0.11 | 0.90 | .399 |
| Rural household has a dacha | 0.06 | 1.06 | .383 | −0.04 | 0.96 | .768 | 0.11 | 1.11 | .076 |
| Household owns a car | 0.04 | 1.05 | .497 | −0.07 | 0.94 | .609 | −0.09 | 0.91 | .138 |
| No money income last month | −0.25 | 0.78 | .072 | −0.24 | 0.79 | .403 | 0.58 | 1.78 | .000 |
| Income deciles (reference is decile 5) | | | | | | | | | |
| Decile 1 | −0.50 | 0.61 | .002 | −0.03 | 0.97 | .917 | 0.48 | 1.62 | .000 |
| Decile 2 | −0.43 | 0.65 | .001 | −0.65 | 0.52 | .016 | 0.45 | 1.57 | .000 |
| Decile 3 | −0.54 | 0.58 | .000 | −0.12 | 0.89 | .614 | 0.16 | 1.18 | .076 |

228

*Table 4.16 (continued)*

| | | | | | | | | | |
|---|---|---|---|---|---|---|---|---|---|
| Decile 4 | -0.32 | 0.73 | .006 | -0.28 | 0.75 | .230 | 0.08 | 1.08 | .404 |
| Decile 6 | -0.03 | 0.97 | .777 | 0.03 | 1.03 | .885 | 0.10 | 1.10 | .299 |
| Decile 7 | 0.19 | 1.21 | .076 | -0.03 | 0.97 | .900 | 0.04 | 1.04 | .693 |
| Decile 8 | 0.22 | 1.25 | .043 | 0.13 | 1.14 | .565 | -0.24 | 0.78 | .023 |
| Decile 9 | 0.51 | 1.67 | .000 | 0.18 | 1.19 | .443 | -0.22 | 0.80 | .037 |
| Decile 10 | 0.78 | 2.18 | .000 | 0.49 | 1.64 | .027 | -0.31 | 0.73 | .005 |
| Log of household money income per head | 0.47 | 1.60 | .000 | 0.29 | 1.34 | .000 | -0.19 | 0.82 | .000 |
| Household non-pension benefit income | 0.02 | 1.02 | .606 | 0.03 | 1.03 | .614 | 0.02 | 1.02 | .671 |
| Household pension income | 0.06 | 1.06 | .031 | -0.04 | 0.96 | .565 | -0.15 | 0.86 | .000 |
| Round (reference is Round 5 1994) | | | | | | | | | |
| 1995 | -0.24 | 0.79 | .001 | -0.16 | 0.85 | .276 | -0.07 | 0.94 | .285 |
| 1996 | -0.27 | 0.76 | .000 | -0.36 | 0.70 | .028 | -0.02 | 0.98 | .735 |
| 1998 | -0.51 | 0.60 | .000 | -0.52 | 0.60 | .003 | -0.13 | 0.88 | .052 |
| 2000 | -0.27 | 0.77 | .000 | -0.47 | 0.63 | .004 | -0.23 | 0.79 | .000 |

Table 4.16 (continued)

Region (Reference is Moscow and St Petersburg)

| | | | | | | | | | |
|---|---|---|---|---|---|---|---|---|---|
| Northern and North Western | 0.44 | 1.55 | .002 | 0.62 | 1.86 | .012 | 0.71 | 2.03 | .000 |
| Central and Central Black-Earth | −0.11 | 0.90 | .375 | −0.30 | 0.74 | .182 | 0.23 | 1.26 | .045 |
| Volga-Vyatski and Volga Basin | −0.45 | 0.64 | .000 | −0.55 | 0.58 | .032 | 0.28 | 1.32 | .018 |
| North Caucasian | −0.21 | 0.81 | .111 | −0.57 | 0.56 | .033 | 0.38 | 1.46 | .004 |
| Ural | −0.16 | 0.85 | .211 | −0.41 | 0.66 | .081 | 0.22 | 1.24 | .068 |
| Western Siberian | 0.04 | 1.04 | .765 | −0.12 | 0.88 | .632 | 0.41 | 1.51 | .001 |
| Eastern Siberian and Far Eastern | −0.03 | 0.97 | .844 | −0.40 | 0.67 | .120 | 0.15 | 1.16 | .252 |
| Constant | −1.06 | | | −1.22 | | | −1.60 | | |

*Notes:* 11 percent of households were lenders, 2 percent of households were both lenders and borrowers and 17 percent of households were borrowers. The coefficient for the log of household income per head is from a separate regression. Household pension and benefit incomes are in thousands of roubles. RRR is the Relative Risk Ratio. All variables are dummies unless otherwise indicated. Standard errors are corrected for panels.

*Number of observations = 18 170. Model Chi Squared = 1 680.1. Prob. > chi2 = .0000. Log likelihood = −15 224.9. Pseudo R2 = 0.0635.*

*For variable means see Table 4.17.*

*Table 4.17: OLS regressions – gross value of help and of loans given and received (RLMS data, 1994–2000, and variable means).*

| | Variable means | Log of help given | | Log of help received | | Log of loans given | | Log of loans received | |
|---|---|---|---|---|---|---|---|---|---|
| | | B | P>|t| | B | P>|t| | B | P>|t| | B | P>|t| |
| Number of adults | 2.10 | 0.09 | .001 | 0.03 | .382 | 0.08 | .041 | 0.23 | .000 |
| Number of children under 7 | 0.23 | -0.06 | .298 | -0.02 | .581 | 0.07 | .279 | 0.06 | .245 |
| Number of children 7–17 | 0.50 | -0.07 | .032 | 0.07 | .049 | 0.04 | .445 | 0.15 | .000 |
| Male-headed household | 0.17 | 0.06 | .233 | -0.02 | .728 | 0.08 | .305 | -0.09 | .244 |
| Single-parent household | 0.05 | -0.02 | .815 | 0.16 | .051 | -0.04 | .760 | 0.25 | .018 |
| Urban household | 0.68 | -0.07 | .517 | 0.01 | .871 | 0.04 | .844 | 0.02 | .900 |
| Proportion of adults: | | | | | | | | | |
| Under 25 | 0.09 | 0.35 | .159 | 0.06 | .771 | 0.55 | .058 | 0.37 | .145 |
| 25–39 | 0.29 | 0.65 | .007 | -0.38 | .054 | 0.70 | .013 | 0.47 | .057 |
| 40–pension age | 0.27 | 0.97 | .000 | -0.60 | .003 | 0.64 | .026 | 0.52 | .038 |
| Of pension age | 0.34 | 0.77 | .002 | -1.00 | .000 | 0.28 | .324 | 0.12 | .643 |
| With higher education | 0.15 | 0.06 | .315 | 0.19 | .003 | 0.23 | .019 | 0.29 | .002 |
| Born in the countryside | 0.49 | 0.02 | .752 | -0.09 | .112 | -0.01 | .942 | -0.08 | .258 |
| Who are disabled | 0.02 | -0.06 | .735 | -0.50 | .006 | -0.32 | .173 | -0.11 | .590 |
| On paid leave | 0.01 | -0.14 | .772 | -0.30 | .307 | -0.33 | .344 | -0.41 | .212 |

*Table 4.17 (continued)*

| | | | | | | | | | |
|---|---|---|---|---|---|---|---|---|---|
| On leave without pay | 0.004 | -0.09 | .782 | -0.69 | .052 | -0.14 | .835 | 0.20 | .574 |
| On maternity leave or housewife | 0.05 | 0.22 | .180 | 0.11 | .359 | 0.22 | .267 | 0.23 | .241 |
| Currently working | 0.51 | 0.20 | .006 | -0.05 | .486 | 0.11 | .327 | 0.22 | .030 |
| With second jobs | 0.03 | -0.12 | .415 | 0.00 | .978 | 0.04 | .848 | 0.03 | .853 |
| With IEA | 0.07 | -0.22 | .005 | -0.16 | .065 | -0.22 | .080 | -0.21 | .064 |
| In self-employment | 0.02 | 0.17 | .326 | -0.10 | .538 | 0.37 | .102 | 0.62 | .009 |
| Owed unpaid wages | 0.32 | -0.04 | .410 | -0.13 | .010 | -0.01 | .909 | -0.05 | .458 |
| Paid in kind | 0.05 | 0.12 | .287 | -0.07 | .514 | -0.28 | .053 | -0.37 | .003 |
| Sent on administrative leave | 0.05 | -0.06 | .482 | -0.13 | .186 | 0.02 | .857 | -0.10 | .287 |
| Urban household has a dacha | 0.37 | 0.15 | .182 | 0.06 | .477 | 0.13 | .491 | -0.05 | .725 |
| Rural household has a dacha | 0.29 | 0.05 | .320 | 0.02 | .694 | 0.08 | .256 | 0.05 | .435 |
| Household owns a car | 0.23 | 0.13 | .004 | 0.23 | .000 | 0.40 | .000 | 0.59 | .000 |
| No money income last month | 0.07 | 0.14 | .192 | 0.16 | .059 | 0.01 | .958 | 0.10 | .350 |
| Income deciles (reference is decile 5) | | | | | | | | | |
| Decile 1 | 0.12 | 0.18 | .171 | 0.09 | .316 | 0.05 | .757 | -0.05 | .703 |
| Decile 2 | 0.08 | -0.07 | .455 | 0.12 | .129 | -0.12 | .389 | -0.19 | .083 |
| Decile 3 | 0.10 | 0.04 | .619 | -0.04 | .658 | -0.11 | .431 | -0.07 | .464 |
| Decile 4 | 0.10 | -0.07 | .416 | 0.02 | .795 | -0.23 | .080 | 0.04 | .711 |
| Decile 6 | 0.10 | 0.08 | .295 | 0.17 | .034 | -0.14 | .208 | 0.12 | .244 |
| Decile 7 | 0.10 | 0.17 | .028 | 0.04 | .654 | 0.17 | .150 | 0.35 | .002 |

Table 4.17 (continued)

| | Mean | Coef. | Sig. | Coef. | Sig. | Coef. | Sig. | Coef. | Sig. |
|---|---|---|---|---|---|---|---|---|---|
| Decile 8 | 0.10 | 0.26 | .001 | 0.03 | .766 | 0.26 | .019 | 0.44 | .000 |
| Decile 9 | 0.10 | 0.44 | .000 | 0.20 | .021 | 0.38 | .001 | 0.65 | .000 |
| Decile 10 | 0.09 | 0.68 | .000 | 0.22 | .019 | 0.80 | .000 | 1.13 | .000 |
| Log of household money income per head | 7.10 | 0.24 | .000 | 0.05 | .051 | 0.35 | .000 | 0.28 | .000 |
| Household non-pension benefit income | 0.14 | 0.02 | .622 | 0.03 | .582 | -0.01 | .844 | -0.02 | .681 |
| Household pension income | 0.90 | 0.04 | .104 | 0.02 | .430 | -0.03 | .307 | -0.02 | .428 |
| Round (reference is Round 5 1994) | | | | | | | | | |
| 1995 | 0.20 | -0.11 | .052 | -0.21 | .000 | -0.21 | .006 | -0.20 | .013 |
| 1996 | 0.19 | -0.02 | .654 | -0.17 | .004 | -0.13 | .102 | -0.19 | .011 |
| 1998 | 0.20 | -0.45 | .000 | -0.52 | .000 | -0.58 | .000 | -0.60 | .000 |
| 2000 | 0.21 | -0.38 | .000 | -0.66 | .000 | -0.44 | .000 | -0.54 | .000 |
| Constant | | 5.25 | .000 | 7.43 | .000 | 5.40 | .000 | 5.92 | .000 |
| N | | 4 614 | | 4 098 | | 2 511 | | 3 507 | |
| R Squared | | 0.124 | | 0.135 | | 0.175 | | 0.221 | |

Notes: The average of the log of help given was 6.35, the average of the log of help received was 6.72. The average of the log of the loan given was 6.26, the average of the log of the loan received was 6.85 (all indexed to June 1992 prices). The coefficient for the log of household income per head is from a separate regression. Household pension and benefit incomes are in thousands of roubles. All variables are dummies unless otherwise indicated. Standard errors are corrected for panels. The regression also included seven regional dummies.

*Table 4.18: OLS regressions – value of all forms of help given and received and variable means.*

| | Variable means | Log of help received | | Log of help given | |
|---|---|---|---|---|---|
| | | Coefficient | P>\|z\| | Coefficient | P>\|z\| |
| Log of household income per head | 6.25 | 0.77 | .000 | 0.16 | .028 |
| Income deciles (reference is decile 5) | | | | | |
| Decile 1 | 0.10 | −0.02 | .947 | −0.05 | .839 |
| Decile 2 | 0.10 | −0.09 | .722 | 0.01 | .960 |
| Decile 3 | 0.09 | −0.30 | .167 | −0.03 | .879 |
| Decile 4 | 0.08 | 0.01 | .966 | 0.04 | .870 |
| Decile 6 | 0.10 | 0.08 | .705 | 0.21 | .363 |
| Decile 7 | 0.10 | 0.18 | .377 | 0.19 | .406 |
| Decile 8 | 0.11 | 0.51 | .010 | 0.18 | .425 |
| Decile 9 | 0.12 | 0.79 | .000 | 0.23 | .332 |
| Decile 10 | 0.12 | 1.14 | .000 | 0.71 | .004 |
| Household pension income | 0.16 | 0.10 | .576 | −0.28 | .364 |
| Household benefit income | 0.05 | 0.33 | .378 | −0.33 | .503 |
| Others help on dacha | 0.11 | 0.16 | .249 | 0.10 | .491 |
| Network contacts per head | 0.46 | 0.12 | .032 | −0.04 | .605 |
| Proportion of friends in network | 0.49 | −0.36 | .005 | −0.14 | .372 |
| Proportion of relatives in network | 0.21 | −0.21 | .143 | −0.11 | .518 |
| Household head | | | | | |
| Male | 0.22 | 0.00 | .991 | −0.06 | .662 |
| Age | 41.81 | 0.04 | .135 | −0.10 | .001 |
| Age squared/100 | 18.84 | −0.02 | .440 | 0.10 | .008 |
| Has higher education | 0.28 | 0.19 | .096 | 0.46 | .001 |
| Has technical education | 0.42 | 0.20 | .056 | 0.16 | .192 |
| Proportion of household members: | | | | | |
| Working | 0.79 | 0.10 | .418 | −0.24 | .141 |
| With secondary employment | 0.20 | 0.10 | .414 | 0.29 | .040 |

*Table 4.18 (continued)*

| | | | | | |
|---|---|---|---|---|---|
| Non-working pensioners | 0.13 | 0.07 | .691 | −0.31 | .211 |
| Owed wages | 0.26 | −0.19 | .175 | 0.04 | .833 |
| On administrative leave | 0.08 | 0.20 | .345 | −0.10 | .671 |
| Paid in kind | 0.11 | −0.13 | .461 | −0.18 | .407 |
| Number of adults in household | 2.17 | 0.18 | .015 | 0.09 | .295 |
| Number of children under 7 | 0.21 | 0.25 | .013 | −0.02 | .890 |
| Number of children 7–16 | 0.48 | −0.12 | .096 | −0.02 | .846 |
| Single-parent household | 0.11 | −0.08 | .641 | 0.17 | .321 |
| **Household:** | | | | | |
| Includes adult children | 0.28 | −0.45 | .001 | −0.01 | .966 |
| Has sold property | 0.14 | 0.00 | .983 | 0.08 | .529 |
| Has a dacha | 0.55 | 0.00 | .994 | 0.06 | .609 |
| Has a car | 0.28 | 0.06 | .499 | 0.22 | .056 |
| Includes infirm member(s) | 0.08 | −0.07 | .684 | 0.30 | .231 |
| Has a non-household carer | 0.03 | −0.10 | .658 | 0.05 | .840 |
| Includes parent(s) of head | 0.10 | 0.26 | .151 | −0.12 | .611 |
| **City (reference is Lyubertsy)** | | | | | |
| Samara | 0.35 | −0.47 | .000 | −0.20 | .208 |
| Kemerovo | 0.26 | −0.35 | .012 | −0.35 | .038 |
| Syktyvkar | 0.22 | −0.25 | .081 | −0.42 | .018 |
| Constant | | 4.96 | .000 | 9.19 | .000 |
| N | | 775 | | 716 | |
| Adjusted R squared | | 0.1888 | | 0.1110 | |

*Notes: The coefficient for the log of household income per head is from a separate regression. Household pension and benefit incomes are in thousands of roubles. All variables are dummies unless otherwise indicated.*

*The mean of the log of the amount received in all forms of help, by those households receiving help was 6.50 and the mean of the log of the amount given, by those households giving help, was 6.96.*

# 5. Do Russian Households have Survival Strategies?

In previous chapters we have seen that secondary employment, subsidiary agriculture and social networks can play an important role in helping the more disadvantaged Russian households to survive in the crisis. However, we have also found that households have relied largely on the means of securing the subsistence of the household that had become traditional by the late Soviet period. The predominant forms of supplementary employment – working in a registered second job and the provision of private services – were those traditional in late Soviet times, with the new activities of trading being of relatively limited importance. Subsidiary agriculture is predominantly a leisure activity of more mature households, continuing to perform its traditional role of securing household subsistence against the threat of inadequate supplies of food in the market. Private transfers continue the Soviet tradition of serving primarily as a means by which parents support their adult children. It would seem that the 'transition to a market economy' has had a devastating impact on the traditional sources of household subsistence – primary wage incomes and social benefits – while providing households with very limited opportunities to develop alternative sources of subsistence.

The market economy has certainly provided opportunities for some. Some of those with capital, connections and the appropriate motivation have been able to establish their own successful businesses, inside or outside the law. Some of those with the qualifications and experience appropriate to the new economic conditions may have been able to find well-paid jobs in the new sectors of the economy, particularly if they work for foreign companies, although many suffered in the wake of the August 1998 crisis. However, most people have neither the inclination nor the social and economic resources required to set up in business, while for most people new private sector employment is the last resort because it offers low wages, long working hours, insecure employment, minimal social benefits and bad working conditions. In the ISITO household survey, those working in manual, clerical or technical occupations in the new private sector worked much longer hours than did their colleagues in traditional sectors of the economy. Despite such long hours, according to Goskomstat's wage data, average earnings in private companies are much less than in state and privatised enterprises and organisations (Goskomstat, 2000f, p.163).

Although we do not have comparable data for the Soviet period, we have found no evidence that the incidence or scale of secondary employment, subsidiary agriculture or private transfers has increased in the period of the 'transition crisis'. This would suggest that households were already mobilising all of their available subsistence and income-earning resources in order to secure an acceptable standard of living in the late Soviet period and so have had very limited possibilities to develop new ways of adapting to the new conditions. This is confirmed by the fact that there appears to be very little tendency for those households that confront financial difficulties to avail themselves of the opportunities to increase their household income offered by these possibilities. This immediately casts some doubt on the notion that such activities constitute significant elements of 'household survival strategies', in the sense of providing a range of opportunities amongst which disadvantaged households can select in order to secure their survival. In this chapter I will question the usefulness of the notion of a 'household survival strategy' to post-socialist societies.

## THE NOTION OF A 'HOUSEHOLD SURVIVAL STRATEGY'

Much recent discussion of household subsistence in the transition economies has centred on the notion of 'household survival strategies' (Voronkov, 1995; Johnson et al., 1996; Yaroshenko, 1999). The notion of a 'household survival strategy' has been widely used in development studies to draw attention to the diversity of sources of household subsistence and in particular to the role of informal and household economic activity, the domain primarily of women, the young and the old. The notion was important in moving away from the narrow perspective of the wage-earning breadwinner supporting a dependent family that is associated with a one-sided view of the young, the old and women as dependants on the wages of men (Pahl,

1984; Chant, 1991; Nelson and Smith, 1998). This approach provided the basis for powerful critiques of development strategies which had single-mindedly pursued the objective of expanding wage-earning or small business opportunities, even if this was at the expense of the contribution of other household members and of other activities to household subsistence. This is particularly important where households are not fully committed to wage-earning in the market economy, so that subsistence production and engagement in the informal economy play a significant role in the reproduction of household members (Tinker, 1990). However, I would suggest that the notion is less appropriate to transition economies for three main reasons.

First, as noted in the first chapter, by the 1980s the vast majority of the adult population of the state socialist countries was fully committed to employment in the wage-earning economy, with a continuing role for subsistence agricultural production in rural districts and a limited amount of moonlighting in the urban economy. Those categories of the population who were not in waged employment (full-time students, the elderly, the chronic sick and disabled, women with young children) were supported by state benefits that, in general, were sufficient to provide for their basic subsistence. Age and gender were significant in determining differential labour market opportunities, not in determining differential commitment to waged as opposed to non-waged employment. With the exception perhaps of Hungary, informal and subsistence activities were of marginal significance to the survival of urban households and the majority of people lacked the skills and resources to engage in such forms of activity.

Second, the notion of a household survival strategy is also misleading in that it implies the determining role of agency (Crow, 1989; Morgan, 1989; Rodgers, 1989, p.20): if survival is a matter of strategy more than of resources then households which adopt the appropriate strategies can survive the destruction of jobs and income-earning opportunities and the erosion of welfare benefits that have been a general feature of the collapse of the state socialist economy. It is only a short step from that view to the current attempts, encouraged by the World Bank, to slash categorical social benefits and to impose punitive systems of social assistance which disqualify from assistance those who are alleged to have income-earning potential: access to a plot of land, a spare room in their apartment which could be rented out, furniture which could be sold, the supposed capacity to establish a small business or even relatives who might support them.[1] While it is important to reject the view of the poor as passive victims, it is equally important not to exaggerate the extent to which the fate of the poor is in their own hands. We therefore need to consider carefully the extent to which impoverished households have or are able to pursue survival strategies. This will be the subject of the second section of this chapter.

Finally, the notion of a household survival strategy presumes that the household is a decision-making unit, making co-ordinated decisions to optimise the deployment of household resources. In the third section of the chapter I will review the available data to consider to what extent this is in fact the case. We will see that it is more plausible to think about household members more or less independently taking advantage of such opportunities as may present themselves within the framework of a limited range of opportunities and quite restrictive constraints. Prosperity, survival, poverty and destitution are not then the results of more or less successful household strategies, but express the greater or lesser good fortune of individual household members in the face of radical economic change. Finally, I will assess the arguments put forward by Michael Burawoy that there are distinctive 'traditional' and 'new' household survival strategies, and that it is women who take primary responsibility for the survival strategy of the household (Burawoy et al., 2000).

## DO HOUSEHOLDS HAVE *SURVIVAL STRATEGIES*?

The notion of a household survival strategy has been employed mostly in ethnographic research. Many people interviewed about how their household makes ends meet will tell a more or less coherent narrative about the various ways in which they have increased their household income or managed to economise on household expenditure. However, such a retrospective rationalisation of the activity of the household is by no means sufficient evidence that what has been done has been the result of a household survival strategy, or of any kind of strategic

---

[1]   See, for example, the Letter of Intent sent by Prime Minister Chernomyrdin to the IMF on behalf of the Russian government (April 30, 1997, No. 1348p-P2), which was linked to the conditionality terms of the $800 million Social Protection Adjustment Loan approved by the World Bank on 25 June 1997. Under the Loan experimental systems were introduced in Voronezh, Volgograd and the Komi Republic to assess need on the basis not only of current income, but also of the 'economic potential' of the household (Ministry of Labour of the Russian Federation, 1999).

decision-making at all. Indeed, many less fortunate respondents will not be able to construct such a narrative, their accounts being tales of woe and successive misfortunes. We have therefore to ask what scope there is for Russian households and their members to adopt strategic responses to their misfortunes.

The Russian Longitudinal Monitoring Survey in the autumn of 1998, soon after the August crisis, asked respondents what they had done in the last year to adjust to the new living conditions. Their responses were as shown in Table 5.1, broken down into groups according to the household income (including income in kind, the value of domestic food production and transfers) in relation to the regional poverty line (Group 1 has an income less than or equal to half the subsistence minimum, Group 2 between that and the subsistence minimum, Group 3 between that and 50 percent above the subsistence minimum, Group 4 up to twice the subsistence minimum and Group 5 more than twice the subsistence minimum). The final column reports the percentage of individuals who reported the particular action who had found it very helpful or somewhat helpful. In general, the more prosperous households had found that the steps they had taken had been more helpful than had the less prosperous households, which was perhaps why they were now more prosperous. More prosperous households were significantly more likely to have taken on additional employment,[2] while less prosperous households were significantly more likely to have asked friends or relatives for help, to have applied for social assistance, spent less on food and clothing or changed their accommodation arrangements. Overall, one-fifth of households had taken one or more of the steps to increase earned income, while one in eight had changed their living arrangements and a quarter had turned to others for help.

However, the majority, almost three-quarters, had adapted to their circumstances by reducing their spending. Even among the most prosperous households, two-thirds had had to cut their spending and one in five to seek help from others. Although three-quarters of respondents believed that their family lived better than they had five

---

2    These households might be in the upper income group because they had succeeded in obtaining secondary employment. Those in the bottom quintile of money income per head net of secondary earnings were significantly more likely than higher income groups to have sought secondary employment, but it was still those in the top quintile who had found it most helpful. Just over a quarter of those who said that they had found additional work had reported secondary employment in the previous round of the survey in 1996. The same was true of the 9 percent of respondents in 2000 who said that they had got an extra job in the last year.

*Table 5.1:* *Actions taken by respondents in the past twelve months (Distribution of individual responses by regional poverty grouping of the household; RLMS 1998).*

| | Regional Poverty Group (1 and 2 are below the poverty line) | | | | | | Found helpful? |
|---|---|---|---|---|---|---|---|
| | 1 % | 2 % | 3 % | 4 % | 5 % | Total % | |
| Percentage of households in each poverty group | 16.4 | 22.4 | 22.4 | 15.5 | 23.2 | 100 | |
| Found Supplementary work# | 5.9 | 6.8 | 6.7 | 7.1 | 8.3 | 7.0 | 91 |
| Changed jobs | 11.4 | 11.7 | 12.0 | 10.9 | 11.4 | 11.5 | 72* |
| Cultivated more on your own personal plot# | 14.9 | 18.4 | 19.9 | 18.0 | 23.4 | 19.2 | 96* |
| Turned to your relatives for assistance# | 24.4 | 24.5 | 19.5 | 16.8 | 16.7 | 20.5 | 95* |
| Turned to your friends for assistance# | 10.1 | 9.4 | 7.6 | 5.4 | 7.0 | 8.0 | 89 |
| Sold your things# | 5.3 | 5.8 | 3.6 | 4.0 | 3.8 | 4.5 | 86* |
| Turned to social security or government organisation for assistance# | 5.3 | 6.1 | 5.1 | 3.6 | 3.4 | 4.8 | 53* |
| Went to work for a private government enterprise | 5.5 | 4.5 | 4.5 | 4.1 | 6.0 | 4.9 | 84 |
| Rented out part or all of your apartment | 1.1 | 0.8 | 1.0 | 1.5 | 1.3 | 1.1 | 91 |
| Travelled for training in order to get a new job | 1.7 | 1.8 | 2.7 | 1.9 | 1.8 | 2.0 | 74* |
| Moved in with relatives to save money# | 3.4 | 4.1 | 4.4 | 2.7 | 2.2 | 3.4 | 92* |
| Ceased living with relatives to save money# | 3.7 | 1.1 | 1.9 | 2.3 | 1.3 | 1.9 | 72 |
| Cut down on buying clothes and shoes# | 64.3 | 67.2 | 66.2 | 61.5 | 55.9 | 63.1 | 67* |
| Cut down on meals# | 59.1 | 61.8 | 55.4 | 53.0 | 40.6 | 53.9 | 65 |
| Spent less money on holidays | 37.9 | 40.7 | 40.4 | 37.5 | 37.3 | 38.9 | 62* |
| Changed your place of residence | 9.7 | 9.4 | 7.3 | 7.7 | 8.3 | 8.5 | 68 |
| N | 1 365 | 2 012 | 1 864 | 1 244 | 1 847 | 8 332 | |

*# Difference between richer and poorer households is statistically significant (p<.05).*
*\* Significantly more of the wealthier than the poorer households found this helpful.*

*Table 5.2:    Actions taken by respondents in the past twelve months (individual responses by regional poverty group of the household; RLMS 2000).*

| | Regional Poverty Group | | | | | |
|---|---|---|---|---|---|---|
| | 1 % | 2 % | 3 % | 4 % | 5 % | Total % |
| Percentage of households in each poverty group | 9.4 | 19.8 | 20.3 | 17.8 | 32.6 | 100 |
| Worked an extra job | 11.5 | 7.7 | 10.1 | 6.9 | 8.3 | 8.6 |
| Raised something on your plot to sell or trade | 6.5 | 6.8 | 8.1 | 5.4 | 10.1 | 7.9 |
| Raised cattle, poultry, fish, and other animals for sale | 7.0 | 7.9 | 7.2 | 3.9 | 10.6 | 7.9 |
| Sold things prepared by yourself at home, for example, knitted and sewn, meat dumplings, or other things | 1.7 | 1.3 | 1.6 | 1.7 | 1.8 | 1.7 |
| Sold food or goods, which you yourself did not prepare, for example, cigarettes, food, clothes | 1.2 | 3.2 | 1.8 | 1.3 | 1.7 | 1.9 |
| Travelled for food and goods which you then sold | 1.7 | 2.4 | 1.3 | 1.9 | 2.4 | 2.0 |
| Rented an apartment, room, summer house, garage, car | 0.9 | 0.6 | 0.9 | 0.5 | 0.7 | 0.7 |
| Placed money in a bank to earn interest, offered money in loans for interest | 0.9 | 0.5 | 0.9 | 0.7 | 2.2 | 1.2 |
| Performed services for pay, for example, offered people a ride in a car, repaired household appliances, cars, took a job remodelling apartments, were involved in coaching, watched children for pay | 4.4 | 4.3 | 5.1 | 3.1 | 4.0 | 4.2 |
| Done any of the above | 25.1 | 24.2 | 26.1 | 18.3 | 27.8 | 24.8 |

years ago, two-thirds of respondents, and over half of those in the most prosperous households, were anxious that they would not be able to provide themselves with the bare essentials in the following year.

RLMS asked a similar set of questions in the autumn of 2000, two years after the crisis of August 1998 (Tables 5.2 and 5.3). In this case, the relationship between actions taken and the level of household income was less clear-cut than it had been in 1998, but whereas in 1998 it had been the richer households who had been most likely to have taken a supplementary job, in 2000 it was the poorest who were most likely to have worked an extra job (which does not appear to have helped them much, because they were still in extreme poverty, despite having done so) while the richest were the most likely to have raised agricultural produce for sale. As in 1998, many more people had responded to difficulties by reducing expenditure than by diversifying their income sources: only a quarter had undertaken any of the income-earning activities mentioned, while three-quarters had reduced one or more of the items of spending. Women and older people were substantially more likely than men and younger people to have reported that they had reduced spending and women and pensioners were substantially less likely to have engaged in income-earning activities (particularly, taking a second job or performing services for pay – women were more likely than men to have engaged in trading or domestic production for sale). Women were also much more likely than men to have taken money from friends or relatives or from state organisations.

*Table 5.3:*   *Actions taken by respondents in the past two years (individual responses by regional poverty group of the household; RLMS 2000).*

| | Regional Poverty Group | | | | | |
| | 1 % | 2 % | 3 % | 4 % | 5 % | Total % |
|---|---|---|---|---|---|---|
| Had to cut down on expenses for clothes and shoes | 69.8 | 74.1 | 69.1 | 64.5 | 53.7 | 64.3 |
| Had to cut down on expenses for food | 60.1 | 64.0 | 54.6 | 53.4 | 37.5 | 51.2 |
| Had to cut down on expenses for vacations | 46.1 | 51.4 | 46.2 | 45.7 | 36.9 | 44.0 |
| Had to appeal more often for monetary help from friends, relatives | 36.3 | 33.4 | 25.4 | 21.3 | 14.5 | 23.7 |
| Had to appeal more often for monetary help from social security and other state organizations | 10.3 | 6.7 | 4.9 | 3.3 | 2.7 | 4.7 |
| Had to sell items because of money shortages | 8.8 | 4.4 | 4.3 | 2.7 | 1.6 | 3.6 |
| Began to raise more on your plot of land | 27.2 | 27.4 | 22.1 | 23.0 | 23.2 | 24.1 |

*Table 5.4:*    *Steps taken by members of households which had*
                *experienced financial difficulties in the past two years.*

What did you do when your household experienced
financial difficulties?

| | Percentage |
|---|---|
| Reduced expenditure on purchase of goods | 77 |
| Reduced spending on food | 68 |
| Cancelled plans for holiday | 48 |
| Got into debt | 48 |
| Had fewer guests, fewer entertainments, met friends less | 47 |
| Resorted to the help of relatives | 34 |
| Reduced savings | 19 |
| Undertook any appropriate work | 17 |
| Worked overtime | 11 |
| Sold domestic property | 9 |
| Rented out an apartment, car, garage etc. | 2 |
| N ≈ 3 660 | |

*Source: ISITO household survey (April–May 1998).*

This data strongly indicates that households survive much more by reducing their expenditure than by increasing their income. This is confirmed by responses to the ISITO survey. Respondents were asked if their household had experienced financial difficulties in the previous two years. The 82 percent of respondents who had experienced such difficulties were then asked which of a series of steps they had taken in that situation. The results are tabulated in Table 5.4, which again shows that the overwhelming majority of responses involved cutting expenditure or seeking help from others, while relatively few respondents had been able to increase their incomes. Household heads were asked if they had sold household property to meet the needs of their household in the previous year. Thirteen percent replied that they had done so. Of these, one-third had received less than a week's household income for the goods, while a third had received more than one month's income from their sale. We also asked all those respondents in work what they would do if they had to increase their earnings, with the results reported in Table 5.5. One in seven would look for another job, one in five would look for supplementary employment, one in five would simply work harder, but almost half the respondents did not think that they had any possibility of increasing their earnings.

*Table 5.5: What you would do if you had to increase your earnings? (Percentage distribution of responses of those in work).*

|  | Percent |
|---|---|
| I would work more at my main job | 17 |
| I would search for other work | 14 |
| I would search for additional work | 20 |
| I would work more at my additional work | 2 |
| I do not have any possibility of increasing my earnings | 47 |
| N | 3 353 |

*Source: ISITO household survey (April–May 1998)*

The extent to which households have had to reduce their spending in order to make ends meet is indicated by the subjective appraisal of their living standards by the heads of households in the ISITO survey shown in Table 5.6, which shows that the majority of households struggle to provide themselves even with the bare essentials.

*Table 5.6: Assessment of the material situation of the household by household heads.*

| How do you assess the material position of your family? | Percent |
|---|---|
| We don't even have enough money for food | 28 |
| We have enough money for food, but it is difficult to buy clothing | 47 |
| We have enough for food and clothing but not for expensive things | 20 |
| We can make long-term purchases but not expensive things | 5 |
| At the moment we want for nothing | <1 |
| N | 4 009 |

*Source: ISITO household survey.*

The conclusion that households have a very limited capacity to increase their income in the face of financial difficulties is strongly reinforced by the analysis in the previous chapters of the data relating to secondary employment, subsidiary agriculture and social networks. We have seen that there is only a very slight and equivocal tendency for those with the lowest incomes to be more likely to engage in secondary employment, while those on the lowest incomes are the least likely to engage in subsidiary agriculture and the lowest income families benefit the least from private transfers. Moreover, there is no evidence that falling income or temporary difficulties, such as administrative leave, short-time working or the non-payment of wages, make people more likely to take a second job, engage in subsidiary agriculture or get help from friends and relatives.

To argue that households do not have survival strategies is not to argue that households are incapable of adapting rationally to their situation, but only to argue that the possibilities of such adaptation are very restricted and that most households have already taken advantage of all the opportunities that realistically confront them. Thus households do not adjust their behaviour in the face of difficulties in order to achieve survival, all households take advantage of such opportunities as are available to them and survival, or even prosperity, is the contingent outcome for those households which are more successful. Those in poverty are not those who have failed to adapt rationally to their situation by taking advantage of additional income-earning opportunities, they are those who have exhausted all the opportunities available to them.

The overwhelming majority of Russian households do survive, but their adaptation to changing circumstances takes place much more on the expenditure than on the income side of the household budget, and this is where we find the essence of the household's survival 'strategy'. Households at every income level cut down on all but the most essential items of expenditure. Goskomstat's retail sales figures show a steady decline in the sale of most items through the 1990s. People hold on to old consumer durables, inherit them from friends and relatives, or buy second-hand. Annual sales of fridges fell by more than two-thirds, of colour televisions, furniture and construction materials by almost half and of washing-machines by more than a third during the 1990s, with only the sales of private cars increasing (Goskomstat, 2000e). Of course, retail sales figures are not very accurate, and many cars and electronic items are imported without being declared, but the tendency is clear. The RLMS data, as well as Goskomstat's consumption data, indicates that consumption of meat, milk and dairy products fell by more than half over the 1990s (Goskomstat, 2001). In the RLMS data, between 1994 and 1998, households spent on average between two-thirds and four-fifths of their total money income on food (expenditure on food comprises 55 percent of the official subsistence minimum), although spending on food fell, in real terms, by almost half, with only a small recovery as incomes rose in 2000. As public funding of the health service declines, those who do not have the money to pay for medical treatment simply have to do without. In the RLMS data, the proportion of those who had not been able to afford to buy prescribed medicines increased from 8 percent in 1994 to 19 percent in 1998, only falling back to 15 percent in 2000 (Zohoori et al., 2001).

One reason that households have been able to survive with very low money incomes has been that they have had to pay very little for their housing and utilities, which have continued to be heavily subsidised. In the RLMS data, between 1992 and 2000 the average proportion of the household budget spent on housing and utilities doubled, but still only amounted to an average of 5.5 percent of household spending, 255 roubles ($9) a month. Under pressure from the World Bank, the Russian government has been seeking to increase the payments made by households for their housing and utilities. Even though such 'cost recovery' programmes are only just beginning, a substantial proportion of Russian households are not able to pay even the modest bills that they receive. In the RLMS data between 22 percent (1995) and 38 percent (1998) were in arrears with their payments. In RLMS 2000, despite the increase in household incomes, 27 percent of households were in arrears in their payments for housing and utilities, the average debt amounting to almost four times the average monthly payments made by those who were not in arrears (Mroz et al., 2001).[3]

## DO *HOUSEHOLDS* HAVE SURVIVAL STRATEGIES?

The household is a budgetary unit, but this does not necessarily imply that income and expenditure decisions are made collectively. According to the ISITO survey data, the vast majority of households have a common household budget, into which household members put the majority of their individual incomes, and in the majority of cases the budget is said to be managed collectively, although one individual, usually a woman, is primarily responsible for shopping and it is plausible to presume that that person takes primary responsibility for

---

[3]  This will underestimate the scale of non-payment since many municipalities have made offset arrangements whereby housing and utility payments are credited against the unpaid wages of public sector employees and even, through more complicated barter arrangements, of private sector employees.

the management of the household budget (Clarke, 2002). In a situation in which most households have incomes barely sufficient to meet the most basic subsistence needs of the household members, management of the household budget primarily involves economising, with little scope for strategic decision-making.

Decision-making on the income side of the household budget primarily involves decisions about employment: whether to take a job or to change jobs, whether to work longer hours or to take up secondary employment. Despite the depth of the economic crisis in Russia, substantial wage inequalities have meant that those with the appropriate qualifications and experience can increase their incomes by changing jobs. Labour turnover has remained at historically very high levels throughout the crisis, with between a fifth and a quarter of people changing jobs each year. Of course, not all of these people are changing their jobs in order to improve their financial situation. A significant proportion have had to leave their jobs because they have been forced out or laid off, while others may change jobs for other than financial reasons. In the ISITO household survey, 45 percent of those who had changed jobs in the previous two years had increased their pay by doing so, but 32 percent had taken a cut in pay, the remaining 23 percent earning exactly the same.

Employment decisions are taken in the first instance by individuals, but if households have survival strategies then we would expect these decisions to be taken in the light of the household's circumstances, as a part of the deployment of the household's resources. In the ISITO survey, we asked respondents about the decision to leave their last job. One-third of respondents said that they had had to leave their previous job, so they had not made a decision. Of those who did make a decision, the majority had consulted with members of their family (Table 5.7), although men were more likely than women not to have consulted anyone else. This data appears to suggest that in the majority of households employment decision-making is a collective process. However, the fact that decisions are taken collaboratively does not necessarily mean that they are taken on the basis of the collective allocation of household resources. To investigate the basis on which decisions are made we have to investigate not what people say, but what they actually do.

According to the standard economists' model of household labour supply, the household member capable of earning the highest wage should work for a wage while the lower-wage-earner devotes her (or his) labour-time to performing the domestic labour required to secure the reproduction of the household, the lower-earner only entering the labour market when the higher-earner is working to the limit of his or her ability. In Russia the vast majority of couple-based households are dual-earner households. In this case, household decision-making dictates that the hours worked by the higher-earner should be insensitive to changes in relative wages, since the higher-earner is already working to the maximum, while those of the lower-earner should be flexible in response to differential earning capacities. Is it the case that changes in the relative wage of the higher earner only affect the hours worked by his or her partner?

*Table 5.7:*   *Did you consult with members of your family when you left your last job? (Percentage distribution of responses by sex for those who chose to leave).*

| | Men | Women | All |
|---|---|---|---|
| Yes, and they insisted that I left the job | 5.5 | 6.6 | 6.1 |
| Yes – we took the decision together | 29.0 | 32.7 | 30.9 |
| Yes, but I took the decision myself and my relatives agreed with it | 20.0 | 24.3 | 22.2 |
| Yes, but I took the decision myself against the advice of my family | 2.3 | 1.9 | 2.1 |
| No, I did not consult, I took the decision myself | 43.1 | 34.6 | 38.7 |
| N | 1 373 | 1 457 | 2 830 |

*Source: ISITO household survey (April–May 1998).*

In Russia there is little flexibility of hours in primary employment, but secondary employment provides a considerable amount of hours flexibility. If we combine primary and secondary employment, then we can investigate the relationship between total hours worked and relative wages of the two partners in dual-earner couple-based households. We assume that, where there is secondary employment, it is the wage in that employment which is relevant because even if wages in primary employment are higher, the fact that the person engages in secondary employment would indicate that there is inflexibility of hours in the primary job.

To test this model we have to take into account a number of other factors which affect decisions regarding hours of work. In particular, the presence or absence of children and the availability of the alternative of working on the garden plot. We also specify the sex of the respondent in the model, to allow for gender differences in working hours, which we do not seek to explain here.

*Table 5.8:    OLS Regression – weekly hours worked by high and low earners, couple-based households.*

|  | High earner | | | Low earner | | |
|---|---|---|---|---|---|---|
|  | Coefficients | T | Sig. | Coefficients | T | Sig. |
| (Constant) | 38.9 | 36.7 | .000 | 43.6 | 32.8 | .000 |
| Ratio of wage of high to low earner | 0.023 | 0.079 | .937 | 2.25 | 5.99 | .000 |
| Male | 6.21 | 7.35 | .000 | 5.81 | 5.41 | .000 |
| Have a dacha | −1.16 | −1.42 | .157 | −0.21 | −0.20 | .839 |
| Have children | 1.29 | 1.16 | .245 | 1.04 | 0.74 | .457 |
| Adj. R squared | | | .062 | | | .057 |
| N | | | 864 | | | 856 |

*Source: ISITO Household Survey (April–May 1998).*

A regression with hours worked as the dependent variable and the size of the relative pay differential as the independent variable, controlling for sex, the availability of a dacha and the presence of children, is entirely consistent with the first part of the economists' proposition: there is no relationship between the hours worked by the highest earner and the relative wage (Table 5.8). When we turn to the low earner, there is a relationship between relative wages and hours worked, which is highly significant, although it is small.[4] However, the relationship is the reverse of that predicted by the economists' household decision-making model: as the wage of the high-earner increases relative to that of the low-earner, so the hours worked by the lower-earning partner increase too. The same relationship holds in the RLMS data (Table 5.9), except that here the hours worked by the highest earner are also sensitive to wage differences, the highest earner working significantly *shorter* hours as the wage differential increases.

This relationship applies equally whether the man or the woman is the highest earner, although men work for pay on average almost six

---

[4]    A linear function fits the data slightly better than a logarithmic function, but the substantive results are the same.

hours a week more than women (seven to eight hours more in the RLMS data), regardless of which partner earns the highest wage. Working a dacha reduces and having children increases the hours worked by both partners, but not sufficiently for the effect to be statistically significant. Finally, the low earner on average works considerably *longer* hours than the high earner (in both the ISITO and the RLMS data), which is completely irrational from the point of view of the economists' model of household decision-making, but is consistent with a model of individual decision-making in which wage-earners work sufficient hours to achieve an earnings' target. Thus the analysis of working hours would seem to suggest that partners make their employment decisions more or less independently of one another.

*Table 5.9:*    *OLS Regression – monthly hours worked by high and low earners, couple-based households (RLMS Panel data 1994–2000).*

| | High Earner | | | Low Earner | | |
|---|---|---|---|---|---|---|
| | B | t | Sig. | B | t | Sig. |
| (Constant) | 134.17 | 32.42 | .0000 | 151.17 | 44.94 | .0000 |
| Ratio of wage of high to low earner | −0.51 | −4.96 | .0000 | 0.32 | 3.52 | .0004 |
| Male | 32.17 | 11.96 | .0000 | 29.53 | 12.53 | .0000 |
| Have a dacha | −2.39 | −0.85 | .3944 | 2.52 | 1.02 | .3056 |
| Have children | 4.94 | 1.77 | .0764 | 1.55 | 0.64 | .5252 |
| 1995 | 3.09 | 0.84 | .4031 | 5.83 | 1.80 | .0718 |
| 1996 | 8.86 | 2.16 | .0309 | 6.94 | 1.93 | .0535 |
| 1998 | 4.36 | 1.07 | .2836 | 4.32 | 1.21 | .2248 |
| 2000 | 11.36 | 2.99 | .0028 | 10.92 | 3.29 | .0010 |
| Adj. R squared | 0.056 | | | 0.057 | | |
| N | 2 819 | | | 2 819 | | |

Not too much weight should be placed on these results, because there is not very much variation in hours worked, the inter-quartile range being only eight hours per week in the ISITO sample and 13 hours per week in the RLMS data, while the data is cross-sectional so we are not studying the response of individual couples. Nevertheless, this finding is supported by the fact, noted in Chapter 2, that household characteristics play very little role in determining the probability of an individual undertaking secondary employment. There does not appear to be a tendency for couples to establish a division of labour in undertaking secondary employment: both men and women are about three times more likely to undertake secondary employment if their partner also does so, so that the tendency is for either neither or both partners to take on additional work. This would suggest that there is some complementarity either in the opportunities for secondary employment faced by partners or in the strength of their motivation to engage in secondary employment.[5]

Although the evidence presented in this section is fairly limited, and cannot be regarded as conclusive, it does suggest that the income-earning decisions of individuals regarding hours of work and undertaking a second job are taken primarily on an individual basis, with little reference to what other household members do. As noted in the last section, it looks as though each individual household member tends to take advantage of all the earning opportunities that present themselves to that individual, 'household decision-making' merely being the aggregate of those individual decisions.

## DO HOUSEHOLDS PURSUE DISTINCTIVE SURVIVAL STRATEGIES?

Criticising the argument presented here, Michael Burawoy and his Russian colleagues insist that household survival strategies can only be revealed by longitudinal ethnographic research, not by 'survey research which homogenizes the heterogeneous, violates the integrity of cases by slicing them into variables, reduces complex process to singular correlation coefficients, and standardizes or ignores context' (Burawoy et al., 2000, n. 2, pp. 61–2). They also argue, on the basis of their ethnographic research, that 'the burden of family survival is born [sic] by women ... working-class men have become increasingly superfluous and burdensome, playing a secondary role in the family and being less informed about the workings of the household (ibid., p.

---

[5]     ISITO respondents were asked what they would do if they needed to increase their incomes. Those who said that they would change jobs or work more in their main or a supplementary job were much more likely already to have secondary employment than those who said that they could do nothing. Moreover there was a significant correlation (Pearson 0.26) between the responses of husbands and wives to this question, although many more women than men said that they could do nothing.

47). In other words, it is not the household which has a survival strategy, but women who take responsibility for the survival of the household as a whole. 'Whether it be the defensive or entrepreneurial household strategies, it is usually women who govern their execution and direction' (ibid., p. 60), and the cited article is a study of four such women.

Michael Burawoy and his colleagues argue that, in the face of the disintegration provoked by the market economy, the household has become the 'dominant organizing unit of survival' (ibid., p. 60), but household resources can be deployed within two fundamentally different household survival strategies. The first, which they call a 'defensive strategy', is based on traditional Soviet practices of diversifying productive activities and sharing household resources as a defence against destitution, combining a primary job, secondary employment, working a dacha, exchanges with relatives and social and welfare benefits. 'These households spontaneously knit together routines of the Soviet period into coping strategies for the new era of uncertainty' (ibid., p. 47). This is opposed to the potentially more lucrative, but more risky 'entrepreneurial strategy' of putting all the household's efforts and resources into the market economy. These two strategies are exemplified by studies of four women who have articulated these strategies with more or less success, although both the strategies adopted and the outcomes achieved are largely explained in terms of the resources available to the respective households rather than the strategic acumen of the respondents.

Burawoy and his colleagues identify these distinctive strategies on the basis of repeat interviews with 48 former employees of a Syktyvkar furniture factory, but generalise from this sample to the condition of Russian society as a whole. While they are right to be sceptical of an excessive reliance on survey data, such data does provide the possibility of testing the generalisability of conclusions reached on the basis of the analysis of singular cases. They make two propositions that we can usefully test. First, that we can distinguish two archetypal 'survival strategies', one based on a diversification of traditional subsistence sources and the other on a wholesale commitment to the market economy. Second, that it is primarily women who take responsibility for the survival of the household, while men are marginalised.

The ISITO household survey data does not support the hypothesis that there is a clear distinction between those households involved in traditional activities and those engaged in the new market economy. The receipt of state social and welfare benefits is determined primarily by the demographic characteristics of the household and those households with members working in entrepreneurial activities or working for new private enterprises do not have significantly different benefit income than those whose members all work in traditional enterprises. Indeed, those who claim to be unemployed but are actually engaged in entrepreneurial activity are three times *more* likely to be claiming unemployment benefit than are those who are unemployed but working for a wage on the side – clearly entrepreneurs are not averse to relying on state benefits to support their activity, and it is often the case that entrepreneurial households rely on pension and benefit income to cushion the risk of their undertakings. In the RLMS data, households in which all working members are engaged in self-employment have, on average, twice as much pension income as other working households.

Households with members engaged in entrepreneurial activity or working in the new private sector as their primary employment are much *more* likely to be involved in secondary employment and there is no difference in the probability of working a dacha. Other household members are much more likely to be working in the traditional sector of the economy than in the new private sector or in entrepreneurial activity.[6] Ninety-four percent of households with more than one working member, in which at least one member is an entrepreneur or working in the new private sector, have at least one other member working in a traditional enterprise or organisation. Thus 'entrepreneurial' households do not have any less diversified sources of subsistence than those that have not committed themselves to the new market economy. Finally, entrepreneurial households do not isolate themselves from their social networks and devote all their resources to their business: households with members engaged in entrepreneurial activities are more likely, and those employed in the new private sector are much more likely, to give money or goods to help others. In the RLMS data, members of households with a member reporting that he or she is engaged in entrepreneurial activity as his or

6    The spouses of entrepreneurs are more likely than others to be involved in entrepreneurial activity, probably because such activity is often based on family businesses, though even spouses are more likely to work in traditional jobs. In the RLMS data, as many spouses of entrepreneurs declare themselves to be housewives (two-thirds of entrepreneurs are men) and more than twice as many work for a wage in an enterprise or organisation as work as entrepreneurs themselves.

her primary employment are more than twice as likely to have second jobs and are much more likely to have given help to others, although they are significantly less likely to work a dacha, than households without anybody engaged in such activity.

The diversification of sources of subsistence appears to be a feature of all households, dependent much more on the socio-demographic characteristics of the household and the opportunities available to the household members than to any strategic decisions taken by the household. In general, the more adult members the household has, the more diversified will be its sources of income. Entrepreneurial activity, or work in the new private sector, for most households provides no more than an opportunity further to diversify their sources of income.[7]

This is not to deny that the decision to try to grasp the new opportunities of the market economy is a radical and fundamental decision that often has implications for the household as a whole. Entrepreneurship is not for everyone. Many people in the ISITO work history interviews said that they did not have the personal skills required to engage in business, and many retained the Soviet association of entrepreneurship with exploitation and speculation. In the ISITO household survey, entrepreneurs were asked how important were various factors to success in business. Much the most important factor cited was 'personal qualities', rated as very important by 69 percent of respondents, followed by 'initial capital' (42 percent) and 'personal connections' (34 percent), with education and qualifications being the least important factor (though still rated as very important by 32 percent of respondents).

Those who commit themselves to the market economy often depend on relatives to provide essential inputs of (unpaid) labour, dragging their families into the market economy in their wake. Almost a third of the ISITO entrepreneurs worked basically with friends and relatives (22 percent hired employees and 47 percent worked alone), and their businesses often involved other household members: just over a quarter of the female entrepreneurs and one in seven of the male entrepreneurs worked in partnership with their spouse, so some

---

[7]    Rose, 1999b similarly stresses that the diversification of income sources and mobilisation of resources is the key to survival. Pickup's ethnographic study of respondents from 83 households in Sverdlovsk oblast found that 'only respondents with influential networks successfully adopted the risky strategy of investing all their resources in entrepreneurial activity' (Pickup, 2002, p. 29) and concluded that 'to straightjacket people's strategies in terms of a Soviet versus market or modern versus anti-modern dichotomy limits our understanding of the rationale behind people's livelihoods' (Pickup, 2002, p. 153).

households are clearly more heavily committed to entrepreneurship than others. But it does seem that those who work in the market economy are no less likely than are those who are confined to more traditional opportunities to seek to maintain a diversity of income sources. Many entrepreneurs depend on other household members bringing in a steady income, whether from waged labour or in the form of a pension, and it is entirely rational for them to do so, because involvement in the market economy is a risky business. Although those engaged in entrepreneurial activity earn, on average, much more than those who work for a wage, the dispersion of incomes is also much greater so that, while a few entrepreneurs prosper, many earn little or nothing for their efforts. Two-thirds of those who told RLMS in 2000 that they had tried to organise their own business in the past said that they had failed. In the ISITO survey, just over half the entrepreneurs earned a regular income from their business, the remainder only making money from time to time. Only one in five had chosen to start their business to make money, almost as many doing it because they could not find any other work, and over a third because it gave them more independence.

## THE GENDER DIMENSION OF SURVIVAL STRATEGIES

Michael Burawoy and his colleagues argue that it is primarily women who take responsibility for the survival of the household, but this argument needs careful examination. There is no doubt that women feel a special responsibility for ensuring the survival of the household, particularly if they have children. Although most households in the ISITO survey claimed that they budgeted jointly, in three-quarters of couple-based households the woman was identified as the person responsible for managing the household budget, so the burden of providing for the household from the meagre resources available tends to fall to the woman. But Michael Burawoy's team's hypothesis is stronger than this, that women are responsible for the management and execution of the household's income-earning activity.

Like Michael Burawoy and his colleagues, we have interviewed many women who have had to compensate for feckless, indolent or, most commonly, alcoholic husbands, working all hours to support their families, and this led us to propose a hypothesis very similar to theirs

(Kiblitskaya, 2000). However, we were not confident that we had not been unduly impressed by what might have been exceptional examples of women's stoicism and courage, and one purpose of our household survey was to try to discover whether we could generalise from these examples.

We have already seen that people's employment decisions are very little affected by the circumstances of the household or by the impact of various misfortunes. We can explore the issue in more detail by examining the responses of husbands and wives to changes in the circumstances of their spouses. If women take the primary responsibility for securing household income, we would expect women to be more likely than men to take steps to compensate for the failure of their partner, for one reason or another, to bring money into the household. We can explore this issue in the ISITO and the RLMS data by asking which spouse is more likely to take positive action to overcome household difficulties. When the subsistence of the household is threatened is it the woman who comes to the fore, while the man is just a 'superfluous burden'?

The data provides us with no evidence that women have taken over responsibility for bringing in an income from men. At the most basic level, although most Russian women work, men are still more likely to work than are women and men work longer hours and earn much more than do women, but the interesting issue is what happens if the man (or the woman) does not bring home the bacon? In general, the analysis of the survey data confirms our previous findings, that individual employment decisions show very little response to household circumstances: there is very little tendency for either husbands or wives to respond to problems confronted by their spouses.

The RLMS data allows us to follow households over time but, comparing responses between rounds of the survey, neither men nor women show any statistically significant change in working hours, primary or secondary employment or individual economic activity in response to a change in their partner's earned income or working hours, loss of a primary or secondary job, or past experience of non-payment of wages, short-time working or payment in kind (the only exception is that men are marginally less likely to undertake individual economic activity the more their wives' employment income has fallen). If we look at the cross-sectional RLMS and ISITO data we again find very little relationship between income-earning decisions and the partner's circumstances.

In both data sets, controlling for age and education, we find that if one partner is not earning, for whatever reason, has unpaid wages, is sent on administrative leave, is working short-time or is paid partially in kind, the other partner is not significantly more likely to have either primary or secondary employment or to work longer hours.

In the RLMS data, if one working-age spouse is not working or unemployed, the other is significantly *less* likely also not to be working or to be unemployed, although in the ISITO data the primary employment status of one partner has no significant impact on the employment status of the other. In both data sets, husbands are more likely to have second jobs than are their wives, but if one partner does not have supplementary employment, the other is also much less likely to have it. This all reinforces the conclusion that households have very little scope for strategic decision-making. If one partner is without primary or secondary work, the other has little chance of compensating by finding a job. It is more likely that both partners will share the disabilities that inhibit them from finding work.

In RLMS in 1998, people were asked explicitly what they had done in the previous year to adjust to new living conditions (see Table 5.1). Men were significantly more likely to have found supplementary work or changed their job, while women were more likely to have asked relatives or the government for help, to have sold things and much more likely to have cut spending on food and clothing. In 2000, respondents were asked directly what they had done in the previous year or two (Tables 5.2, 5.3). Men were significantly more likely than women to have taken an extra job, raised livestock for sale and much more likely to have performed services for pay, while women were significantly more likely than men to have sold home-made or other goods, to have cut spending on food, clothing and vacations, to have taken money from friends, relatives or government organisations or to have sold possessions. Overall, men were much more likely to have sought some additional income-earning opportunities, while women were much more likely to have sought help from others or cut spending. This all strongly suggests that the traditional division of household roles persists, with the man taking responsibility for bringing in the income and the woman taking responsibility for the management of the household budget.

The survey data does not really allow us to test Michael Burawoy's team's thesis that the women of the new bourgeoisie, by contrast to working class women, have been pushed 'into subordinate, often decorative positions within the household' (ibid., p. 44),[8] because the phenomenon is confined to a small stratum of the population – in both data sets, since 1998 only about one in a hundred men earned more than $500 a month and one in a thousand earned more than $1000 a month from all sources. Nevertheless, we can look at the survey data to see how widespread the phenomenon of the 'trophy wife' might be. Controlling for other variables (age, education, location and household composition), in the RLMS data the labour force participation of the wives of the top 20 percent of male wage-earners falls off steadily as their partner's earnings increase (the decline is not statistically significant in the ISITO data, and there is no significant overall relation between the participation of men and their wives' earnings in either data set). However, more than two-thirds of the wives of even the top 10 percent of male wage-earners were still working. In the RLMS survey, almost one in five of women in that stratum describe themselves as housewives, against one in ten of all wives (almost a quarter of the wives of men who described themselves as entrepreneurs categorised themselves as housewives).[9]

The survey data does not at first sight appear to support Michael Burawoy's team's hypotheses. In order to approach the question from another direction, we used our survey to explore the question, who is the breadwinner in the Russian household?

**Who is the breadwinner in the Russian household?**

As in many societies, the ability to support his family is an important aspect of the gender identity of the Russian man. However, in the Soviet period the role of 'mere housewife' was politically devalued and economically discouraged: Soviet wage scales and pensions were not designed to support a family of dependents on the income of a single breadwinner (Lapidus, 1988, pp. 92–3) and most women worked outside the home for a substantial proportion of their lives. Moreover, the state provided many of the things that the husband

---

[8]   Elena Meshcherkina's interviews with new Russians suggest that the reality is rather more complex. While new Russian men might want their wives to return to the home, their wives are often not willing to be pushed into 'subordinate, often decorative positions' (Meshcherkina, 2000).

[9]   The predominantly male entrepreneurs in Pickup's sample displayed very traditional attitudes to the gender division of labour and the majority of their wives stayed at home to care for the children, although this was at least partly explained by the high cost of childcare (Pickup, 2002, pp. 129, 197), a factor which inhibits many mothers (and a few fathers) of pre-school children from going out to work.

could not, including many things that money could not buy. The dominant model was therefore that of the two-earner family, with women combining waged work with their domestic tasks and taking a break from work only for the period of statutory maternity and child-care leave. With the state assuming a large part of the male gender role, the responsibility of a man for his family and his ability to provide for it were quite restricted. The ideology of the male breadwinner was nevertheless preserved in Soviet society in the form of the expectation that a man should earn more than his wife and put most of his income into the household budget (Kiblitskaya, 2000), although a Soviet woman was expected to be, in the words of one of Kiblitskaya's male respondents, 'a sort of second-order breadwinner' (ibid., p. 91).[10]

With the 'transition to a market economy', the responsibility for supporting the family has suddenly been thrown back on to its individual members, at the same time as employment reductions and falling real wages have made it increasingly difficult to make ends meet. Wage inequality has increased dramatically so that many men and women are trapped in low-paid jobs with few opportunities to earn higher wages. In order to discover to what extent men were living up to the expectations of their manhood and taking responsibility for providing for their families, in the ISITO household survey we asked every adult member of the household, 'who would you call the breadwinner (*kormilets*) in your family?' For analytical purposes we identify the breadwinner of the household by majority vote of all household members.

The breadwinner would prima facie be expected to be the person with the highest income in the household, and in 85 percent of our households this was the case, but this still leaves one in seven households in which the person nominated as the breadwinner was not the highest earner.[11] In a monetary economy, an income is a

[10] In a current project on gender and employment directed by Sarah Ashwin, funded by INTAS, 76 percent of respondents thought that a man *should* be responsible for providing for the family and 21 percent thought the man and the woman should both be responsible. In the 2000 RLMS, 42 percent of men and 35 percent of women agreed that 'it is usually bad for a family if the wife works' and 56 percent of men and 43 percent of women disagreed that 'if the wife works then she is held in higher respect in the family than if she were simply a housewife'.

[11] See Potuchek, 1997 for a recent analysis of the notion of the breadwinner in dual-earning US families, based on the idea that the notion of the breadwinner is a key boundary in the social construction of gender as a dynamic process of negotiation, related both to outside experience and to complementary boundaries such as 'mother' and 'responsible for housework'.

prerequisite for performing this role, but this is not a sufficient condition. The breadwinner is not simply the person who feeds the household, but more fundamentally, the person who assumes or is assigned the obligation to ensure that the household is fed. Thus, for example, we might expect the role of breadwinner to be culturally assigned to prime-age male members of the household, who are expected to get a job and provide for their families, so they may be nominated as breadwinner even if they do not bring in the largest income. On the other hand, women tend to take on the responsibility for feeding their family and for preparing food, so that in this respect they also have a claim to the breadwinner role (the Russian word '*kormilets*' literally means the person who feeds). Men and women may have correlatively different conceptions of the role of breadwinner.

The impression given by our qualitative work-history interviews was not that men are not committed to working to support their families, but that men and women have rather different priorities. Our interviews indicated that for men a high money income was the key indicator of their social status, while for women the important indicator was the provision of the basic means of subsistence. It was noticeable in our work-history interviews that it was more often the women than the men who stressed the obligation of the man to provide for his family.

> My husband is still earning normally. If there is not enough money, it is up to him to think about money (Nadezhda, deputy shop chief, engineering factory).

The following respondent's husband appears not to be as clear as his wife about his obligations, since she expects to have to 'prepare him morally':

> A man should take a second job, but not a woman... And if it got absolutely awful here with wages or whatever, my husband would leave, I would prepare him morally for this. It is more difficult for a woman to get a job, it is easier for a man (senior department forewoman, engineering factory).

Some men were clearly quite willing to allow their wives to serve as the main providers for the family, rather than making an effort to increase their own incomes.

> Now it is also possible to earn additionally here, doing repairs, for example, but there is hardly any point, since there isn't any money. My wife, on the whole, gets her salary on time (fettler, engineering factory).
> – *How do you earn additionally?*

I don't, there is no time. And my husband does not want to. Another man with such hands would earn additionally, but mine does not want to. And we live (Female bus conductor. Her husband is unemployed. Her salary is the sole material support for her family).

In rare cases we found families with fairly equal relations between the husband and wife, in which the decision as to which partner would be the main breadwinner was the result of a conscious family strategy in which the man was ready to adapt his work routines to the needs of his wife, particularly if she has a well-paid job:

I worked, then married, then my son was born. At first my wife stayed at home with him (until he was three, as one is supposed to do), and then we decided not to send him back to the kindergarten – he was frequently ill. My wife had to leave work and I began to look for a job myself, one that involved shift work with a schedule that would let me take my turn looking after our child. I immediately remembered Plastic, I knew that they worked shifts and the pay was not bad (at that time it wasn't).

— *And you are not going to leave?*

Yes and no. The work schedule suits me, they have put me on permanent nights. The pay is certainly no good, but at the moment I cannot simply leave for a better-paid job, though I have had some offers, but I would have to work only during the day. My wife has a good job. She works as an ITR in Kuzbassenergo. Though I shall certainly leave if I can find shift work with worthwhile pay. But the first condition is obligatory (operative, plastics factory).

We found many female respondents who were ready to take on any work, out of a feeling of responsibility for their families:

It was all the same to me what I worked at, I just wanted to work. Life has forced me to take any job (woman janitor, printing works).

It took a long time to decide to leave school. There were a lot of reasons. Well, the main one, of course, was material, I have two children. And my husband is in the same profession.

— *Were you ready to do any work?*

Basically yes, any work (woman storekeeper, formerly a Russian teacher, chocolate factory).

Another school teacher was ready to take work as a market trader:

There is nobody to help me, and I have to bring up my son. At school I was paid very irregularly and little, so I had to overcome my unwillingness and decided last summer to come here and trade as a hired worker (seller, retail market).

It is much more difficult for a man to take on 'any work', because for a man the public status of his profession is often at least as important as his status as breadwinner of the family and he will do all in his power not to lose his professional identification.

I sat at home for a year and a half. Of course, I didn't just sit there, I worked. I tried to register as unemployed, but at the Employment Service they humiliated me by telling me that I was an old man. That's at forty-odd. I began to work for myself. I set myself the goal of not losing my qualifications and to work in my specialism. It cost me a lot that saving of my face (male design engineer, electrical factory).

Men who were not able to make a worthwhile contribution to the family budget suffered this as a demoralising and degrading experience, but nevertheless some did not regard it as sufficiently degrading to impose on themselves the even greater humiliation of taking on work beneath their dignity and status. Even if unemployed, a man retains the status, if not the income, of his profession, which he immediately loses if he takes a low-status job. Nevertheless, although we found many men who were torn between their obligation to provide for their family and their desire to maintain their masculine self-respect by earning good money in a good job, in the end most men reconciled themselves to their domestic responsibilities, however painful it might have been.

I worked there until the summer of 1996, but I was forced to look for work again because they stopped paying completely and the family had to be fed, our parents needed help, I was bringing absolutely nothing home and they began to pay my wife at school really badly. In my soul two principles struggled: I absolutely did not want to leave my specialism, but I could not find a job in my specialism (male bus conductor).

If a man in the end agrees to take 'anything', it is often a real life tragedy for him. His professional identification is the core of his masculinity and a threat to it may be a threat to his psychological equilibrium. Here, for example, is the story of a high-skilled worker who has become a loader:

I worked conscientiously and my qualifications were appropriate, and for three months the pay was reasonable, but then the stoppages began. I hung on for all of two years, but was already constantly looking for work. It reached the point at which it did not matter whether or not it corresponded to my specialism, as long as it was not fetching and carrying, not servile work, as long as they paid money. I am a man, I have two babies at home, they must be clothed and fed. Although I know my job very well and I love it, I was ready to make a sacrifice. And I wanted to eat too, and not only black bread. Now I feel myself a total beast of burden, an ox, a beast who is of no use to anybody. My dignity suffers, and though personally nobody troubles me, I feel as though all around are shouting: 'Nobody needs you!' Such a time has come when we work in order to eat, that is to say that we live in order to eat (loader, milk factory).

The impression from our qualitative interviews was that, although women in particular felt that it should be the obligation of the man to provide for his family, in reality women would often assume this responsibility, sometimes because of the demoralisation of their husbands but often simply because they were better placed to do so. This impression is confirmed by the analysis of our survey data. Although men on average earn much more than women, in both the RLMS and the ISITO data, in almost a third of couple-based households the wife earned more than her husband. In the ISITO data, sex is not a directly significant factor in determining which household member is identified as the breadwinner (Kozina, 2000).[12] In the relation between couples, relative income is overwhelmingly the most important factor, followed by age and occupational status, but other things being equal the husband is no more likely to be identified as the breadwinner of the household than is his wife.[13] Over 60 percent of breadwinners are men because men tend to earn substantially more than women.

Although men are expected to be the breadwinners, men often find it very difficult to live up to those expectations and in a substantial minority of households a woman plays the breadwinner role. However, the fact that women sometimes play the breadwinner role is a long way from saying that men 'have become increasingly superfluous and burdensome, playing a secondary role in the family'. Certainly this is true of some men, but many men have been able to keep or find jobs that enable them to reconcile the conflicting pressures to which they are subject, and many of the men we interviewed had confronted their anxieties and even taken jobs that they regarded as demeaning in order to continue to support their families. In well over half the couple-based households in the ISITO survey the husband earned more than

---

[12]   In the ISITO survey data, men are twice as likely as women to nominate themselves as the breadwinner. In VTsIOM surveys, almost three-quarters of male respondents and almost half of female respondents characterise themselves as the person 'bringing the main income into the household'. In September 1994 respondents were asked the sex of the breadwinner and 62 percent identified a man, 38 percent a woman, exactly the same proportions as in our survey. If we compare the responses of married men and women in two-earner families in the VTsIOM data, we find that over one-third of women without children and over a quarter of those with children say that it is they who provide the main income, although 80 percent of men declare that they are the main earner, whether or not there are children.

[13]   It is noteworthy that the presence of children in the household does not in itself have any significant impact on the probability of a man filling the breadwinner role. This would suggest that a woman is more likely to be responsible for childcare if there is another breadwinner in the household, rather than childcare responsibilities preventing a woman from being the breadwinner.

his wife and the husband was almost three times as likely as his wife to be identified as the breadwinner.[14] So, although women undoubtedly make a very substantial contribution to household subsistence, in the majority of households it is still a man who plays the breadwinner role.

While the husband still tends to be the breadwinner, we have seen that the burden of adjustment to deteriorating economic conditions falls primarily on the expenditure rather than the income side of the household budget, and it is this burden that falls preponderantly on women. In this sense it is true that it is primarily women who take responsibility for the survival of the household.

In the ISITO household survey, the household head was identified at the beginning of interviewing as the person mainly responsible for the management of the domestic economy, and the wife was identified as the household head in three-quarters of couple-based households (in VTsIOM surveys, about two-thirds of female respondents but only one-fifth of male respondents identify themselves as the person responsible for managing the domestic economy). Ninety-six percent of households had some kind of common budget, and both male and female household members put the vast majority of their income into the budget or spent it for common household needs. In over 80 percent of households the budget was reported to be controlled collectively, but we would still expect that the 'head of household' would normally take primary responsibility for budgetary management. This supposition is supported by the fact that in over three-quarters of couple-headed households it was a woman who was identified by the household head as being primarily responsible for doing the shopping (in over 95 percent of these cases it was the wife, otherwise usually a daughter, Clarke, 2002). So we can safely presume that the burden of making ends meet falls predominantly on women.

This is a heavy burden with shrunken household incomes and the shops awash with things to buy at unaffordable prices. In the ISITO household survey, almost three-quarters of heads of households said that they did not have enough money to feed and clothe their households. On average, necessities accounted for 97 percent of total household spending, and accounted for 84 percent of the spending even of the top expenditure decile. Over 80 percent of households had

---

[14]     In 40 percent of couple-based households, the husband and wife agreed that the husband was the breadwinner and in 12 percent both agreed that the wife was the breadwinner. In the remainder they each nominated themselves (3 percent), or the other (1 percent), or at least one of them nominated somebody else (44 percent), most often a son or daughter.

nothing left to put aside at the end of the month as savings or for larger purchases or vacations, and for only 10 percent of households did such discretionary spending account for 10 percent or more of their monthly household expenditure. Control of the household budget is a position of responsibility much more than being a position of power.

We have already seen that three-quarters of respondents in both the ISITO and the RLMS surveys reported that they had responded to difficulties by cutting expenditure and the burden of cutting expenditure falls disproportionately on the women who have to struggle to make ends meet. This is where the heaviest burden of securing the subsistence of the household tends to fall and this is the sense in which 'the burden of family survival is borne by women'.

## CONCLUSION

Russian households still rely overwhelmingly on their traditional sources of subsistence: income from waged primary and secondary employment, social benefits, private transfers and, particularly for rural households, the produce of their garden plots. Our analysis of the data suggests that the various income-earning activities are complements rather than substitutes: neither individuals nor households rationally allocate their labour-time between alternative uses in order to maximise the household income. This is not because people are not rational, but because their decision-making is severely constrained by the circumstances in which they find themselves.

Despite the catastrophic fall in wages and employment, income from primary employment is still the most important source of household money income, while social benefits, and particularly pension income, have become even more important than they were in the past. In the four large cities covered by the ISITO household survey, income from primary employment comprised on average 60 percent and pension income comprised 32 percent of household money income. In the RLMS data, wages contributed an average of 53 percent and pensions 33 percent of the total household money income of urban households over the period 1994–2000. Rural households were less dependent on wages, which contributed an average of one-third, while pensions contributed a massive 40 percent of household money income.

We have seen that supplementary employment tends to pay better than primary employment and can make a substantial contribution to the household budget of those who have such work on a regular basis, but these are only a small minority of households, the majority of people being unable to undertake additional jobs on top of their main work. Thus, secondary earnings contribute on average only 6 percent to household money incomes. Moreover, those with the best paying secondary employment tend to be those who are already comfortably off, so secondary employment does not make much contribution to the relief of poverty. Nevertheless, two-thirds of the heads of households which had secondary earnings in the ISITO household survey considered that this was important for the security of their household.

Two-thirds of the heads of the ISITO households which had a dacha considered that the products of their plot were important for the security of their household, but we have seen that the dacha makes an insignificant contribution to the household money income of urban households and that urban households with a dacha spend no less on food than those without. Moreover, the poorest households are the least likely to have a dacha. The dacha certainly contributes to the sense of security of the urban household and can be a vital resource for those families with no other source of income, but in general it is not a significant source of household subsistence and does not result in significant savings in monetary outlay. The situation is obviously very different with rural households. In the RLMS surveys, net cash sales of agricultural produce contributed 15 percent of the money income of rural households, while many rural households are self-sufficient in their staple foodstuffs.

Private transfers can provide a substantial supplement to the household income. Almost half the ISITO households received help from friends and relatives and half of these considered that help important for the security of their household. However, we have seen that private transfers are dominated by the regular exchange between parents and children, rather than being a form of charitable assistance, with parents continuing to support their children until they are well past pension age, the flow of resources only being reversed when the parents have actually retired from their main employment. Although there is a weak tendency for resources to flow from richer to poorer households, the richest families both give and receive the most. The patterns of giving increase the significance of pension income for the subsistence even of those households that do not contain a pensioner, since pensioners tend to be donors of help.

We have found that households that have suffered economic

difficulties as a result of unemployment, lay-offs, short-time working, falling wages and the non-payment of wages are not, in general, more likely than others to engage in secondary employment, to work a dacha or to receive help from friends and relatives. We have also seen that there is no evidence that the incidence of these phenomena has increased as the crisis has deepened through the 1990s, or even since the Soviet period. This led us to doubt that these phenomena could be considered to be the elements of household *survival* strategies. We suggested that this was not because households and household members did not seek to adapt to their straightened circumstances by looking for alternative sources of income, but because most household members had already mobilised all of the possibilities that were open to them so that they had only a very limited ability to compensate for the loss of one source of income by finding an alternative. The most deprived households have the most limited opportunities to find a job that pays a living wage, to find secondary employment, to start their own business or to work a dacha and are not able to compensate for failure in one field by picking up compensatory activity in another.

While appropriate skills, education and experience are important qualities in the primary and secondary labour markets, social connections are a key to success in all spheres of economic life. The most deprived households are those that are the most socially isolated. People need connections to find a decent primary or secondary job, to start their own business or to get access to land if they do not have their own plot. Those with close social and kin connections are more likely to receive help and more likely to be able to borrow to tide themselves over hard times, but social connections are built up over a lifetime and cannot be constructed suddenly in times of need. Moreover, we surmised that the emergence of persistent and systematic inequality might put such social connections under increasing strain as the prospects of the reciprocation of assistance deteriorated, a contention that is supported by Pickup's study (Pickup, 2002, pp. 246–55).

The fact that the opportunities that confront household members are quite restricted is probably also the reason why we find that household members do not appear to co-ordinate their decisions about the allocation of their labour-time in order to maximise the welfare of the household as a whole, in the ways that economists' models of household behaviour suggest they should. Again, there is no reason to believe that household members are behaving irrationally. It is more likely that the opportunities available to household members are very limited, so that each individual takes advantage of any acceptable opportunities that present themselves: everybody makes do as best they can. It is not that people do not make rational choices, but that the choices available are far more restricted than the economists presume.

Several commentators have suggested that the optimum survival strategy for households is to diversify their income sources, and certainly households with the most diversified sources have the best chances of surviving the vicissitudes of the 'transition to a market economy'. However, we have seen that the employment decisions of individual household members are little affected by the circumstances of their partners or the rest of the household, so it is not clear to what extent the diversification of income sources is a matter of strategic choice, rather than the contingent outcome of the independent employment decisions of individual household members.

We have found no evidence to support the idea that the burden of supporting their families has been taken on disproportionately by women. Men continue to have higher labour-market participation rates than women and earn substantially more than women so that a man remains the breadwinner in the majority of households. There is some evidence that the failure of men to provide for their families is a source of household breakdown (Kiblitskaya, 2000), but although the divorce rate increased slightly in the early 1990s, it has been falling since 1995. Several commentators have remarked on the strength of the family as an invaluable resource in surviving transition (Pickup and White, 2002; Vannoy et al., 1999). On the other hand, the limited capacity of members of disadvantaged households to increase their incomes in the face of adversity means that adjustment to crisis has been primarily on the side of expenditure, and it is here that the burden of adjustment does fall primarily on women, since it is women who are usually responsible for the management of the depleted household budget so that it is women who are in the front line in the struggle to make ends meet.

The review of the data provides no grounds for complacency. There is absolutely no evidence that secondary and informal employment, domestic agriculture or private transfers have played a significant role in reducing the impact of the collapse of the traditional economy on the vast majority of Russian households. The transition to a market economy has opened new opportunities only to a very small fraction of the population, work in the new private sector for the vast majority of its employees being unstable and insecure, involving long hours of work for low wages in unhealthy conditions with minimal social benefits and without even the minimal protections provided by the law. The living standards of the mass of the Russian population will not be improved by the further growth of small businesses, usually operating on the margins of legality, but only by the recovery of investment in the traditional economy and the restoration of the real value of social benefits. This, rather than any expansion of the new private sector, has been the basis of the limited improvement in living standards since the August 1998 crisis.

# References

Alasheev, S., Varshavskaya, E. and Karelina, M. (1999). 'Podsobnoe khozyaistvo gorodskoi sem'i', in Kabalina, V. and Clarke, S. (eds) *Zanyatost'i povedenie domokhozyaistv: adaptatsiya k usloviyam perekhodnoi ekonomiki Rossii.* Moscow: Rossiiskaya politicheskaya entsiklopediya (ROSSPEN).

Blau, P.M. (1964). *Exchange and Power in Social Life.* New York: John Wiley.

Burawoy, M., Krotov, P. and Lytkina, T. (2000). 'Involution and destitution in capitalist Russia'. *Ethnography* 1: 43–65.

Chant, S. (1991). *Women and Survival in Mexican Cities: Perspectives on Gender, Labour Markets and Low-income Households.* Manchester and New York: Manchester University Press.

Chernina, N.V. (1996). 'O novoi modeli zanyatost'i'. *Rossiiskii ekonomicheskii zhurnal,* 11–12.

Clarke, S. (1999a). 'Poverty in Russia'. *Problems of Economic Transition* 42: 5–55.

Clarke, S. (1999b). *The Formation of a Labour Market in Russia.* Cheltenham: Edward Elgar.

Clarke, S. (2000). 'The household in a non-monetary market economy', in Seabright, P. (ed.) *The Vanishing Rouble: Barter Networks and Non-Monetary Transactions in Post-Soviet Societies.* Cambridge: Cambridge University Press: 176–206.

Clarke, S. (2001). 'The measurement and definitions of poverty in Russia', in Gordon, D. and Townsend, P. (eds) *Breadline Europe.* Bristol: Policy Press: 307–56.

Clarke, S. (2002). 'Budgetary management in Russian households'. *Sociology* 36 (3): 535–53

Clarke, S. and Kabalina, V. (1999). 'Employment in the New Private Sector in Russia'. *Post-Communist Economies* 11: 421–43.

Commander, S. and Yemtsov, R. (1995). *Russian unemployment: its magnitude, characteristics and regional dimensions.* Washington DC: EDI, World Bank.

Cox, D., Zereria, E. and Jimenez, E. (1997). 'Family safety nets during economic transition', in Klugman, J. (ed.) *Poverty in Russia: Public Policy and Private Responses*. Washington D.C.: World Bank: 211–48.

Crow, G. (1989). 'The Use of the Concept of "Strategy" in Recent Sociological Literature'. *Sociology* 23: 1–24.

Donova, I. (1998). 'Faktory, opredelyayushchie povedenie individa v sfere vtorichnoi zanyatosti'. Kemerovo: ISITO.

Donova, I. and Varshavskaya, L. (1996). 'Secondary employment of employees of industrial enterprises', in Clarke, S. (ed.) *The Restructuring of Employment and the Formation of a Labour Market in Russia*. Coventry: Centre for Comparative Labour Studies, University of Warwick.

Earle, J. and Sabirianova, K. (1999). 'Understanding wage arrears in Russia'. *SITE Working Paper* 139.

Emerson, R.M. (1976). 'Social exchange theory', in Inkeles, A., Coleman, J. and Smelser, N. (eds) *Annual Review of Sociology*, 2. Palo Alto, CA: Annual Reviews.

Garsiya-Iser, M., Golodets, O. and Smirnov, S. (1995). 'Chto skryvaet skrytaya bezrabotitsa'. Moscow: *Segondya*, 22 December.

Goskomstat (1996a). *Metodolicheskie polozheniya po statistike*. Moscow: Goskomstat Rossii.

Goskomstat (1996b). 'Rynok truda Rossiiskoi federatsii v 1996 godu'. *Informatsionnyi statisticheskii byuulleten'* 13: 45–64.

Goskomstat (1996c). *Trud i zanyatost'v Rossii*. Moscow: Goskomstat Rossii.

Goskomstat (1996d). *Maloe predprinimatel'stvo*. Moscow: Goskomstat Rossii.

Goskomstat (1996e). *Rossiiskii Statisticheskii Ezhegodnik*. Moscow: Goskomstat Rossii.

Goskomstat (1997). *Rossiya v Tsifrakh*. Moscow: Goskomstat Rossii.

Goskomstat (1998a). 'O zanyatosti naseleniya'. *Statisticheskii byulleten'* 9 (48): 59–156.

Goskomstat (1998b). *Rossiiskii Statisticheskii Ezhegodnik*. Moscow: Goskomstat Rossii.

Goskomstat (1998c). *Sotsial'lno-ekonomicheskoe polozhenie Rossii*, VI. Moscow: Goskomstat Rossii.

Goskomstat (1998d). 'O razvitii individual'nogo sektora sel'skogo khozyaistva'. *Statisticheskii byulleten'* 5: 19–52.

Goskomstat (1999a). *Rossiya v Tsifrakh*. Moscow: Goskomstat Rossii.

Goskomstat (1999b). 'Osnovnye pokazateli vyborochnogo obsledovaniya byudzhetov domashnikh khozyaistv po Rossiiskoi federatsii v 1998 godu'. *Statisticheskii byulleten'* 1 (51): 9–182.

Goskomstat (1999c). 'Osnovnye pokazateli vyborochnogo obsledovaniya byudzhetov domashnikh khozyaistv po Rossiiskoi federatsii v 1998 godu'. *Statisticheskii byulleten'* 5 (55): 49–182.

Goskomstat (1999d). 'Osnovnye pokazateli vyborochnogo obsledovaniya byudzhetov domashnikh khozyaistv po Rossiiskoi federatsii vo II kvartale 1998–1999 godu'. *Statisticheskii byulleten'* 11 (61): 113–88.

Goskomstat (1999e). *Rossiiskii Statisticheskii Ezhegodnik.* Moscow: Goskomstat Rossii.

Goskomstat (2000a). *Rossiya v Tsifrakh.* Moscow: Goskomstat Rossii.

Goskomstat (2000b). *Dokhody, raskhody i potreblenie domashnikh khozyaistv v 1999 godu.* Moscow: Goskomstat Rossii.

Goskomstat (2000c). *Obsledovanie naseleniya po problemam zanyatosti, noyabr' 1999 goda (vypusk 2).* Moscow: Goskomstat Rossii.

Goskomstat (2000d). *Obsledovanie naseleniya po problemam zanyatosti, mai 2000 goda.* Moscow: Goskomstat Rossii.

Goskomstat (2000e). *Rossiiskii Statisticheskii Ezhegodnik.* Moscow: Goskomstat Rossii.

Goskomstat (2000f). *Sotsialnoe polozhenie i uroven' zhizni naseleniya Rossii 2000.* Moscow: Goskomstat Rossii.

Goskomstat (2000g). *Obsledovanie naseleniya po problemam zanyatosti, noyabr' 2000 goda.* Moscow: Goskomstat Rossii.

Goskomstat (2001). *Rossiya v Tsifrakh.* Moscow: Goskomstat Rossii.

Granovetter, M. (1973). 'The strength of weak ties'. *American Journal of Sociology* 78 (May): 1360–80.

Hervouet, R. (2001). '"Etre à la datcha": Recherche exploratoire sur un phénomène multidimensionnel au Belarus'. *Département de sociologie.* Bordeaux: Université Victor Segalen.

Iarskaia-Smirnova, E. and Romanov, P. (1999). 'At the Margins of Memories, 1940–1953: Provincial Identity and Soviet Power in Oral Histories'. Mimeo. University of North Carolina, Chapel Hill.

ISEPN RAN (1998). *Rossiya 1997, sotsial'no-demograficheskaya situatsiya.* Moscow: ISEPN, RAN.

Johnson, S., Kaufmann, D. and Ustenko, O. (1996). 'Household Survival Strategies'. *Ukrainian economic review* II: 112–116.

Khibovskaya, E.A. (1995). 'Vtorichnaya zanyatost' kak sposob adaptatsii k ekonomicheskim reformam'. *Voprosy ekonomiki*: 5: 71–79.

Khibovskaya, E.A. (1996). 'Vtorichnaya zanyatost' v raznykh sektorakh ekonomiki'. *VTsIOM: Ekonomicheskie i sotsial'nye peremeny: monitoring obshchestvennogo mneniya*: 3 (23) 24–27.

Kiblitskaya, M. (2000). 'Russia's female breadwinners: the changing subjective experience', in Ashwin, S. (ed.) *Gender, State and Society in Soviet and Post-Soviet Russia*. London and New York: Routledge: 55–70.

Klopov, E. (1996). 'Vtorichnaya zanyatost' kak forma sotsial'no-trudovoi mobil'nosti' in Gordon, L. and al., (eds.) *Trudovye peremeshcheniya i adaptatsiya rabotnikov*. Moscow: IMEMO: 21–40.

Kosonen, R. and Salmi, A. (1999) (eds). *Institutions and Post-Socialist Transition*. Helsinki: Helsingin Kauppakorkeakoulun Julkaisuja.

Kozina, I. (2000). 'Chto opredelyaet status "kormil'tsa" sem'i?' *Sotsiologicheskie issledovaniya*.

Lapidus, G. (1988). 'The interaction of women's work and family roles in the USSR'. *Women and Work: An Annual Review* 3: 87–121.

Ledeneva, A. (1998). *Russia's Economy of Favours*. Cambridge: Cambridge University Press.

Lonkila, M. (1997). 'Informal exchange relations in post-Soviet Russia: a comparative perspective'. *Sociological Research Online*, <http://www.socresonline.org.uk/socresonline/2/2/9.html> 2.

Lonkila, M. (1999a). *Social Networks in Post-Soviet Russia: Continuity and Change in the Everyday Life of Saint Petersburg Teachers*. Helsinki: Kikimora Publications.

Lonkila, M. (1999b). 'Post-Soviet Russia: a society of networks?', in Kangaspuro, M. (ed.) *Russia: More Different than Most*. Helsinki: Kikimora Publications.

Lovell, S. (forthcoming). *Summerfolk: A History of the Dacha, 1710–2000*. Ithaca, NY: Cornell University Press.

Maleva, T. (1998). 'Rossiiskii rynok truda i politika zanyatosti: paradigny i paradoksy' in Maleva, T. (ed.) *Gosudarstvennaya i korporativnaya politika zanyatost'*. Moscow: Carnegie Centre.

Meshcherkina, E. (2000). 'New Russian men: masculinity regained?' in Ashwin, S. (ed.) *Gender, State and Society in Soviet and Post-Soviet Russia*. London and New York: Routledge: 105–17.

Ministry of Labour and Social Development and Goskomstat Rossii

(1997). *Monitoring of the Socio-Economic Potential of Families for the Fourth Quarter of 1996. Statistical Report.* Moscow.

Ministry of Labour of the Russian Federation (1999). 'Pilotnye programmy po vvedeniyu adresnoi sotsial'noi podderzhki maloimushchikh semei v Respublike Komi, Voronezhskoi i Volgogradsckoi oblastyakh: Predvaritel'nye Itogi', Moscow: Ministry of Labour of the Russian Federation.

Mitrofanov, A.V. (1989). *'Sovetskii tyl v period korennogo pereloma v velikoi otechestvennoi voine'.* Moscow.

Morgan, D.H. (1989). 'Strategies and Sociologists: A Comment on Crow'. *Sociology* 23: 25–29.

Mroz, T. and Popkin, B. (1997). 'Monitoring economic conditions in the Russian Federation: the Russian Longitudinal Monitoring Survey, 1992–96'. Chapel Hill, NC: University of North Carolina at Chapel Hill.

Mroz, T., Henderson, L. and Popkin, B. (2001). 'Monitoring Economic Conditions in the Russian Federation: The Russian Longitudinal Monitoring Survey, 1992–2000. Report submitted to the U.S. Agency for International Development.' Chapel Hill, NC: Carolina Population Center, University of North Carolina at Chapel Hill.

Nelson, M.K. and Smith, J. (1998). 'Economic Restructuring, Household Strategies and Gender: A Case Study of a Rural Community'. *Feminist Studies* 24: 79–114.

OECD-CEET (1991). *The Soviet Agro-Food System and Agricultural Trade: Prospects for Reform.* Paris: OECD-CEET.

Ofer, G. and Vinokur, A. (1992). *The Soviet Household Under the Old Regime.* Cambridge: Cambridge University Press.

Ovcharova, L. (1997). 'The definition and measurement of poverty in Russia' in Clarke, S. (ed.) *Poverty in Transition.* Coventry: Centre for Comparative Labour Studies, University of Warwick, 1–30.

Pahl, J. (1980). 'Patterns of Money Management within Marriage'. *Journal of Social Policy* 9: 313–35.

Pahl, R.E. (1984). *Divisions of Labour.* Oxford: Basil Blackwell.

Perova, I. (1999). 'Dopolnitel'naya zanyatost': masshtaby, struktura, kharakter'. *VTsIOM: Ekonomicheskie i sotsial'nye peremeny: monitoring obshchestvennogo mneniya* 4 (42): 31–34.

Perova, I. and Khakhulina, L. (1997). 'Neformal'naya vtorichnaya zanyatost': masshtaby, struktura'. *VTsIOM: Ekonomicheskie i sotsial'nye peremeny: monitoring obshchestvennogo mneniya*: 6 (32) 30–32.

Perova, I. and Khakhulina, L. (1998). 'Estimate of incomes from informal secondary employment'. *VTsIOM: Ekonomicheskie i sotsial'nye peremeny: monitoring obshchestvennogo mneniya* 3: 29–31.

Pickup, F. (2002) *Local Level Responses to Rapid Social Change in a City in the Russian Industrial Urals*, PhD thesis, London School of Economics.

Pickup, F. and White, A. (2002). 'Sverdlovsk Region in the Year 2000: livelihoods in "transition"', *BASEES Annual Conference*. Fitzwilliam College, Cambridge.

Popov, A. (1995). 'Predlozhenie i spros na rynke truda v Rossiiiskoi federatsii: kolichestvennaya otsenka'. *Voprosy statistiki*: 6 26–28.

Potuchek, J.L. (1997). *Who Supports the Family? Gender and Breadwinning in Dual-Earner Marriages*. Stanford: Stanford University Press.

Rodgers, G. (1989). *Urban Poverty and the Labour Market: Access to Jobs and Incomes in Asian and Latin American Cities*. Geneva: ILO.

Rose, R. (1998). 'Getting things done with social capital: New Russia Barometer VII'. *Studies in Public Policy*, 303. Glasgow: Centre for the Study of Public Policy, University of Strathclyde.

Rose, R. (1999a). 'What does social capital add to individual welfare? an empirical analysis of Russia'. *Studies in Public Policy*, 318. Glasgow: Centre for the Study of Public Policy, University of Strathclyde.

Rose, R. (1999b). 'Modern, pre-modern and anti-modern: Social capital in Russia'. *Studies in Public Policy*, 324. Glasgow: Centre for the Study of Public Policy, University of Strathclyde.

Seeth, H.T., Chachnov, S. and Surinov, A. (1998). 'Russian poverty: muddling through economic transition with garden plots'. *World Development* 26: 1611–1624.

Shlapentokh, V. (1989). *Public and Private Life of the Soviet People. Changing Values in Post-Stalin Russia*. Oxford: Oxford University Press.

Shvetsov, Y.G. (1989). *Differentsiatsiya rabochego vremeni i formy vtorichnoi zanyatosti*. Tomsk.

Simagin, Y. (1998). 'Ob otsenkakh masshtabov dopolnitel'noi zanyatosti naseleniya'. *Voprosi ekonomiki* 1: 99–104.

SOTEKO (2000). *Osnovye napravleniya i prioritety gosudarstvennoi sotsial'noi politiki po povysheniyu dokhodov i urovnya zhizni naseleniya.* Moscow: Kompaniya sotsial'nykh tekhnologii i ekspertizy.

Srubar, I. (1991). 'War der Reale Sozialismus Modern?' *Kölner Zeitschrift für Soziologie und Sozialpsychologie* 43: 415–32.

Tinker, I. (1990). *Persistent Inequalities.* Oxford: Oxford University Press.

Vannoy, D. et al. (1999). *Marriages in Russia: Couples During the Economic Transition.* Westport, Conn. and London: Praeger.

Varshavskaya, E. and Donova, I. (1998). 'Vtorichnaya zanyatost' naseleniya'. Mimeo. Kemerovo.

Varshavskaya, E. and Donova, I. (1999). 'Vtorichnaya zanyatost' naseleniya' in Kabalina, V. and Clarke, S. (eds) *Zanyatost' i povedenie domokhozyaistv.* Moscow: Rossiiskaya politicheskaya entsiklopediya (ROSSPEN).

Varshavskaya, E. and Karelina, M. (1998). 'Sotsial'nyi fenomen sibirskoi "fazendy"'. Mimeo. Kemerovo and Samara: ISITO.

Voronkov, V. (1995). 'Poverty in Modern Russia: Strategies of Survival and Strategy of Research' in Segbers, K. and de Spiegeleire, S. (eds.) *Post-Soviet Puzzles: Mapping the Political Economy of the Former Soviet Union.* Berlin: Nomos Verlagsgesellschaft, Vol. 3: 23–38.

Vychislitel'nyi tsentr (1994). 'Dvizhenie rabotnikov i nalichie svobodnykh rabochikh mest, Jan-December'. Moscow: Goskomstat.

World Bank (1995). *Poverty in Russia: An Assessment.* Washington, D.C.: World Bank.

Yakubovich, V. (1999). 'Sotsialnye vozmozhnosti i ekonomicheskaya neobkhodimost': vklyuchennost' gorodskykh domokhostyaistv v seti neformalnoi bzaimopomoshi' in Kabalina, V. and Clarke, S. (eds.) *Zanyatost' i povedenie domokhozyaistv: adaptatsiya k usloviyam perekhodnoi ekonomiki Rossii.* Moscow: Rossiiskaya politicheskaya entsiklopediya (ROSSPEN).

Yaroshenko, S. (1999). 'Domashnie khozyaistva v usolviyakh perekhodnoi ekonomiki v Rossii: Tipy obespecheniya pitaniya v gorodskikh sem'yakh', in Kabalina, V. and Clarke, S. (eds.) *Zanyatost' i povedenie domokhozyaistv: adaptatsiya k usloviyam perekhodnoi ekonomiki Rossii.* Moscow: Rossiiskaya politicheskaya entsiklopediya (ROSSPEN).

Yemtsov, R. (1994). 'Masshtaby i formy bezrabotitsy'. *VTsIOM: Ekonomicheskie i sotsial'nye peremeny: monitoring obshchestvennogo mneniya*: 5 40–43.

Zohoori, N., Gleiter, K. and Popkin, B. (2001). 'Monitoring health conditions in the Russian Federation: the Russian Longitudinal Monitoring Survey, 1992–2000. Report Submitted to the U.S. Agency for International Development.' Chapel Hill, NC: Carolina Population Center, University of North Carolina at Chapel Hill.

# Index

1998 crisis 4, 43, 81, 87, 117,
    165, 191, 208, 236, 240,
    242–3, 270

administrative leave 3, 29, 54,
    62, 64, 143, 154, 171, 198–
    9, 207, 246, 258
agency 238–9
agricultural production 116,
    118–22, 125, 171

breadwinner 77, 237, 259–65,
    269
    definition 77
    loss of 1, 139

charity 152, 195
child care 1, 75, 77, 95
communality 7, 206
co-operatives 2, 35
    agricultural 119

dacha , 7–9, 12, 21, 113–77,
    181, 199, 238, 269
    and hours worked 162
    and educational level 139
    and gender 132
    and household composition
        130, 138–9, 151, 159
    and income 142, 144, 154
    and primary employment 167
    decision to use 125–31, 153,
        160
    dynamics 158–9

overproduction 164
returns to working 159–66
sales income 17, 146–7, 176
turnover 158
using others' land 161
decision-making 266
    employment 61, 85, 89, 248,
        262
    household 8, 89, 239, 249–
        52
    individual 90, 251
    strategic 240, 248, 258
domestic labour 11, 77, 132,
    162, 163, 249

employment
    casual 42, 44, 68, 96
    family firms 6
    informal 12, 87, 95–6, 269
    new private 6, 144, 236, 270
    on leave 15
    part-time 17, 26, 27, 36, 87,
        129
    private individuals 6
    short-term 17
    Soviet conception 12
    unregistered 6
    unregistered 5
entrepreneurs 15, 109, 111,
    123, 280–1, 285
entrepreneurs' spouses 254, 259
ethnography 8, 151–2, 179,
    181, 239, 252, 255

gender 18, 28, 31, 38, 40, 49,
  51, 53, 55, 59, 69, 75–6, 78,
  132, 146, 182, 201, 243,
  253, 256–9, 268
gender roles 259–66
gifts 123–4, 150–1, 189, 190,
  192–3, 195, 196, 198, 199,
  200
  and loans 207
  food 150, 161, 188
  New Year 185
  under valuation 191

household network
  definition 68
household resources 7, 9, 89,
  114, 121, 130, 143, 147, 153,
  159, 176, 185, 196, 199,
  201, 236–9, 248, 253–6
household subsistence 7, 237,
  265, 267
  sources 7, 8, 9
  traditional forms 236
household survival strategy 7–
  9, 83, 85, 125–6, 150, 152–
  3, 164, 206, 236–70
  defensive 253
  entrepreneurial 253–5
  expenditure   reduction   9,
    240–7, 266
  gender  dimension  253, 256–
    9

individual economic activity 2,
  6, 14, 20, 37, 63
inflation 2–4, 189, 200, 207
informal connections 178–9
informal economy 5, 10, 41, 96,
  238

kinship 178, 183, 186, 193,
  196, 202, 206–7, 268
*kolkhoz* markets 2, 121, 169

labour book 6, 12
Labour Code 13, 33, 64
labour shortages 27, 42, 87,
  169
labour turnover 248
lay-offs 3, 7, 8, 10, 63, 129,
  130, 142, 268
loans 82–3, 95, 180–1, 187,
  189–92, 195–6, 198–9, 202,
  204–05, 207, 242
low  wages 6, 7, 10, 28, 42, 60,
  236, 260

maternity leave 6, 15, 95
minimum wage 3
multiple employment 23
mutual assistance
  Soviet period 178

non-payment 3–4, 8, 10, 83,
  129, 142, 151, 166, 175,
  189, 198–9, 207, 246–7,
  257, 268

overtime 13, 34, 35, 87, 94,
  129, 244

payment in kind 13, 14, 39, 40,
  158, 176, 189, 221, 283
pensions 1, 4, 128, 144, 266
perestroika 2, 10, 35, 126, 158,
  179
personal subsidiary agriculture
  115, 118, 158
  Soviet period 119, 121

poverty 1, 4–5, 141, 157, 170, 174, 176, 181, 189, 192, 193, 196–7, 206, 239, 243, 246, 267
private transfers 7, 8, 9, 142, 178–235, 237, 246, 266–7, 269
  and household composition 130–1, 140, 151, 202
  and age 193, 202
  and income 193
  and new private sector 204
  and pension income 205
  and reciprocity 195
  and relief of poverty 193, 205
  and social transfers 205
  between parents and children 182
  changes over time 189
  contribution to budget 188
  crowding out 205
  impact on inequality 193

reciprocity 151–2, 185–8, 193, 195–200, 202, 204–07
  exchange of services 36
  expectations of 186, 207–08
  gender dimensions 182, 201
  parents and children 181–6
  pensioners 182, 201
  symmetry 185–8, 195
  unemployed 182
savings 1, 2, 4, 244, 266

secondary employment 7–8, 10–112, 128–9, 132, 139, 143, 146, 148, 158–9, 163, 167, 203, 236–7, 240, 245, 248, 252, 258, 266–8

  and 1998 crisis 87
  and administrative leave 13, 20, 24, 39, 60, 63–5, 72
  and age 69
  and domestic labour 13, 77, 78
  and education 69
  and hours worked in first job 71
  and household budget 81
  and household composition 13, 76–8, 91
  and household survival 85–96
  and income 79–80, 83, 85–6, 88–9, 93, 95
  and job tenure 69
  and labour mobility 57–61
  and lay-offs 65, 80, 87
  and low-pay 27, 29, 42, 95
  and non-payment 60, 63, 65, 81, 87
  and occupational status 48
  and payment in kind 60, 63, 65
  and primary jobs 94
  and primary wages 90, 91
  and qualifications 70
  and short-time 39, 80, 87
  and social networks 78
  and socio-economic status 13, 56, 70
  and survival strategies 87
  and unemployed 12–13, 24, 38, 40, 56, 72
  and unpaid leave 37
  branch distribution 41–7, 74
  casual 18, 21, 26, 33, 37, 49, 51, 56

secondary employment
(*continued*)
changes over time 23, 45, 60,
    87, 89
constraints on primary
    employment 36
decision-making 89–93
definition 11, 14
demand for 17–8
deskilling 58
    gender differences 59
domestic constraints 75
earnings 54–6
    gender differences 55
economic significance 79–85
entrepreneurs 38
formalisation 13, 16–17, 23,
    27, 32, 49–51
gender differences 49, 51,
    69, 75–6, 78
helping friends and relatives
    39, 44
home-working 26
hours worked 52
    gender differences 53
impact on poverty 85
incentives and constraints
    26, 47, 61–6, 68, 70–4
incidence 61
individual economic activity
    21, 51, 53
industrial workers 23, 28
intensity of work 59
international comparison 26
*kalym* 13, 30–4
labour contract 13, 32–6
    professionals 36
    rates of pay 35–6
multiple employment 12
negative consequences 95–6

new private sector 32, 41,
    51, 56, 68, 74, 95, 96
occupational distribution 46–
    9
official estimates 16
opportunities 68–70
personal connections 66
poverty 76
professional demands 57
public services 27,–8, 32,
    41–2, 46
recruitment 66
regularity 15, 22, 24–6, 32,
    44, 47, 51

scale 16–26
sectoral distribution 74–5
self-employment 13, 18, 24,
    37, 41, 47, 50–1, 64
services 11, 14, 18, 21, 36–7,
    43, 47, 56
    gender differences 38
    rates of pay 37
shabashniki 35
skill demands 58, 73
small business 29, 47
Soviet period 2, 10–11, 16,
    26–7, 36, 43, 62, 73, 84,
    86
*Sovmestitel'*, 10, 13, 16–17,
    27–30, 32, 41–3, 46–7, 49,
    50, 56, 67, 75
    and low pay 28
    public services 29
    sectoral differences 29
stability 20–1, 24
statistical reporting 16
street trading 26, 40–1
    gender differences 40
subjective factors 78–9

survey data 17
time constraints 72
time demands 51–4
trading 21, 33, 37–40, 44, 56, 75
    barter goods 39–40
under-reporting 18, 25
urban centres 23, 25, 70
working hours 54
self-employment 13–14, 128
self-interest 185
self-sufficiency 113, 118, 123, 125, 154
shortages 2, 170–1, 178

short-time 3, 7–8, 10, 54, 62–3, 129, 142, 154, 246, 257–8, 268
single-parent 151, 201
social assistance 177, 238, 240
social networks 9, 61, 68, 78, 152, 160, 178–9, 183, 196, 199–200, 202–04, 207, 236, 245, 254

and secondary employment 179
social norms 185, 203
social support 151, 208
    Soviet period 206
speculation 2, 255
subsistence crisis 6, 7, 86

theft 13, 30
transition crisis 2–6, 86–7, 113, 129, 158, 168, 208, 236, 248, 268, 269

unemployment 3, 10, 143, 198, 207, 258, 263, 268
    benefit 3, 139, 144
unpaid leave 64, 198
unregistered employment 12, 84, 85

wage delays 63, 143, 154, 159
wage inequality 3
World Bank 24, 63, 177, 181, 205, 238, 239, 247